Housing the Aging

HOUSING

THE

AGING

Edited by Wilma Donahue

with a Foreword by Everett J. Soop

GREENWOOD PRESS, PUBLISHERS
WESTPORT, CONNECTICUT

Library of Congress Cataloging in Publication Data

Conference on Aging, 5th, University of Michigan, 1952.
    Housing the aging.

    Reprint of the ed. published by University of Michigan,
Press, Ann Arbor.
    Bibliography: p.
    Includes index.
    1. Aged--Dwellings--Congresses. 2. Old age homes--
Congresses. I. Donahue, Wilma T. II. Title.
[HD7287.9.C55   1952a]   362.6   76-26114
ISBN 0-8371-9043-6

Copyright 1954
University of Michigan

Originally published in 1954 by University of Michigan Press, Ann Arbor

Reprinted with the permission of The University of Michigan Press

Reprinted in 1976 by Greenwood Press,
a division of Williamhouse-Regency Inc.

Library of Congress Catalog Card Number   76-26114

ISBN 0-8371-9043-6

Printed in the United States of America

FOREWORD

In some of the older sections of the United States it is still common to find that generation after generation has lived in the same house. Rumors are abroad that sometime in the near future houses may be bought and sold like new and used automobiles are today. When a new type comes out, or improvements involving more comfort are available, or housing needs change, the old one will be turned in on a new or different model.

What changes do we look for in housing as we grow older? The adequacies of one period of our lives are often the inadequacies of another. The common problems of design, type of construction, location, and method of financing are always involved. Our personal needs dictate the values we put on each of these factors. Moreover, the values shift as needs change.

In recognition of the variations in needs of older people, the focus of the 1952 conference on problems of the aging, conducted at the University of Michigan, was on housing.

This volume, *Housing the Aging*, is the fifth in a series based on similar annual conferences. Major responsibility for planning the program and editing the proceedings was carried by the Division of Gerontology of the Institute for Human Adjustment. Other responsibilities were borne by the Summer Session and the Extension Service. Also, appreciation is due and is hereby expressed to the Horace H. Rackham School of Graduate Studies for the grant from Rackham funds that made this publication possible.

Everett J. Soop
Director of Extension Service

PREFACE

THIS VOLUME is a report of the University of Michigan Fifth Annual Conference on Aging which was held in Ann Arbor, July 24-26, 1952.

"Housing the Aging" was selected as the topic for the Conference in recognition of the growing interest and concern of many people in finding solutions for this difficult problem. Objectives of the Conference, and hence of this volume, included the following:

To provide opportunity for an integrated review of present knowledge about the housing of healthy, frail, sick, and disabled older people.

To promote interest in active support for good housing and neighborhood planning for the aging as important community resources.

To assess the housing desires and needs of aging individuals of varying socio-economic and health status.

To study the resources of investment capital for financing better and more integrated housing in desirable neighborhoods within the reach of all income groups of the aging population.

To encourage local government to take a leading role in the planning, initiation, and operation of community services for the aged in their own homes or immediate neighborhoods in order to improve and prolong independent living arrangements.

The University was joined in the sponsorship of the Conference by the Michigan State Medical Society, and by two federal agencies: the Housing and Home Finance Agency, and the Committee on Aging and Geriatrics of the Federal Security Agency. The guidance of these groups in the development of the Conference program and in their participation in the Conference was of inestimable value to the University. Special appreciation must be expressed to E. Everett Ashley III, chief, Housing Economics Branch, Division of Housing Research, Housing and Home Finance Agency, for his assistance in the early development of the outline; for his continued help throughout planning stages of the Conference, and in the preparation of a *Fact Book on Housing the Aging* which was made available to all Conference participants. To Clark Tibbitts, chairman of the Committee on Aging and Geriatrics, Federal Security Agency (now Department of Health, Education, and Welfare) and to other members of his committee, we wish to express our thanks for special assistance given in identifying and bringing together at the Conference the leaders in the field. The members of the Michigan State Medical Society, under the leadership of Dr. Hazen Price, chairman of the Geriatrics Committee of the Michigan State Medical Society, are due our special thanks for bringing the Conference to the attention of physicians throughout the state and for soliciting the help of members of the medical profession in the deliberations of the Conference. Leonard G. Haeger, director of Technical Service Department, National Association of Home Builders, made many helpful suggestions which assisted us in our efforts to interest private builders in the problem of housing for old people.

Within our own University we were assisted and joined in sponsorship by the University of Michigan Medical School, the College of Architecture and Design, the School of Business Administration, the School of Public Health, and the School of Social Work. In addition, the University of Michigan Extension Service and the Summer Session gave financial assistance and presented the Conference as a part of the regular summer session activities. To all these groups and to the individual staff members who gave unstintingly of their time, we are grateful.

To the contributors to this volume and to the leaders of the several housing clinics presented at the Conference, we owe much, for it was these people who furnished the content of the Conference and helped in the achievement of its goals. This volume will, I hope, provide them with the satisfaction of feeling that they have made a concrete contribution to one of the most challenging problems facing the United States today.

WILMA DONAHUE

CONTENTS

Financing Housing for the Aging PART IV

Getting Community Action PART V

The Problem

PART I

WHO ARE
THE AGED? *Chapter I*

BY HENRY D. SHELDON

Henry D. Sheldon, Ph.D., is chief of the Demographic Statistics Section, Population and Housing Division, of the United States Bureau of the Census. Before this he was an instructor in sociology at the University of Rochester. He has published "Correctional Statistics," Chapter II in Contemporary Correction, and with Clark Tibbitts, "Introduction: Philosophy of Aging," in The Annals of the American Academy of Political and Social Science, January, 1952. He is a member of the Population Association of America.

THE CURRENT FOCUS of attention on the place of older persons in our society arises, in part, from the increase in their number. Now it is well known that the proportion of persons sixty-five years old and over in our population has doubled since 1900. In 1950 the twelve million persons sixty-five and over constituted about 8 per cent of the total population, whereas, in 1900 the three million in this age group represented only 4 per cent of the total.

The Changing Age Structure of the American Population

The increase in the number and proportion of persons aged sixty-five and over is, of course, but one facet of the fundamental changes in the age structure of our population which have been in process throughout a large part of our history. In 1790 the median age of the white male population was about sixteen years: that is, one half of that population was older and one half younger than sixteen. In 1950 the corresponding figure, about thirty, was almost twice as large. Similar figures for the total population from 1820 on indicate that, at least since the early nineteenth century, the population of the United States has been an "aging" population and that this process has been going on at an accelerating rate.

Trends 1900 to 1950. Between 1900 and 1950 this process of aging is reflected in the larger increases in the proportions of the population at each successive age interval from thirty-five upward. The proportion of persons thirty-five to forty-four years old in 1950 was 1.2 times as large as the corresponding proportion for 1900, and this excess increased with age until, for the group age seventy-five and over, the 1950 proportion was 2.1 times as large as that for 1900.

Sources of change. The increase in the absolute number of persons sixty-five years old and over between the years 1900 and 1950 is the result of several factors. Native persons sixty-five and over in 1900 represent, for the most part, survivors of persons born between 1815 and 1835. Similarly, native persons sixty-five and over in 1950 represent survivors of births in the period 1865 to 1885. Since the number of births in the latter period was considerably greater than the number in the earlier period, the same relationship is to be expected among their survivors.

The same type of argument applies to the increase in the number of foreign-born persons sixty-five and over from 1900 to 1950. Although the exact periods of immigration of foreign-born persons sixty-five years of age and over at the two dates cannot be specified, it is clear that there was a greater volume of migration in the forty to sixty years prior to 1950 than in the corresponding period prior to 1900.

Finally, there are differences in the causes of death rates to which the two populations were exposed in the course of attaining the age of sixty-five. Although the data on mortality in the nineteenth century are extremely sketchy, it is clear that the conditions to which the population aged sixty-five and over was exposed in 1950 were more favorable than those to which the population attaining age sixty-five and over was exposed in 1900. The effect of this improvement in mortality was, for the most part, to permit larger numbers of persons to survive to age sixty-five and over, rather than to permit larger numbers of persons who had attained age sixty-five to live longer. The declines in mortality rates for the age groups above sixty-five have been rather modest.

On the other hand, the increase in the proportion of persons sixty-five and over is primarily a matter of declining fertility. The available evidence shows a consistent pattern of declining birth rates throughout the nineteenth century and in the first three decades of the twentieth century. This decline in the birth rate simply means that the proportion of children in the population decreased continually throughout the period, and conversely, the proportion of adults increased. It should be noted that, although the birth rate declined throughout the period, the actual number of births continued to increase until the early nineteen twenties. That is, although women, on the average, were having fewer children, the number of women having children continued to increase. By the early nineteen twenties, however, the decline in the birth rate caught up with the increase in the number of women, and there were fewer children under five in 1930 than in 1920, and in turn fewer such children in 1940 than in 1930. These changes are reflected in the age distribution for 1940 which shows, for ages under twenty, a progressive decline with descending age at each five-year interval. The figures on births, however, for the decade from 1940 to 1950 indicate a reversal in this trend.

Future prospects. Since the population which will become sixty-five and over in the next several decades is now alive, and since there seems, at present, little reason to believe that future immigration will be a significant factor in population growth in the near future, it is possible to estimate with some assurance the size of the population aged sixty-five and over at future dates.

On the basis of current mortality rates, the number of persons sixty-five and over in 1960 would be about sixteen million; and in 1975, about twenty-one million. If the trend toward declining mortality observed in the past continues, these numbers will be appreciably higher, and if real gains are made in the reduction of mortality from those diseases characteristic of later and middle life such as cancer and heart disease, the growth in the older population will be substantial.

The future trends in the proportion of aged persons in the population will depend not only on future trends in mortality, but also on future trends in fertility, and, at the present writing, there is a certain strain of ambivalence in demographic thinking on this point.

Projections made in the late nineteen thirties and early forties shared the common assumption that the continuous decline in fertility observed in the past would continue, and thus produced figures which showed a declining total population in the latter part of the twentieth century and a sharp increase in the proportion of persons aged sixty-five and over. One such set of projections, for example, shows for the year 2000, under the assumptions of "low" fertility and "low" mortality (the assumptions calculated to maximize the proportion of older persons) a population aged sixty-five and over of more than twenty-five million would constitute about 18 per cent of the total population. Under the assumptions of "high" fertility and "high" mortality the corresponding figures were about twenty million and 11 per cent.[1]

The sharp upswing in fertility during the decade 1940-50 has given rise to the ambivalence in demographic thinking previously mentioned—on the one hand it raises serious doubts as to the reliability of the earlier projections based as they were on an assumption of a continuous decline in fertility. On the other hand, most demographers would regard the assumption of a long continuation of the relatively high birth rates of the past decade as an extremely bold one. On balance it seems reasonable to expect some increase in the proportion of persons aged sixty-five and over in the decades to come, but an increase somewhat below those indicated by the earlier projections.

[1]Warren S. Thompson and P. K. Whelpton, *Estimates of Future Population of the United States, 1940 to 2000*, Nat. Resources Planning Bd. (Washington, D.C.: Govt. Printing Office, 1943), pp. 43, 102.

Geographic Distribution

Distribution by states. Among the states the percentage of the population age sixty-five and over in 1950 ranged from 4.9 in New Mexico to 10.8 in New Hampshire. The states in which the proportions of older persons were relatively high (9 per cent or more) fell into two groups: Maine, New Hampshire, Vermont, and Massachusetts in New England; and Indiana, Wisconsin, Minnesota, Iowa, Missouri, Nebraska, and Kansas in the Middle West. The states with relatively few older persons (less than 7 per cent) were Virginia, West Virginia, North Carolina, South Carolina, Georgia, and Alabama in the Southeast, and Louisiana, Texas, New Mexico, Arizona, Utah, Nevada, and Wyoming in the Southwestern and Mountain States.

Differences in the age composition among the states, like differences in the age composition of the population of the United States at different dates, are attributable to the combined effects of past trends in fertility, mortality, and migration. Since the combination of effects is relatively unique from state to state, a detailed analysis of these trends for the past sixty to eighty years would be necessary to determine precisely the reasons for differences.

It is possible, however, to make inferences as to the factors involved in certain states. New Mexico, for example, with the lowest percentage of persons aged sixty-five and over has long been a state with extremely high fertility and mortality. It seems reasonable to suppose that the low proportion of elderly persons in this state is directly related to these factors. This type of explanation would seem to apply also to Arizona and Utah as well as to those states in the Southeast having small proportions of their population at the upper age levels.

The effects of fertility and mortality on the age structure of the population of a state are overlaid, of course, with the effects of migration. In 1940, for example, about 20 per cent of all persons in the United States were living in a state other than the state in which they were born and about 9 per cent were foreign born. Statistics on migration from the current population surveys indicate that interstate migration rates for persons eighteen to thirty-four years old are from two to three times as high as those for persons thirty-five years old and over. On this basis, a heavy outmigration from a state would tend to increase the proportion of the population in the upper age levels, and conversely, a heavy inmigration would be expected to halt or at least to temper the increase in the proportion of older persons.

In the decade from 1940 to 1950, the effects of the heavy net outmigration from Arkansas and Oklahoma are apparent in increases in the proportion of persons sixty-five and over. The estimated net outmigration, during the decade, for Arkansas was 434,000 and the percentage of persons sixty-five and over increased from 5.5 to 7.8. For Oklahoma the corresponding figures were 446,000, with increases of 6.1 per cent and 8.7 per cent. The effects of heavy inmigration appear to be reflected in age statistics for the Pacific Coast states in which the gains in the percentage sixty-five years and over were only one half of 1 per cent or less.

It is not, however, merely a matter of migration in the past decade. Although the immediate effect of a large inmigration is to retard the aging of a state's population, these migrants will eventually attain age sixty-five and over and at that point will increase the population aged sixty-five and over. There is some evidence, for example, to suggest that a part of the increase in the population sixty-five years of age and over in Florida between 1940 and 1950 can be accounted for by the surviving relatives of the young adults who migrated to Florida during the "boom" of the nineteen twenties.

Although, in general, it would appear that heavy inmigration tends to dampen the trend toward an older population, there are exceptions. The most outstanding exception is the state of Florida. Although there was an estimated net inmigration of 561,000 during the decade, 1940-50, the percentage of persons sixty-five and over increased from 6.9 to 8.6. Here it appears that inmigration has been selective and that the proportion of older persons among inmigrants has been sufficiently large to have a real impact on the age structure of the state.

Urban and rural residence. In 1950 the percentage of persons aged sixty-five and over was 8.1 in the urban population, 8.6 in the rural nonfarm population, and 7.6 in the rural farm population. This pattern is essentially similar to that of 1940 even though the 1950 figures are based on the new definition of urban and rural residence which allocates some eight million persons to the urban population who, under a definition comparable to 1940 would have been classified as rural, and, for the most part, rural nonfarm. The net effect of this shift has been, in all probability, to decrease the proportion of older persons in the urban population and to increase the proportion in the rural nonfarm population, since, in general, the population involved is that of urban fringe areas which on the average is a younger population than that of the central cities which these areas surround.

The pattern of distribution of the proportion of persons aged sixty-five and over by urban and rural residence, however, was by no means uniform among the states. In seventeen states the percentage of persons aged sixty-five and over exceeded the corresponding percentages for the rural farm and urban population— in nineteen states, however, this percentage was highest in the rural farm population, and in twelve states, in the urban population.

Standard metropolitan areas. Another type of area for which statistics on the number and distribution of elderly persons are of significance is the standard metropolitan area. These areas are composed of a county, or group of counties, which contain one or more cities of fifty thousand or more inhabitants and which approximate a single integrated social and economic unit. In their entirety, they account for more than half of the total population of the United States. As among states, and for the same reasons, there is considerable variation in the proportion of elderly persons among individual standard metropolitan areas. Among the seven standard metropolitan areas of Michigan, for example, the percentage of persons aged sixty-five and over ranges from 5.4 in the Detroit area to 9.0 in the Jackson area.

In general, however, the figures for the standard metropolitan areas that are now available indicate that the percentage of persons aged sixty-five and over is greater in the central cities than in the remainder of the area or "ring." This difference reflects, in most instances, the fact that the suburban ring is an area of more recent settlement by younger persons. It also means, however, that older persons are found in greater concentrations living in the older structures of the central cities. /

Characteristics of the Population Aged Sixty-five and Over

Sex and marital status. In the United States there were 5.8 million males sixty-five and over as compared with 6.5 million females of the same age, or about ninety males per one hundred females.

The larger number of women among older persons is reflected in their distribution by marital status. In 1950, the percentage of single men and women was around eight; slightly more than one third of the women, but almost two thirds of the men, were married; and more than one half of the women, but about one fourth of the men, were widowed. The large proportion of widows among women aged sixty-five and over, which reflects the higher mortality of males, the greater tendency of widowers to remarry, and the lower average age of women at marriage is, from the point of view of planning for the welfare of elderly persons, the most significant fact to emerge from the statistics of marital status.

Household relationship. In our culture, normal, or at least modal, living arrangements involve membership in a household. A household, for census purposes, is a person or group of persons occupying a single dwelling unit. The term "dwelling unit" refers to ordinary living quarters such as a house or apartment. It is bounded at one extreme by a room occupied by a lodger, which is not regarded as a dwelling unit, and at the other by the larger lodging house, hotel, dormitory, institution, or other special types of congregate living quarters designated in census terminology as "quasi-households." In short, the term "household" implies the situation of what is ordinarily regarded as a family living in a home, whereas the term quasi-household implies specialized mass living arrangements.

In these terms the population aged sixty-five and over is not materially different from the total population. About 98 per cent of the total population, and 96 per cent of the population sixty-five and over live in private households. It is true, of course, that the proportion of elderly persons in quasi-households is about twice as great as the corresponding proportion for the total population, and this situation emphasizes the need for specialized facilities for the care of elderly persons with special disabilities. On the other hand, however, it indicates with equal clarity that, at the present time, institutions and other types of congregate living arrangements account for only a very small fraction of the older population.

Within households, the membership may be classified by relationship to the head of the household. The membership of what is ordinarily conceived to be a normal household is composed of a man and wife and their children. No great violence is done this concept if we add other relatives such as aunts and uncles, occasional lodgers, or servants, or if, on the other hand, we contract the membership to merely a husband and wife, a widow and her child, or a single individual occupying a house or apartment. In the ordinary husband-and-wife household, census statistics somewhat arbitrarily designate the husband as the head, and use him as a reference point for assigning relationship. In households in which the configuration of membership does not permit this simple Victorian solution, the person regarded as head by the membership is designated as head.

If persons who are household heads and women who are wives of heads may be regarded as maintaining their own households, then for the United States as a whole, about 72 per cent of all persons aged sixty-five and over maintain their own households. In short, nearly three fourths of the older population live in what might be regarded as a normal family setting for adults.

The next largest group of persons aged sixty-five and over—about 20 per cent of the total—lives as relatives of the head of the household. For persons sixty-five and over in this group, the most common type of relationship to the head of the household is that of parent. In general then it is this group—about one fifth of the total—that is found in the three-generation family setting. It does not, however, include the relatively small number of heads and wives of three-generation households who are sixty-five and over. The remaining 4 per cent of the older population live in private households primarily as lodgers.

Type of household. Households may be classified into three types: husband and wife households which are ordinarily regarded as the normal household, other households with a male head in which a married couple does not constitute the central core of the household, and households with female heads. Among all households in the United States about four fifths are husband and wife households. Among households headed by persons aged sixty-five and over, however, only slightly more than one half are husband and wife households. This situation is a natural consequence of the process of aging in which, at advanced ages, the death of husband or wife leaves the household incomplete. The excess of widows over widowers is also reflected in these statistics. Among other than husband and wife households, there are twice as many households headed by women as by men.

Although statistics at the national level are useful in the general consideration of the living arrangement among older persons, planning and action, of necessity, must go on at the level of the local community. Since the standard metropolitan area provides an approximation of the "real" urban community independent of the vagaries of corporate limits (but not of county lines) it represents a natural unit for analysis and planning. In view of this situation, it may be of some interest to examine, briefly, advanced statistics in the general field under consideration for a specific standard metropolitan area by way of illustrating the kinds of materials which will be available from the 1950 census. The Grand Rapids, Michigan, standard metropolitan area has been selected for this purpose simply because advanced figures were readily available.

Kent County, Michigan, with a population of about 290,000, constitutes the Grand Rapids standard metropolitan area. In 1950 the central city contained about 60 per cent of the total population. The percentage of persons sixty-five and over was 8.9 for the entire area, 9.9 for the central city, and 7.3 for the ring.

The statistics for this area indicate that the distributions of the older population by marital status and household relationship are, in general, not essentially different from those at the national level. Two exceptions should be noted:

The percentage of persons sixty-five and over in quasi-households was about twice as high in the Grand Rapids standard metropolitan area as in the county as a whole, owing largely to the presence of several fair-sized institutions in the area. This percentage may be expected to vary considerably from area to area depending on whether or not large institutions happen to be located in them.

Again, in contrast to the county as a whole, the statistics for the Grand Rapids standard metropolitan area show a slightly higher percentage of the older population maintaining their own households and a lower percentage living as other relatives. These differences are not large, however, and in all probability reflect the fact that the figures relate to a predominantly urban area.

An examination of partly complete figures from the nonfarm housing tabulation of the 1950 census for the Grand Rapids standard metropolitan area indicates that, although the proportion of home ownership is higher among household heads sixty-five and over than it is for all household heads, the income of the older heads is considerably below that of the general population. In the older population there are also appreciable differences by type of household. The income level of the heads of husband and wife households is considerably higher than that of the female heads of households and the remaining group falls into an intermediate position. There is also evidence in these advanced data that in comparison with all households, those headed by elderly persons have, on the average, a smaller number of members, but, at least for home owners, have, on the average, a greater number of rooms. The figures on dilapidation are inconclusive but suggest a higher incidence of dilapidation among the dwelling units of older renters than among those of renters in general. These findings are far from startling but there is, nevertheless, some satisfaction in the confirmation of common-sense expectations by statistics.

Summary

In summary, then, the number and proportion of elderly persons in our population has increased in the past and may be reasonably expected to do so in the future. A relatively small number of these persons live in institutions, hotels, lodging houses, and as lodgers in private households. A larger number live as relatives in the households of other persons—in many cases the households of their children. The great majority of older persons, however, live in their own households—households, among which, in contrast to all households, the income of the head is lower, the membership is smaller, there are fewer complete husband and wife households, and more households headed by women. In any comprehensive program for improving the housing of our older population, it is this group which becomes a matter of primary concern.

WHERE AND HOW OLDER
PEOPLE LIVE TODAY *Chapter II*

BY E. EVERETT ASHLEY III

> *E. Everett Ashley III, M.B.A., is chief of the Housing
> Economics Branch, Division of Housing Research, of the
> Housing and Home Finance Agency, Washington, D.C.
> From 1947 to 1950 he was director of the Construction
> Division of the National Housing Agency and from 1942
> to 1947 was chief of the Surveys and Special Studies Sec-
> tion of this organization; from 1941 to 1942, he was con-
> sultant to the Defense Housing Co-ordinator at Washing-
> ton. His publications include* Government Housing Activity
> *(1941),* The Housing Situation, The Factual Background
> *(1948), and* How Big is the Housing Job? *(1951). He is
> chairman of the Interdepartmental Committee on Housing
> Adequacy, a member of the Federal Security Agency Com-
> mittee on Aging and Geriatrics, and chairman of the
> Advisory Committee on Business and Commercial Develop-
> ment to the Arlington County Planning Commission.*

IN CONSIDERING the problem of housing the aging it is appropriate
that we begin with a common understanding of what the underlying situation is. For our purposes we will use the term "aging"
to mean those over sixty-five years; but in the case of housing, just
as in the case of most other aspects of the problem of the aging,
it is not chronological age alone that should be the principal
determinant. We are all familiar, I am sure, with the story of
Justice Holmes when he was about eighty. Walking past the
Capitol one morning his eye caught a beautiful girl flouncing
down the street. Holmes turned to his companion and said with
a sigh, "Oh, to be seventy again!" Age, then, is not a disease but
a stage of wisdom and experience. The problems of the aging

become our problems insofar as we have failed to provide for them those basic necessities and supports that they were once able to provide for themselves in their prime of life.

All told, we have more than ten and one-half million persons over sixty-five years of age living in the nonfarm areas of the United States. Of these ten and one-half million, some seven and one-half million live in their own households. There were about five and six-tenths million of these households in 1950. The balance live either with relatives or friends, in hotels or boarding houses, or in institutions.

While it would be desirable to' evaluate the housing arrangements of the entire population over sixty-five years of age, for the present we must content ourselves with the five and six-tenths million older families and individuals who maintain their own quarters. In making my observations on the living arrangement of this group, I will lean heavily upon special sample tabulations prepared by the United States Bureau of the Census under an agreement with the Division of Housing Research, Housing and Home Finance Agency.[1]

Statistics on Living Arrangements

To me the most striking thing about the living arrangements of older families is the high concentrations of one- and two-person families. This situation is largely the result of the maturing children leaving their parents' home and of the deaths of spouses. Over 68 per cent of the group under study was made up of either single individuals or couples—25 per cent single individuals, 43 per cent couples. In fact, the over-sixty-five group accounted for two fifths of all one-person nonfarm households. In contrast, only 33 per cent of the younger families contained two persons or less. In absolute numbers, there were in nonfarm areas 1,405,000 single individuals over sixty-five years of age who maintained their own separate homes or apartments in 1950. Of these, 985,000 were women, while only 420,000 were men. In addition, there were

[1] These tabulations are recorded in *Facts for Housing the Aging,* a handbook prepared at the University of Michigan in 1952.

2,402,000 two-person families maintaining their own households, the head of which was over sixty-five.

As a result of the smallness of family groups among the aging there is noticeably less congestion in their homes. Over 80 per cent of them had an average of less than three-quarters persons per room. Among younger families only a little over one half had an average of that much elbow room. At the other end of the scale, only 2 per cent of the older families, contrasted with over 6 per cent of the families under sixty-five, were seriously overcrowded, that is, with an average of more than one and one half persons per room.

Much of this lack of crowding among older families, no doubt, results from the fact that they do not contract the size of their quarters as rapidly as their families dwindle in numbers. Houses bought to meet the needs of a family with several children are frequently retained even after all the children have married and set up homes of their own.

In fact, the census figures show that older families tend to have larger quarters than do younger families. Nearly three fifths of the aging had quarters containing five or more rooms, whereas less than half of the families under sixty-five years of age had units that large. Even in occupying units of eight or more rooms, the aging hold a definite edge over the younger families (11 per cent compared with 5 per cent).

Home Ownership

That older families do not give up their larger homes just because the children have gone off on their own is due in part, at least, to the fact that 68 per cent of the households headed by persons sixty-five or older own their own homes. In fact, the proportion of home owners among this age group exceeds that for all others in the population.

For many older families, ownership of a home, no doubt, represents part of their own social security program, assuring them of a roof over their heads in their declining years. A large group of the nearly four million home owners of over sixty-five find in their homes a satisfactory shelter, at least as long as they are able to take care of it and are fit enough to fend for themselves. This is at least suggested by the fact that two thirds of our older families live in dwellings, which, in 1950, had all modern conveniences and were not dilapidated.

For an indeterminate share of the group, however, home ownership is undoubtedly more or less of a burden. Because of sentiment, inertia, or economic necessity, elderly men and women continue in some cases to struggle with a house beyond their physical and financial means to carry.

Undoubtedly, it is these situations which contribute to the fact that a somewhat larger share of our older families (8.4 per cent) live in substandard housing than is true of younger families (6.9 per cent). With failing strength and diminished income, some older household heads find the problems of house maintenance more than they can cope with. As a result, the structures gradually deteriorate to the point where they fall into the census classification of "dilapidated." Thus, in 1950, almost 7 per cent of the dwellings owned by persons over sixty-five years of age were in poor condition, compared with slightly over 4 per cent of the owner-occupied units headed by persons under sixty-five.

Rental Housing

All of the poor housing occupied by the aging, however, cannot be attributed to the senility of its occupants. For instance, in the case of rental housing the situation is far worse than that for owned homes. In contrast with the 7 per cent of dilapidated units among aging owners, we found that nearly 12 per cent of the dwellings rented by the aging were dilapidated. But the disparity among rented homes between the quality of the units of the older and younger families is not so great. Of the families whose head was under sixty-five, nearly 10 per cent also lived in dilapidated rented dwellings in 1950.

The heavier concentration of low quality units among renter-occupied than among owner-occupied units is reflected in the comparative figures on rents and values. In contrast with the rest of the population, a heavy concentration of older families (40 per cent compared with 21 per cent for younger families) rent quarters for less than $30.00 a month. Whereas rents of older families tend to concentrate at the lower end of the rent scale (75 per cent paid less than $50.00), the values of the homes owned, while not quite as high as those of younger families ($6,000 *vs.* $7,400), are better distributed.

Evaluation

This is but a quick sketch of how our aging are housed. There are, of course, many gaps in our data which need to be filled. We need to know more, for example, about living arrangements in rural areas. We need to be able to measure and to evaluate the housing situation of those aging families and individuals who do not have homes of their own. We need, especially, to have facts on housing conditions in nursing homes and in institutions. All this will take time and effort and money. But despite the many gaps in our knowledge about how the aging are housed, we do have enough facts to identify some aspects of the situation.

It should be obvious, though I fear we sometimes lose sight of it in our anxiety over the plight of the aging, that every family does not become a housing problem when its head reaches sixty-five. As statistics bear out, a considerable number of old families are well housed in their own homes and neither need nor want to make a change. Hence, the often quoted forecast of a three million increase in our population over sixty-five in the next decade is not a reliable measure of the magnitude of the housing problem for the aging during that period.

Economic Aspects

Although much of the public interest in the problems of housing the aging has been centered around the infirm and the chronically ill, numerically, a bigger need for thought and action is in housing for generally healthy but aging persons. In this group, especially among those who are renters, the problem is often largely economic. For instance, as the heads of families pass sixty-five they tend to retire or at least to curtail their work. This, in turn, results in a decline in income. As a result, many aging renters find themselves no longer able to afford the quarters which previously had satisfactorily housed them.

About 94 per cent of the aging live out their lives in a conventional house, not necessarily their own, but at least in a home of relatives or friends. It is obvious that any way in which their homes can be made safer, healthier, and more pleasant to live in will ease the economic burden on the aging themselves and on those who ultimately must care for them. This is particularly important for countless aging couples and single individuals who for economic reasons are doomed to live out their remaining years feeling themselves to be a burden upon relatives or friends. Equally significant, it will ease the burden on the taxpayers by substantially reducing the number of aging who might otherwise have to be cared for in institutions at public expense.

Psychological Aspects

The aging who live in the homes of relatives or friends comprise a segment of the older population about whom, unfortunately, we have no statistics. But I have a strong suspicion that many in this group, both couples and single individuals, would dearly love the independence of separate quarters if they were available at rents or costs within their means. Were statistics available for this group their present housing accommodations might show up well from a physical standpoint—living in good conditions and with all modern conveniences. But there is more to the problem than merely having a sound roof over one's head. There are, for example, psychological and emotional factors, to say nothing of the whole train of human relations aspects of their status. On these counts much of the otherwise satisfactory housing for those who must live with relatives or friends probably ranks among the least appropriate. We all know scores of elderly men and women in our communities who are too proud or too poor to go to institutions or nursing homes and are thus forced to work out makeshift housing arrangements that are satisfactory neither to themselves nor to their would-be benefactors. For them, perhaps, the solution may be along the lines of the English "mother-in-law annexes" or some other compromise between their present enforced doubling and institutional housing. Community action may be called for in some instances to see to it that local zoning regulations will permit the provision of such quarters in all residential areas.

Developing Suitable Housing

Means also need to be devised to make it easier for the elderly home owner who desires to do so to dispose of a house too large for his current needs and to acquire more suitable accommodations. Many an old couple desperately hangs on to an eight-room house merely because the legal and financial complexities of disposing of it and acquiring a smaller, more manageable unit seem too formidable. For the same reason many retired people suffer through cold northern winters rather than move south.

It is apparent that many older families would welcome better units within their means. Of course, it must be borne in mind that in 1949, nearly half of the group over sixty-five had cash incomes of less than $1,000 a year. Here I might suggest that section 213 (the so-called co-operative housing section) of the National Housing Act seems to offer substantial possibilities, particularly if co-operative groups recruit a reasonable proportion of older persons into their membership. Such arrangements would appear to have merit over schemes for projects exclusively for aging persons. Anyone who is seriously interested in providing low-cost housing accommodations for older persons might also explore the possibility of financing them with mortgages insured by the Federal Housing Administration under Title I, section 8, of the National Housing Act.

I have heard of some developers who have shied away from housing for aging persons because they felt that it would involve special design problems. Actually, however, many of the features which are desirable for aging persons are equally suitable for younger families with small children—for example, space all on one floor, no stairs to climb, absence of drafts, automatic heat, nonslip floors, and many more items of this nature. Hence, in actual practice, housing designed for the aging can provide desirable facilities for families in all age groups. Units for the aging, therefore, can be integrated appropriately in housing developments aimed at younger age groups. This will not only make for greater flexibility in management and operation but will also avoid the creation of undesirable segregation of aging families.

The whole burden of providing housing for aging need not fall upon the building industry alone. Community groups, churches, foundations, and fraternal organizations can play an important role, particularly in meeting the housing needs of the aging at the lower end of the income scale. In the past, community groups have tended to place their major emphasis in this area upon the care and shelter of the infirm and chronically ill aging persons. As I have tried to point out, however, an even bigger need among the aging healthy persons exists. Some of the religious and fraternal organizations are already re-examining their approaches to the problem. It is to be hoped that this process of reappraisal among the groups already active in the field will continue, and that community groups which have thus far remained on the sidelines will also accept the challenge. But we must never lose sight of the fact that the physical aspect of housing is only one facet of a difficult and many-sided problem. We will do a disservice to the aging whom we seek to help if we fail properly to orient their needs in terms of a total human complex.

In the Housing and Home Finance Agency, as we address ourselves to the whole problem of housing for American families, the specific question of housing the aging is being given active study and consideration not only in the Office of the Administrator but in the constituent agencies as well. In our Division of Housing Research we are doing all we can to encourage industry to explore the whole question of housing for the aging. This is just one part of our work to help all branches of the industry in their efforts to make it possible to achieve our national housing policy of "a decent home in a suitable living environment for every American family."

WHERE AND HOW OLDER
PEOPLE WISH TO LIVE *Chapter III*

BY WILMA DONAHUE

Wilma Donahue, Ph.D., is research psychologist and chairman of the Division of Gerontology, Institute for Human Adjustment, and lecturer in psychology at the University of Michigan. She is director of the annual University of Michigan Conference on Aging; chairman, Governor's Inter-departmental Committee on Aging; and vice-chairman of the Committee on Aging, Adult Education Association, U.S.A. She is a member of the Council of the Gerontological Society and a member of the editorial board of Geriatrics. Her publications include many articles in the field of aging.

THE HOUSING problem has been and still is a perennial and critical one for families of all ages in our society. Through the combined efforts of private enterprise and government, however, significant progress has been made in housing younger families, especially since the Second World War. But what has been done to house the aging during this and earlier periods has been negligible in comparison to the need. As it concerns the elderly, the housing problem today is still large and complex and is one of the most pressing that faces older people and those who are concerned with their welfare.

Traditionally, religious, fraternal, and philanthropic societies provided most of the specialized housing for the more able-bodied older people. Public hospitals and infirmaries sheltered the poor and the indigent sick. Older persons who continued to live independently remained in their own homes without reference to whether these homes provided arrangements essential to their well-being as old people. Recent developments have improved the situation to some extent. During the last ten years, there has been a marked increase in the number of nursing and convalescent homes; there has been a growing tendency for chronic disease hospitals to be built in conjunction with general hospitals or as separate facilities; and some public and some private housing especially designed for the use of older people has been developed.

Also, modern trends have brought about a deeper understanding of the requirements of older people for housing which offers more than the elementary needs of shelter—safety, security, and health. It is now understood by increasing numbers of people that living arrangements for old people must provide satisfactions for their desire to continue as active members of a community, that hospitals must become centers for the rehabilitation of the disabled and sick older persons rather than mere domiciliary facilities, and that dwellings which suit the physical and financial circumstances of the aging must be provided to enable them to live in independence, safety, and comfort.

This does not mean that all major questions concerned in housing the aging have been settled. Indeed, as we come to recognize the true dimensions of the problem, new and urgent questions present themselves. Is there any one best way of housing old people? Are we seeking one or many solutions? What types of housing do older people want? Can we rely upon their stated wishes? What special features should be built into houses which will meet the special requirements of the older age group? Are architects and builders interested in an undertaking to house the aging and do they consider it financially feasible? What are the attitudes of different lending agencies toward the older person as a prospective borrower? To what extent are government resources for housing available to old people? To what extent can communities be expected to provide more than shelter and minimum nutritional and medical care in the housing of public charges? What steps can be taken to ensure that the concepts of rehabilitation will be adopted as an essential aspect of all housing plans for the chronically ill or disabled older people? Who will establish standards and who will have responsibilities for maintaining them? What patterns of interrelated community and professional services will best ensure maximum care for all older people irrespective of where they may be housed?

These and a multitude of other questions need immediate consideration. In this book, many of the most competent people in the country in the field of housing will give them attention, suggest solutions, and point to needed next steps. In it, the needs of the well, able-bodied, and frail older people will be considered separately from the needs of those who are already ill or in need of protection. Basic to all types of housing is the question of how it can be financed, and this problem will be considered with respect to all classes of housing. Finally, the responsibility of the community and society to take steps to ensure to the aging not only adequate physical shelter but also the maximum of comfort, safety, and personal satisfaction will be examined.

Where Older People Want to and Should Live

It has already been implied that there is no single answer to even so simple a question as where older people wish to live. The period of later maturity extends over twenty or thirty years and during this time the needs and the desires of the aging person change even more than during an equivalent period of earlier adult life. The healthy, able-bodied, active individual may change during this time to one who is frail or chronically ill and in need of sheltered care and nursing services.

Not only are there profound changes in the capacity of the individual as he grows older and older, but there are marked changes in the external circumstances which must be considered. Companionship may become a scarce commodity when the spouse dies, when children become progressively more absorbed in their own families and affairs, and when friends move away and can no longer be visited or entertained. Financial resources are more likely than not to become depleted or to prove insufficient to meet the mounting costs of medical care or maintenance of a home deteriorating with the passing of the years.

We are forced to conclude that if the goal of housing every aged person in circumstances best suited to his need is to be realized it will be necessary to have a wide variety of housing and living arrangements. Furthermore, we will have to adapt our practices to take account of the changing needs of the aging person during the several decades of later maturity.

It would be relatively easy at this time for the "experts" to write a prescription for housing older people which would take into account the changes in physical status, health, and social circumstances which accompany aging. To do so, however, without knowledge of the consumer's wants, would be short of folly. Failure to get instructions from older people or disregard for their preferences are likely to result in the proverbial horse refusing water to which it is led. For example, in England, many older people refused to move from their dilapidated dwellings to the fine modern apartments provided for them. They preferred their old familiar homes to those designed for their safety and comfort but built in new and strange neighborhoods.

If we turn to the consumer and try to explore his wishes we will find that old people, like those of younger ages, are not prepared to answer the question. Asking an individual directly about his desires is not enough because the conscious consumer-wants are limited by experience and knowledge. An individual can only want what he knows. What we really need is to know what people would want if they understood the full range of possibilities on the one hand and all the practical limitations on the other.[1]

A better approach to learning what the housing needs of old people are would be through livability studies which tell exactly what families do in their homes and what they would do if they had different or better facilities.[2] Such studies would afford opportunity for exchange of ideas between the housing expert and the people he is trying to serve. In this way the older people could be educated to know what they can get and to understand the alternatives of design available to them within their purchasing power.

To date, few studies of this type have been made, and needless

[1]Catherine Bauer, "Social Questions in Housing and Community Planning," *Journ. Social Issues,* 7(1951):35-46.

[2]Svend Reimer, "Architecture for Family Living," *ibid.,* 7(1951):140-51.

to say, none at all have been reported for the older age group. Therefore, if we wish to take consumer preferences into consideration in the planning of housing for old people, we must content ourselves at present with the testimony of experts, the results of a few questionnaire studies, and the expressed opinion of a few individual older people.

Advice of Experts

Those expert in the knowledge of old people have concerned themselves largely with establishing the principles which should underlie good housing and living arrangements to meet the requirements of aging people. They have generally pointed out the basic needs of the older generation and the changes that take place as a result of growing older which call for special housing and living arrangements. They have been concerned with the question of family responsibility and three-generation living, with the advisability of continuing in old homes and neighborhoods as compared with moving to more benign climates, and with the degree of privacy older people want and should have. Their interest has been with the most suitable types of communal housing, with the problems of segregation by age within communities or into special retirement communities, and with plans for providing auxiliary services in order to widen the choice of feasible living arrangements.

The American Public Health Association has a committee charged with responsibility for establishing guiding principles for healthful housing of the aging. The National Committee on Aging of the National Welfare Assembly sponsored a project on standards for sheltered care. The report of this project includes information about practices in relation to standard setting and contains a statement of standards for institutional care of older people and of services by public and private agencies in establishing and maintaining standards.[3] A number of other standard-

[3] Edith Alt, "Suggested Standards for Homes for the Aged and Nursing Homes," Sec. 1, and "Methods of Establishing and Maintaining Standards in Homes for the Aged and Nursing Homes," Sec. 2, in *Standards of Care for Older People in Institutions* (New York: Nat. Comm. on Aging, Social Welfare Assembly, Inc., 1953).

setting agencies have published manuals and guides for the use of their own organizations.[4]

Another source of expert opinion is to be found in the deliberations and recommendations made by the First National Conference on Aging held in Washington, D. C., in 1950. This conference stressed the importance of standards for health and safety in living arrangements and for the personal needs of older people for privacy, companionship, and independence.[5]

The opinions expressed in these publications, based as they are upon theoretical knowledge of good public health and social practices and upon outcomes of experience, are of great importance because they incorporate the best thinking of a large number of informed individuals.

Perhaps Ollie Randall is the only person able to command the status of expert who has also the intimate knowledge gained from living in a special housing unit for old people during a period of more than two decades. She has pointed out that:

The old tendency to plan for the older person and to decide for him what he wants or what is good for him, imposing standards of our own age upon him, for good or woe, is a hardy perennial which persists in plaguing us. One of the special considerations in planning for older people is that of knowing that there is strength in the person's own drive for what he may want and for evaluating his ability to carry out his own plan, and along with that, the strength of the forces which may exercise definite control upon that drive or may even counteract it completely. These modifying controls are to be found in the social, health, and economic needs of the individuals which cannot be denied attention.

Studies made of large numbers of older people will give objective evidence of the range of housing accommodations which will be needed if we are to take into consideration the modifying con-

[4]*Approved Standards and Suggestions for Homes for the Aged of the Methodist Church*, Bd. of Hospitals and Homes of the Methodist Church, Chicago; *Kansas Law and Standards, Rules and Regulations for Adult Boarding Homes, 1952,* Kan. Dept. Social Welfare; *Standards for Maintenance and Operation of Nursing Homes—Including Construction Standards for Existing and New Structures, 1952,* Wis. Bd. Health.

[5] *Man and His Years* (Raleigh, N.C.: Health Publications Institute, Inc., 1951).

trols which Miss Randall enumerates. We need to classify with great care the housing expectations of a wide range of people in order to arrive at a more complete view of those essentials which should be incorporated into planned housing for elderly people of different cultural levels and interests.

Studies of Housing Preferences

It has already been pointed out that only a few studies have been made of the housing preferences of older people. The most salient fact emerging from those studies which have been reported is the almost universal desire for continued independence in living arrangements.

In Manhattan, Kansas, a survey of fifty older families revealed that their first preference was to continue living in their present homes. Poor health did not alter their desire for independent living arrangements. In the event of illness, they indicated that they would want to continue to live in their own homes under the care of a nurse or companion. If this arrangement were not possible, they would, as a last choice, live with their children but would want separate quarters in their children's homes.[6]

The same wish for independence was shown in a survey of 6,000 people who had retired or were approaching retirement. This group, composed largely of families in the higher income brackets, also wanted the privacy of living in their own homes. Two thirds preferred a single-family detached dwelling with two or more bedrooms built on a larger than average lot.[7]

At the University of Illinois a survey was made of 130 retired faculty members to determine their housing preferences. The oldest members of the group wanted elevator apartments and all members preferred individual renting. A campus site was preferred and such special services and facilities were stipulated as community dining rooms, drugstore and small grocery, commu-

[6]Elinor M. Anderson, *Existing and Preferred Housing of Aged Couples of Moderate Income in Manhattan, Kansas* (unpublished master's thesis, Kan. State Teacher's Coll. of Agriculture and Applied Science, 1951).

[7]*Housing Preferences of Older People* (Minneapolis: Investors Diversified Services, Inc., 1952). (Mimeographed.)

nity lounge, social and recreational rooms, community laundry, hobby and study areas, and parking space. These people would like to have maid service but do not want a nurse or a physician in residence, preferring instead to make their own arrangements for medical care.[8]

A study of retired people in St. Petersburg, Florida, indicates that both men and women wish to live in self-owned detached dwellings. The next most preferred arrangement would be to live with another person of the same sex in a single dwelling. In no instance was a choice made of a facility of the rooming-house type with a central dining service.[9]

The same disinterest in communal types of housing was evidenced in a recent survey made of the needs expressed by older people in Grand Rapids, Michigan. Almost half of the sample interviewed reported some dissatisfaction with present living arrangements, and almost a quarter wanted to change their housing; no one indicated a desire to move into an old age home or other type of congregate arrangement, including the homes of sons and daughters.[10]

On the other hand, in a survey of the aged in the state of Rhode Island, approximately one third of the 2,400 persons admitting dissatisfaction with their housing indicated that they would like a congregate arrangement in which they could maintain their own quarters and yet be near other old people and have access to communal facilities for recreation, housekeeping, and the like. Half of the 2,400 dissatisfied people said that they would prefer to live independently rather than with children

[8]Jack Baker, "The Student Looks at Emeritus Housing," A part of a discussion-demonstration at the University of Michigan Fifth Annual Conference on Aging, Ann Arbor. More detailed information can be obtained from Professor Baker, School of Architecture, Univ. Ill.

[9]Irving L. Webber, *The Retired Population of Florida: Its Characteristics and Social Situation* (Tallahassee: Fla. State Improvement Comm., 1950).

[10]Woodrow Hunter and Helen Maurice, *Older People Tell Their Story* (Ann Arbor: Div. Gerontol., Instit. Human Adjustment, Univ. Mich., 1954).

or relatives.[11] It may be that if more studies were made of the desires of the very old people or of those who are in poor health, we would find a stronger trend toward a preference for communal and sheltered care facilities. Also, we might find that there would be less resistance to becoming a member of the household of a son or daughter.

Reasons why older people reject living with other members of their families were reported in a study of old age security recipients in Los Angeles County. The study reports "an overwhelming majority of these recipients living with relatives are not particularly happy due to such factors as uncongenial relatives, crowded conditions in the home, and/or annoyances of small children in the home. There has also been some feeling among recipients living with relatives that they are not wanted, that they are in the way, or that they are a burden on their relatives." It would appear that the aged person would prefer to live alone, but health reasons or limited income make such arrangements impractical or impossible.[12]

In a study of the adjustment of women living under various arrangements, it was found that a larger percentage of those living in their own homes or living in rooming houses or old age homes made better adjustment scores on a test of interests and attitudes than of those living in the homes of other people.[13] Findings such as these make imperative the provision of living facilities in which the older person may continue in independent status and in which he is able to have some self-determination about the extent of his dependency on others.

Pertinent to housing preferences of older people is the question of the extent to which migration may be expected to take place among them after their retirement from the labor force. Accord-

[11]*Old Age in Rhode Island,* Gov.'s Comm. to Study Problems of the Aged, Providence, 1953.

[12]"Housing Conditions Among Recipients of Old Age Security Living in Los Angeles County," Unpublished rept., Bureau of Public Assistance, April, 1950. Quoted in *Report of Subcommittee on Housing for the Aging,* Welfare Counc. Metropol. Los Angeles.

[13]Ruth S. Cavan, "Family Life and Family Substitutes in Old Age," *Amer. Sociol. Rev.,* Feb., 1949, p. 83.

ing to the United States Census, in 1949 only one half of 1 per cent of people aged sixty-five and over moved to a state that was not contiguous to them. In a study of a typical midwestern city, in 1942, it was found that of the people aged fifty-nine, 40 per cent moved at least once during the ensuing six years, and about half of these moves involved change of residence to a different community. Only 2 per cent of the group sixty-five and over migrated to the south or southwest during the six-year period.[14]

A study of 223 retired employees (men and women) of a large metropolitan department store was made to determine the extent of migration among the group and to isolate any factors related to this tendency. Only about 15 per cent of the group migrated. Factors found to favor this changing of residence included a weekly pre-retirement income of $70.00 or more, a company retirement benefit of at least $40.00 or more a month, a preretirement residence in the suburbs, a medium pay mobility index (based upon the number of changes in rate of pay within the period of service), and a tendency to move frequently after retirement.[15]

The Upholsterers' International Union of North America has made a study of the preferences of their members for retirement to Florida as a part of the Union's preparation for establishing a retirement village in that state. Union members were interviewed in Chicago, Kankakee, and Milwaukee. The outcomes varied according to the city in which the worker lived. Those interviewed in Chicago were more favorable to migrating to Florida after retirement than were those interviewed in the other two cities. The differences in reaction have been interpreted to mean that the workers in Chicago were normally a more mobile group than those in Kankakee and Milwaukee. It is assumed that the people in the latter two cities have struck their roots more deeply in their communities.[16]

[14]Robert J. Havighurst and Ruth Albrecht, *Older People* (New York: Longmans, Green and Co., 1953), pp. 164-65.

[15]Charles R. Manley, Jr., "The Migration of Older People," *Amer. Journ. Sociol.*, 59(1954):324-31.

[16]"Evaluation of Upholsterers' International Union Group Discussions on Proposed Florida Retirement Village" (Chicago: The Industrial Relations Center, Univ. Chicago, 1953). (Mimeographed.)

Although the Kankakee and Milwaukee union members may have chosen to remain in their home cities in the belief that they would be happier than if they moved to a new locality, this may not necessarily be true. Actually, individuals who have migrated appear to be as well adjusted as those who remain in their home communities.[17] Of course, one might assume that those people who do migrate are those who can find just as great satisfaction in a new community as in their old ones.

What Older Individuals Recommend

A few older people have been articulate in stating with some specificity the type of living arrangement they prefer and why. For example, one man makes a plea for what he calls a new kind of old people's home.[18] He says:

A cottage for two with room for twenty, that's what my wife and I are looking for, a big living-kitchen plus a bedroom is all that we need for ourselves. But when the young ones come, that is something else again. So we are in rebellion against the doll house (dog house) our solicitous children think would be just wonderful for the old dears. . . We have designed the kind of retirement home *we* think we need. . . . It consists of three parts: that living-kitchen and bedroom on the main floor, a basement playroom for family parties below, an attic dormitory for as many of the offspring as can be happily huddled together. . . We are crusading for 12,000,000 other oldsters who want some years of *living* at the end.

It is interesting to note that this plea is made for all oldsters and yet the plan outlined as the ideal old people's home does not suit the desires of another elderly gentleman in any respect. In discussing the changing conditions and their effects upon the housing needs of older people, he says: "I am myself a perfect example of the (changing) situation. I am eighty-two years of age. My wife died six years ago, and I am living alone and having all my meals by myself. I am often very lonely. Each of my children

[17]A'delbert P. Sanson and William G. Mather, *Personal and Social Adjustment of 49 Retired Rural Men*, Progress Rept. No. 19 (State College: Pa. State Coll., School of Agriculture, 1950).

[18]Frank A. Cooper, "Wanted, a New Kind of Old People's Home," *Amer. Home*, Jan., 1952, p. 18.

has asked me to live with him or her—no one of them has the room or the quiet an old fellow like me requires, and there would be nothing for me to do."[19] His ideal old age home is one which would be built on a college campus where educational and cultural advantages would be readily accessible. He recommends a central building housing about 150 old people and with offices, special rooms such as auditorium, clubrooms, classrooms, parlor, library, music room, infirmary, kitchen, and dining room. Around the central building would be enough smaller buildings housing about fifty people each to provide for a total of three or four hundred. Most of the rooms would be singles with baths, some would also have grills and refrigerators. But the major requirement for this home is that it should be under the supervision of someone who has a liking for old people and who is able to develop friendliness and co-operation among the residents. Self-government, sharing of cars, planned activities, and the establishment of family-type relationships would provide the incentives for helping to fill the gap of loneliness.

The major differences between the exponents of these two plans are immediately apparent. In the first instance the wife is living, and there is still a solid family core from which major satisfactions and affectional needs are satisfied. The man who has lost his wife and is growing frail besides has the same need for companionship and happy participation in things he considers important. But to satisfy these needs it is necessary for him to find the kind of living arrangement in which he can make new friends and can establish family substitutes.

Some older people have already put their dreams for a retirement home into material form. One such home was described at the conference reported in this book and has since been reported upon in the literature a number of times.[20] The Strongs were determined not to be slaves to a home. Their idea of retirement was to give up the large old home built to accommodate their

[19] Henry S. Curtis, "Homes for Retired Teachers," *Nat. Ed. Assn. Journ.*, Nov., 1952, pp. 530-33.

[20] Jack Pickering, "A Home Tailored for Two," *Lifetime Living*, Feb., 1953.

family of five children, and to move into a neat, small house just big enough for two. They wanted a place that would not cost much to run nor require hours of drudgery to maintain. With the assistance of an architect, they designed and built a three-room house which provides ample space for them and which meets the requirements of low-cost upkeep, easy housekeeping, one-story living, ample space to store the treasures kept from the past, and room to sleep overnight guests. After living in the house for more than two years, the Strongs have found that it is costing them less than $8.00 a week to occupy it, including taxes, water, gas, electricity, telephone, heat, and upkeep.

There are a number of other couples in the country who have made the same kind of careful analysis of their needs and have built retirement homes to meet them. The houses are as different as the tastes of the individuals living in them, but all of them are permitting their owners to have the kind of houses they want to live in, an important factor in the total adjustment to the changes taking place with aging.

Housing the Aging

Even a brief review of the opinions and recommendations of the experts and of the preferences of older people makes it evident that much is already known which, if applied, would go far toward solving the problems of housing older people. Why then has not such housing been provided? What are the missing ingredients?

In part, the difficulty lies in the fact that the information which is available has not been widely disseminated. The present poor status of the housing of old people and the extent of the need for better housing in this group are largely the knowledge of specialized groups such as welfare workers and government officials dealing with the elderly. Although the physical features needed in housing especially designed for old people have been defined by a few research groups, this information is not generally known by builders and planners of housing developments.

Often, questions colored by emotion, such as whether special housing of the aging will constitute segregation or discrimination against this minority group, loom large in the thinking of a community or group and interfere with taking action.

Another deterrent to action has been the debate centering about the topic of what constitutes the best type of housing for the aging. Some people advocate the establishment of retirement villages, others point out that the separate old people's towns built in the Scandinavian countries have been given up as undesirable. Most planners in this country advocate the inclusion of old age housing within the limits of a community, but so far there is little agreement upon what is to be included in such facilities.

Lack of recognized standards for the building of old people's homes and hospitals and for the care of old people has been an inhibiting factor to the building of these facilities because each group had to carry out research and establish standards before work could be started. The determination and acceptance of approved standards would greatly simplify the task of planners and builders.

The failure of builders and contractors to recognize that older people represent a market potential of considerable size has left the private market for individual dwellings virtually unserved. It has been commonly assumed that housing the aging is a matter of concern only to those who have responsibility for the poor and the sick. Also, three-generation housing and the provision of houses for young people which are flexible enough to serve as lifetime homes are still fairly new concepts among modern builders.

Older people, although wanting to remain independently in their own homes, have done little to provide themselves, even when financially able to do so, with new housing adapted to their changed needs. This is surprising when they are aware that frailty and illness are always imminent in old age and that few communities have services such as housekeeping, nursing, and home medical care, which make it feasible to continue living in their own homes until they are very old.

The major barrier today to providing housing for the aging, public or private, has been the unavailability of the usual sources of housing capital. The Federal Housing Acts of 1937 and 1940 providing federal funds for public housing projects were limited to the construction of dwellings to be occupied by families. Although an elderly couple qualifies as a family unit, local authorities tended to discriminate against the older couple because of the probability that one of the pair would soon die and leave the other as a single individual who would then have to be asked to move to make way for a family. State and local funds have also been intended largely for the housing of young families. Even in the few instances in which special provision has been made to serve the older age group, the amount of housing allocated to their use has been woefully inadequate. Insurance companies have considered it inadvisable to undertake low-rent housing projects requiring more than a twenty-five year amortization period, a condition difficult to meet if rents are to be kept within the range which older people can pay. Venture capital has not been interested in housing projects for the aged because the financial status of the majority of older people does not make it possible for them to pay rents high enough to ensure the high rate of interest required by the private investor and to retire the initial loan in a relatively short time.

In general, in the past, housing for old people has been financed by philanthropy and by public funds spent for poor farms and almshouses and hospitals. Only a very limited amount of private capital has been employed. The result has been a few good old age homes, a large number of substandard facilities, and almost no homes built specifically to serve the large mass of the old age group.

Conclusion

In summary, we find that we already have a sufficient amount of information from which to draw conclusions about where and how older people want to live. Old people and experts agree that a prime requisite of housing is one which provides for maximum of independence and privacy regardless of whether it is a communal- or individual-type dwelling. This does not mean, however, that older people are seeking isolation. On the contrary, they want housing of an appropriate type situated in close proximity to community services, to members of their families, and to the homes of their friends. Most of them want to continue to live in their home communities, but if they migrate they want to live as independent families. This independence is a strong characteristic which is not forfeited until frailty or illness necessitates the security of sheltered care. Although there are many factors which have delayed the building of adequate numbers and kinds of housing for old people, the greatest of barriers have been, first, the lack of education of old people, builders, and planners regarding what is already known about housing, and second, the failure to make financial resources available for the purpose of building homes for older people.

Housing Well Older People

PART II

PLANNING CONSIDERATIONS
IN URBAN COMMUNITIES   *Chapter IV*

BY EDMOND H. HOBEN

Edmond H. Hoben, M.Sc., is urban studies specialist, Division of Housing Research, of the Housing and Home Finance Agency, Washington, D.C. His experience in housing and community planning goes back to 1932 when he was executive secretary of the Mayor's Housing Commission in Milwaukee, Wisconsin. From 1948 to 1950, he was executive director of the Minneapolis Housing and Redevelopment Authority. He was coeditor of the Housing Year Books, National Association of Housing Officials, *from 1935 to 1943; author of the annual housing and planning article for* Encyclopedia Americana, 1941-1944, *and of numerous articles in periodicals such as* The American Journal of Economics, Journal of Land and Public Utility Economics, *and* The Annals of the American Academy of Political and Social Sciences. *He is a member of the American Society of Planning Officials, the National Association of Housing Officials, and the National Housing Conference.*

IN PLANNING the physical development of a community one cannot neglect the social aspects. In fact, there is no such thing in today's cities as dwellings that constitute adequate housing in themselves. Only when a pattern of the various services for health, safety, education, recreation, and so forth is laid over the fabric of land and buildings is there created the garment of good environment which we call housing in the fullest sense.

Thus a broad attack on the problem of housing well older people will lead us into the whole battlefield of community planning, theory, and practice. Here, even before we are challenged by the specialized needs of our senior citizens, we are subject to a barrage of doubts about the validity of some of the predominant patterns of urban growth.

Perhaps it is not right to use the word "pattern" to describe the arrangement of land use in much of urban America—at least, if the word "pattern" is taken to indicate the result of conscious design and direction. It was the lack of pattern, with its resulting damage to economic and human values, that constituted a prime motive for the development of means for guiding land use. These means include formulation of an over-all scheme (sometimes called a master plan) and the implementation of this scheme through such devices as subdivision regulations, zoning ordinances, and building codes. But the master plans have given scant attention to the needs of the older population, and even have been antagonistic.

Trends in Residential Growth

Of the various regulations for controlling building developments, the zoning function is of particular importance in considering housing arrangements for older people. Originally, zoning was looked upon largely as a device to prevent one type of land use from damaging another. Thus, industries and commerce were banned from residential areas. As zoning practice developed further, there was considerable trend toward further subdividing the kinds of residential uses. So we have in many places several classes of areas for single family homes, areas for two-family homes, and areas for structures for three or more families.

This increasing segregation of dwelling types, by law, plus the inclination of like families to group together, and the inclination of builders operating in unregulated areas to build the easiest way, have lead to pronounced stratification in newer residential areas. We now see frequent cases of entire areas devoted to homes uniform in age, size, and price, and, all too frequently, in design. Into these homes are supposed to fit most of our families who, for one reason or another, are in the housing market. These persons who constitute the market range, in terms of size, from the single person to the family with a half dozen children; in terms of income, from the $3,000-a-year clerk to the tycoon; and in terms of age, from the young newlyweds to the golden wedding couple.

Concurrent with the growth of the single-type subdivision has been an increasing tendency toward the exclusion of stores from residential areas and the grouping of new stores in large concentrations in outlying sections. The disappearance of the neighborhood stores may work a hardship on the older people, particularly, on those of limited mobility. We know, of course, that changes in retailing practice are shaped by forces much stronger than the convenience of the relatively small group of purchasers represented by the elderly. Nevertheless, the community planners would do well to blend with their enthusiasm for gigantic regional shopping centers some concern for designating locations for small and less widely spaced commercial facilities.

The corner store has a very useful function. It has been classed as a bad companion for homes usually because of its obtrusive position on the lot and its unsightly appearance. There is no reason why local shopping areas cannot be fashioned to be harmonious with good residential neighborhoods. The aged are not the only people who would like to be able to get a loaf of bread or an aspirin within a short walking distance.

While these changes have been taking place on the outskirts of the city, the center, because of creeping blight, has been becoming less habitable. By and large, the first occupants of the vast recent additions to our housing supply are families that have not reached their maximum size. They experience a series of moves—just ahead of or behind the stork.

Effects of Residential Growth on Housing

Our chief interest here, of course, is in how these trends in residential growth and housing supply affect the housing opportunities of the older population. Let us take first the largest single group of the old people—the couples maintaining their own households. The chances are that many of them own houses that are larger than necessary, and that are located in an older part of town subject to actual or incipient blighting. Many of these will continue to live out their lives in reasonable comfort in such a situation. Yet, there are many others who will find the old homestead too much of a burden. Their first necessary choice, then, would be between staying in town or joining the exodus led by the families seeking green pastures for their children. In an "in town" location there is rarely anything suitable in size to buy—even if they could get enough from the sale of their old house to undertake buying another. The probable other "in-town" choices, then, are to reduce the size of their home by subdividing it, or to rent a small unit in an older building—probably in a walk-up apartment building or in a large old house that has been converted to small units.

Unfortunately, at present such conversion of large houses into smaller units is clandestine. Frequently, the zoning ordinance does not recognize the impossibility of the continued use of the grand old mansion by a sole surviving matriarch or even by an aging couple. The house becomes a sort of unofficial rooming house, or it is devoted to housing several families without making any adequate changes in structure or equipment. But some communities are now aware of the need for permitting and guiding orderly transition; and while the general appearance of the neighborhood is protected by limitations on exterior alterations, they require basic provisions for safety and sanitation.

Possibly one of the deterrents to legal conversion, even when zoning permits, is the common requirement of building or health codes that an entire structure be brought up to the standards of new construction when substantial alterations are made. There might well be considered, for conversion purposes, some standards between the scant ones for existing housing and the extensive ones for new housing.

The prospect of renting anything new in an "in-town" location is not good. Even an efficiency apartment in a newer building is likely to be too expensive for Mr. and Mrs. Average Old Folks. Anyway, there is doubt about the adequacy of such condensed quarters for an elderly couple.

The Senior Companion Apartment

A need for some form of accommodation better suited in terms of design and price is indicated. Dr. Hertha Kraus of Bryn Mawr has suggested a form of group dwelling which she calls the "senior companion apartment." It would house seven persons, some of whom would be couples. Because it does not afford complete food preparation and bathroom facilities for each of the seven units, it could be constructed for less than a regular apartment building. There is a further possibility that such accommodation could be made available by remodeling the ground floor of a large house.

Zoning problems. Where could such a building be located in the community? In Los Angeles, it would probably be classed as a lodging house and, therefore, would be permitted in the same zone as large multifamily dwellings, small hotels and apartment hotels, and institutions of a philanthropic nature. It could not be in a single family zone, because in Los Angeles a family consisting of unrelated persons cannot have more than five members. Up the coast in San Francisco, the group of seven persons envisioned in the Kraus plan might be defined as a family and therefore admissible to a single family dwelling zone.

The same sort of structure in Des Moines could not even class as a boarding house, because there a boarding house must serve not more than six people. It might be considered a club, however, and thus could be located in the same area as hospitals, clinics, and hotels for transients.

Regulations in St. Petersburg are quite accommodating— probably reflecting the locality's financial interest in caring for the inactive elderly. There, if classed as a guest house, it could go into the best residential districts. As a boarding house it would be permitted in two-family districts. If the city authorities, however, deemed that the proposed unit was devoted to "housing and caring for the aged, convalescents, physically unfit, except persons suffering from mental ailments and persons so ill as to require regular hospitalization" it would be classed as a "restorium."

As such, it would go into the zone which includes hotels, clubs, and so forth.

In general, our zoning ordinances show a common tendency to view as harmful to a residential neighborhood accommodations for persons with mental or marked physical disabilities. As we strive to give the elderly a wider choice of how and where to live, this view should be re-examined. Apparently, one or two physically incapacitated or mentally deficient persons can be cared for as relatives in the best family homes in the most exclusive districts. The reasons for excluding structures for the organized care of such people from almost all one- or two-family districts should be reviewed. There are many degrees of mental or physical incapacity. It could well be that some form of group dwelling which started out with a relatively "normal" clientele of oldsters would become, because of deterioration of the occupants, a place for rendering nursing care. Would it then become a nonconforming use in its district?

It is worth considering whether giving greater attention in our planning regulations to density of land use, parking provisions, and provision for privacy would be an adequate substitute for the present emphasis on the exact nature of the use to which a building is put.

Community Considerations

What are the conclusions from this abbreviated review of the applicability of local controls to particular types of group living arrangements? It is clear that one of the first things to do in considering a type is to see how it would be classified as to permissible locations within the city. It may turn out that available locations are largely in blighted areas. This suggests the possibility of relating to urban re-development activities part of a program for housing the aging in new central areas. Through redevelopment, large blighted or slum areas can be cleared and the land can be made available for new uses at prevailing market prices that do not have to include the costs of eliminating the accumulated errors of the past. The major promise of urban redevelopment as regards the elderly is not that its site cost write-down mechanism alone will bring the cost of housing within reach of this group. Rather, the promise is availability of a good environment in near central locations which are desirable for many of the old people. Here could be built new housing of several types, including some units for the senior population.

If our average oldsters decide to go out to the edge of town they find miles of two-bedroom houses that have been produced in vast quantities during the record-breaking period of the past three years. These, while they are adequate in size for an aging couple, are often too expensive. Further, these new houses usually are beyond the criss-cross single-fare network of public transportation which, in the more central areas, affords an opportunity to travel in any direction at low cost and in relatively short time. Dependence upon friends or relatives with cars, even for daily shopping, might result in a degree of isolation particularly undesirable for the elderly. The typical two-bedroom house, which is somewhat large or beyond the means of an aged couple alone, is too small for the full life cycle of most families with more than one child. It is certainly too small for a family with children that would like to share its home with the older generation. Yet the sharing arrangement is one under which the second largest group of our elderly persons live.

The Three-generation Household

Some of the psychologists and sociologists may view with alarm the three-generation family. Nevertheless, there are good reasons for seeing what could be done to make such a household more workable. The provision of an annex or wing for grandpa and grandma is worthy of trial. Such a subdwelling unit would presumably not have complete facilities for food preparation. It might well have access to the principal family unit at some point like the dining or living space. Even a free-standing subunit or one attached by a breezeway would afford an opportunity for sharing the facilities of the principal unit.

Experimentation with homes designed specifically for three-generation use will raise certain problems of community planning. First, this type of building, consisting of a usual one-story home plus a one-story wing, would require a lot larger than normal or would require some scaling down of yard requirements. Second, a determination would have to be made as to whether it constituted a one-family or two-family dwelling. The legal restrictions of uses in districts of single-family detached dwellings find their counterpart—or perhaps their origin—in the strong feeling that variation in dwelling types represents a depreciating influence. This feeling probably stems from observation of the ravages wrought by uncontrolled intrusion of multifamily and commercial uses into residential areas.

Need for Comprehensive Planning

Perhaps the controls that we have set up are forcing such compartmentalizing of land uses that they are rendering a disservice to all age groups. One of the difficulties in seeking to achieve more varied neighborhood composition, both as regards structures and people, is the use of the lot as a unit of control. Regulations have to be such, that even when each lot is put to its most intense use, the health, safety, and welfare of the community are not endangered. In recent years, our courts are evincing an inclination to consider the protection of amenities as well. This makes the lot-by-lot method of control even more difficult.

Community planning for the aged, as for the younger elements in our cities, calls more and more for positive design on a neighborhood scale. Such neighborhood designs, particularly when they incorporate large projects of rental housing, do not lend themselves to testing by the specific requirements of our usual ordinances. Rather, they call for evaluation in terms of the objectives instead of the specifics of our land use and housing regulations. The city planning commission or other body charged with review of neighborhood development proposals that do not fall in the mold set by codes must develop an acute sense of the values that comprise a good urban environment. In turn, our municipal legislative bodies will have to be prepared to stand up for some departures from piecemeal city building.

We should not expect, however, that specific proposals for housing for oldsters are going to originate in city planning commissions or city councils. Such plans will usually be the product of private groups that have an extraordinary combination of vision and realism. It is likely that financial support of some foundation or trust will be required, not only to keep rents low, but to sustain a proposal through the long and trying period required for "adjustments" to anything different in city building. Few, if any, private profit seeking organizations—financial or building—are likely to be willing to sustain the cost of the pioneering that is required.

Like most city planners I have fallen into the error of talking largely in big-city terms. My plea, however, for avoiding extreme compartmentalization of land uses and building types might well be heard in smaller places that are tempted to copy the big city. The town of 5,000 has a personalized set of relationships which could well be maintained when seeking means of housing the aged. In these places, the man sitting on the park bench is likely to be known as "Grandpa Jones" and not as an aging statistic.

Summary

I would summarize the main points in the planning program as follows:

1. The basic objective of keeping a place for our older citizens in the main parade of life requires providing housing that is distributed widely throughout the community.

2. Zoning ordinances and related land use controls should be examined critically to see whether they are creating a stratification of population which not only freezes out the old people but also creates neighborhoods suitable for use by a family during only a very short part of its life cycle.

3. Development of varied neighborhoods will require a large-scale rather than a lot-by-lot method of city building.

4. Current emphasis on large widely spaced shopping centers should not cause us to overlook the importance of the smaller convenient shopping center—particularly for the aged.

5. Private groups usually will have to undertake the pioneering work in developing and carrying out proposals for better housing for the aging.

THE BUILDING INDUSTRY AND
HOUSING THE AGING *Chapter V*

BY EARL C. DOYLE

> *Earl C. Doyle is executive vice-president of the Builders Association of Metropolitan Detroit and, as such, is the chief full-time staff officer of this organization. He has been connected with the Builders Association since 1945.*

THE NEW CHALLENGE before the home building industry is the problem of housing the aging. Up to the present the industry has largely ignored the problem. But the need is now critical, and private builders must demonstrate that this need can be met. This chapter is concerned, then, with how the problem might be approached.

Present Position of the Industry

But, first, to understand the nature of the problem that confronts home builders, it is necessary to briefly review the present position of the industry. The volume of home building in recent years has been unusually high. For example, in 1950, in the Detroit metropolitan area alone, home builders took out building permits for 42,880 dwelling units. The average replacement cost of these units was about $8,500. The total dollar volume of home building that year in the Detroit area was in excess of $364 million and far exceeded the volume of commercial, public, and industrial construction. For the Detroit area, in terms of both units and dollar volume, that was the highest volume of home building of all time. The previous high total in one year was reached in the early 1920's when a total of 33,000 units were built. But since the Korean trouble started, volume has dropped because of restrictions and limitations put on the use of steel, copper, and aluminum. In 1951, the total was about 33,000 units; while in 1952, although total figures are not yet available, the volume will probably be no more than 26,000 units.

Yet even this relatively low figure of 26,000 units is large: it is equal to the number of homes standing in a town of sixty to sixty-five thousand population. When one builds in such volume it is like adding, in dwelling units, a Saginaw or a Lansing each year to the Detroit metropolitan area. And building on so large a scale means also that we are building homes mainly for purchase by families of average means. We are building for a mass market. Significantly enough, the buyers are mainly young wage earners. In terms of social values, we are building to meet the housing needs of the most numerous group of the population, that is, the wage earners in industry and commerce.

Special Problems

We build for the market. But if it is to be a healthy market, it must be defined in terms of the two traditional elements of private industry, the desire for profit, and the necessity to meet a need in order to do business. This is the way we must look upon the problem of housing the aging. On first glance it would seem that one of these conditions, the incentive of profit, is absent. Since the earning power of most aging people is seriously reduced, they are not usually able to pay as much for adequate housing as the young and active wage earner. Here is the crux of the whole matter. Who is to finance these homes for the aging? Who will insure and who will buy the mortgages? But the problem is by no means insurmountable provided that the construction and financing parts of the building industry, our educational institutions, research agencies, and the community in general, recognize the problem and have a will to find the answers.

It should be recognized at the outset that the aging have specialized housing needs. These involve not merely the physical and economic factors of shelter but sociological and particularly psychological factors. What are these specialized needs and how do they differ from the requirements of other kinds of housing? It is not the purpose of this chapter to discuss this problem. But it is important to note here that, according to recent sociological investigation, these needs do not differ essentially from the housing needs of newly married persons.

Cycle of Housing Needs

One of the most significant factors that all must consider, if we are to understand the problem of housing the aging, is the cycle of need for housing that the typical family undergoes. This cycle is not a new human experience. It has been present as long as there have been families, although many of us today appear to see it for the first time. The author became aware of it about fifteen years ago when a close friend sold the large home he had acquired from his father and built a much smaller home for himself and his wife. The story of these transactions exemplifies the nature of the cycle.

It begins with the marriage and the first small home the couple bought to start their lives together. Then came the children, three of them. They grew up, went to school, and the small home bustled with activity. But as the children reached high school age their sphere of interests grew, their personal tastes diverged, they entertained their friends continually, and the father soon realized that the little home where he first brought his bride was no longer big enough for his active family. At the same time, very conveniently, the parents of the author's friend began to feel that the large home where they had raised their family was too much for them, now that their children had gone and they were alone. Here was the solution to both his problem and that of his parents. He bought his father's house on its two and one-half acre lot for his own use, remodeled it and built a new, smaller house for his parents. He and his family found the breathing space that they needed in the ample quarters of the big home, while the grand-parents were better satisfied with the new, smaller home.

Maintaining the home was no problem with everyone pitching in and doing part of the work. The two girls helped their mother with the housework; the son helped the father keep up the lawns, the gardens, and the tennis court. And there was the added help of a man and a woman who worked for them part time. Then the children graduated from college, married, and left the home of their parents. About the same time, the occasional help went away and it seemed impossible to replace them. The mother and father were now alone. The position that the father's parents were in many years before, when they had sold him their home, was now his position—living alone with his wife in a home that had been built for a growing family. In turn, they, too, moved into a new, smaller home which needed less energy to keep up and was more befitting the fewer needs of old age. The pattern of life was approaching full circle.

Here is a typical example of the cycle of housing need. There are first, the needs of the young husband and wife at the beginning of married life. Then, as the husband and wife become parents and the family grows, their housing needs grow correspondingly. And finally, when the children grow up and leave their parental home and the husband and wife are again alone, the needs are reduced. It is a three-phase cycle.

Certain observations on this cycle may be made here. First, the conditions that motivate the changing need are social rather than economic. The cycle operates whether the people involved are poor or rich or in moderate circumstances. Second, the main determining factor is, simply, the size of the family. Third, the minimum of housing facilities can suffice, if necessary, in both the first and last phases. Fourth, granted the need, the degree to which the need can be satisfied in our society is determined by the degree to which it can be paid for. And fifth, it is in the last phase of the cycle, that of old age, where the financial problems are generally most acute. Once again the whole crux of the matter is reduced to the economic.

The Need to Provide Lifetime Housing

And once again we must ask the question, how is this housing need to be financed? Whether or not it can be paid for, the need remains and must be satisfied. How is the building industry to meet the challenge of housing the aging? There is one method which may go far to alleviate the financial obstacles in the way. Since the cycle of need is normal, or usual, it would be wise for people to plan their lives accordingly. Even while they are paying for the home in which they are raising their family, they should be looking ahead to meet the ultimate needs of their old age. When you plan for the future you are less likely to be caught short.

Most of us have neglected to plan for our later years simply because we have scarcely thought of this last stage of housing need. There are many reasons for this neglect. Mainly, the reason is that people just live from day to day. Life in the present is enough to preoccupy them without concerning themselves with the future. When it is hard to meet the payments on the mortgage or pay the bill for the washing machine, it is understandable why people are not seriously concerned with planning to get enough money for the home of their old age.

Yet awareness of the cycle, and particularly of its last phase, should sharpen the home buyer's vigilance so that even while buying the parental home he should be concerned with its liquidation when the time finally comes. If a long-trend inflation of real estate prices continues, it will probably require ready savings as well as the net proceeds from the liquidation. Thus the necessity for prudent saving for this purpose is ever present. Too many people have the mistaken notion that their parental home will yield enough when liquidated to provide the purchase price of the final dwelling. And there are many who even expect their parental home to be suitable for the older years. It becomes obvious, then, that a program of education is needed to explain some of the physical, social, and economic factors that determine housing needs today.

Need for Education About Housing

The home-building industry favors such educational endeavor, and will give it moral and even financial support. For the people must be alerted and informed if the problem of housing the aging is to be solved.

There are various forms which the education program might take. There is the curricular form. For example, Wayne University has a course in the art of living. The Detroit Builder's Association has contemplated providing a typical, moderate-priced home for use on the campus for this course. Educational institutions can also provide information through adult classes, and through extension courses. The home-building industry and related industries can do much by offering publicity to the press. Speakers can expound this subject. The Builder's Association of Metropolitan Detroit can do much through its annual builders show.

But to succeed with the educational approach there must be much fact-finding, which calls for research, based on case histories and indisputable first-hand facts. The data furnished by the Housing and Home Finance Agency from census sources is helpful. The HHFA should be encouraged to further research in this field. The Detroit Builder's Association might be persuaded to undertake financing such research on a modest scale.

These are some of the ways that the home building industry might approach the problem of housing the aging. They are by no means conclusive. In fact, the industry has only begun to consider the problem. But there is one approach, however, which the builders will vigorously oppose. That is public housing. Public housing may appear to some persons as the quick and easy solution; but it is the socialistic answer and out of harmony with the basic concepts of American life. Therefore, it cannot be considered as a solution at all. The way of free enterprise may be more indirect and more difficult, but maintaining a free society is always a difficult job, and is becoming more so. The only way to solve the problem of housing the aging must be the American way. And that way will be found by the builders of America.

Conclusion

In conclusion, I want to add that the problem of housing aging people is important and urgent, but it is comparatively new. Consequently, there are housing problems affecting other elements of the population that are ahead of it, at least as far as the home-building industry is concerned. We, for instance, are greatly interested in slum rebuilding through private enterprise working with government. Also, we are confronted by the need for suitable new housing for Negroes. All this is, of course, superimposed upon the building problems which spread over a wide range. There is, therefore, much need to bring the problems of housing the aging to the attention of the builders and to help them find methods for meeting the need.

DESIGNING HOMES
FOR THE AGING *Chapter VI*

BY I. S. LOEWENBERG

> *Israel Sidney Loewenberg, B.S., is architect and partner of Loewenberg and Loewenberg, Architects and Engineers, Chicago. He is also a member of the Board of Directors and treasurer of the Welfare Council of Metropolitan Chicago, a member of the Board of Directors of the Jewish Federation of Chicago, and chairman of the Council on the Care of the Aged and Chronic Sick of the Jewish Federation. His publications include the articles "Architectural Aspects of Housing for the Aged" and "Ideal Home for the Aged." Mr. Loewenberg is a member of the American Institute of Architects and the Illinois Society of Architects.*

The Approach

THERE IS A considerable shortage of adequate housing facilities of all types, independent and congregate, for aging people. This is the compelling basis from which the whole problem of housing the aging must be viewed.

In approaching the problem, the architect should be guided by several principles. First, in the design of homes for the aging, he should remember that older people have the needs that are common to all people, but they also have special needs owing to the fact that they are old people. Second, he should recognize the fact that older people are individuals, human beings—not a group of people—and need various types of housing and living arrangements. He should know and understand their physical and psychological status, their economic level, and their own preferences.

The housing needs of the comparatively well, older person may be met through regular community housing facilities, both public and private, or through special housing projects in which people of any age group might live. Older people with varying degrees of disability may be able to remain in their own homes with provisions for home services. A relatively small percentage of older people need housing especially designed for them, such as institutional homes for the aged, nursing homes, and chronic sick hospitals.

In the design of regular community housing, both public and private, we should recognize the fact that aging is accompanied by physical decline, that there is a greater frequency of illness and physical handicap, that life is less active. While, in terms of comfort and healthful living, old and young people should have the same type of housing, it is quite evident that the physical needs of the aging demand that these factors be given more careful consideration.

Special Needs

What are some of these special needs in the design of homes for the aged? First, and most important, is that the design of their special provisions be incorporated in the plan in as thoughtful and unobtrusive a way as possible. The living arrangements should be normal in every way, but embodying everything that recognizes the human needs of an older person. The living arrangements should be on one floor with no steps or ramps. Every multiple story building should be provided with an elevator. The building should have a ground floor entrance. Because older people are more housebound, it is desirable that the building be oriented so that at least the bedroom and living room have some sunshine during the day. Rooms should have large glass areas to increase the sense of expansion of horizon. Windows should be placed to obtain good exposure to prevailing summer breezes. Large windows will also secure more daylight. The building should be heated approximately 8° higher temperature than required for younger people. It should have increased artificial lighting and be more uniformly distributed. Doors and partitions should be wider to accommodate a wheelchair if it becomes necessary. Floors should be nonskid. Bathrooms should have grab bars at water closet and bathtub. Thresholds at doors should be eliminated. Shelving should be lowered to avoid the use of stepladders. Kitchens should be all electric, and designed so that housekeeping is simple and no steps wasted, no bending over, climbing, or excessive reaching. They should have laborsaving devices such as garbage disposers, and should be large enough for eating purposes. Rooms, generally, need not be large. Closet space should be ample. All surfaces should be readily washable and there should be no dust-catching projections.

Statistical Considerations

While these and many other characteristics are advisable in homes for the aging, we need to have more factual information about the home and living arrangement needs of older people who wish to remain in their own homes; and considerable research is needed to develop standards that will meet the special problems of adequate housing for them.

Of the statistical data available on housing for the aging, there are two points of particular significance: (1) that approximately 70 per cent of households with heads sixty-five years or more are owner-occupied, and (2) that 64 per cent of all households with heads sixty-five years or over have annual incomes under $2,000.

On an individual basis, L. S. Silk says: "Over 80 per cent of the urban and rural non-farm families of people 65 years of age and over maintain independent households. Generally speaking, their housing circumstances are worse than those of the rest of the population. The aged tend to occupy relatively very low rent dwelling units and low value structures and their housing is relatively more dilapidated and deficient in plumbing facilities."[1]

Mr. Wilber J. Cohen has reported that "the income of 2,100,000 aged is under $500 per year, 2,300,000 aged have

[1] L. S. Silk, "Housing Characteristics of the Aging in the United States." *Journ. Gerontol.*, Suppl. No. 3, 6 (1951). (Abstract.)

incomes from $500 to $999, and 1,600,000 aged have incomes from $1,000 to $1,999."[2]

The above data clearly indicate: *(a)* that the majority of the people in the older age group prefer to live in some kind of family household, if possible; and *(b)* that the majority of people in the older age group are in the lower income group and cannot pay an economic rent for private housing that is being built today. Building costs are too high and incomes are too low. This problem is not a new one and exists among the lower income group of all our people, but because of the very large percentage of older people who are in the very low income group, the distress created by poor housing for them is more widespread.

Public Housing

Public housing should help solve part of this problem. At present, housing authorities, because of the general housing shortage, have given first consideration to families with children. Also, under present legislation, federal housing projects have been unable to admit the single older person. But it is important that the tenant's selection policy be modified and the law be changed to accommodate the ever-growing number of single older people. With the large public housing projects now being undertaken, it is essential that planning for these projects take into consideration the inclusion of a proportional number of smaller units specifically designed to meet the needs of older people, with provisions for the operation of special home services where necessary. Local housing authorities already have a background of experience in management of large-scale rental housing and some experience in housing older people. They should be encouraged to develop various experimental types of dwelling units and services as pilot jobs for extensive study and research. It would offer a real opportunity for experimentation in a limited way, before assuming a large-scale program of national scope.

[2]Wilber J. Cohen, "Income Maintenance for the Aged," *Ann. Amer. Acad. Pol. and Soc. Sci.*, 279 (1952):154-63.

Independent Congregate Housing

There is a great need for progressive, administrative planning to provide independent congregate living arrangements for older people, with provisions for special services, such as friendly visiting and counseling, homemaker service, recreation, library, and hospital extension services. A small number of projects of this type have been organized throughout the country.

Tompkins Square House in New York City has a long-established and successful program in this area of housing. A few of the other examples are the apartment house project of the Home for Aged and Infirm Hebrews and the Fort Green housing project, both of New York City, the co-operative residences in Washington state, and a few other smaller projects in various sections of the country. Sweden, Denmark, and England have gone much farther in developing housing projects with various types of home services than we have. We have barely scratched the surface in this very important field of housing for our older people.

The development of adequate domestic living arrangements for our aging will help to solve many community problems. It would, for example, relieve the tremendous pressure for institutional care and, at the same time, save capital investment for costly institutional construction.

Institutional Homes for the Aged

Only a small part of our aged population need special social service assistance as well as medical care. But while their percentage is not great, numerically they represent a very large group of people. Our homes for the aged, therefore, should plan their programs toward meeting a community need in place of functioning as isolated little islands. A modern, progressive home for the aged is a social agency and should be a part of the community's network of services developed for the care of people who need help. The design of a home for the aged will depend entirely on the program of care contemplated, the admission policy of the home, and the social attitude of its board of directors in its relationship to the total community. A modern, progressive home for the aged should admit:

1. The sick, aged person who does not need general hospital care but does need a certain amount of nursing and medical care, to whom we generally refer as a person whose illness is irreversible.

2. The comparatively well, aged person who is unable to adjust with his family and friends, in his own home, or in a boarding home.

3. The chronically ill, aged person who, from a social and psychological point of view, needs protective care and help.

The home might be a structure or a group of structures with provisions for segregation of the comparatively well, aged, the temporary sick, and the custodial and chronic sick. Yet a resident in the home, if transferred from one section to another, should not have the feeling of being uprooted. The home should be affiliated or have a working agreement with a general hospital for acute illness of the residents. If possible, the medical program of the home should be supervised by the medical staff of the general hospital.

Location. The home should be located in a neighborhood which is easily accessible to transportation, church, shopping facilities, movies, and libraries, and, if possible, near a general hospital. The grounds should be large enough to contain a garden area for the use of the residents.

The design for a home for the aged will be determined to a large extent by the number of residents it will contain. A small home of fifty or sixty beds will not be able to plan the all-inclusive program of the larger home. For the purposes of this paper, I have assumed a home with a capacity of approximately 150 to 175 residents and located in a temperate climate.

Building. The building should contain the following: mechanical plant and service area, this part of the building containing the heating plant and such other mechanical equipment as pumps, fans, refrigeration machinery, etc.; incinerator room; laundry; a small laundry for use of residents who are able to do their own personal work; general storage rooms; storage rooms for seasonal clothing of residents; sewing and linen room; storage rooms for provisions, china, blankets, trunks, etc.

Administrative and communal. This part of the building should contain administrative offices, the executive director's office, other offices in accordance with the program and needs of the home, board of directors' room, general waiting room, main dining room and other small dining rooms as needed. I should like to suggest one small dining room for the use of the residents for special parties. There should be a small kitchen in connection with this room so that residents may prepare special foods that they particularly desire for various occasions. There should also be a main kitchen with refrigerator rooms, dishwashing rooms, service pantries, etc. The kitchen should have ceramic tile walls and floor, acoustical ceiling, and stainless steel equipment. Kitchen and dining room should be mechanically ventilated.

There should be a chapel for religious services, which might be also used as an auditorium for entertainment purposes. If the policy of the home does not permit such a combination, an assembly room should be provided. The assembly room should have a stage where various programs for and by the residents may be given. There should be a library and rooms for recreational and occupational therapy classes. There should also be a barber shop, beauty parlor, and chiropodist's office. These facilities should be provided for hygienic reasons as well as for morale building.

Residential. This part of the building, which is to house the moderately well and ambulatory residents, should be designed to include a certain number of single rooms as well as two-bed rooms, each with its own or adjoining toilet room. There should be well-located bathrooms. The bathrooms may have supervision if necessary. Bedrooms should be light, airy, and, in addition to the bedroom furniture, should have room for an easy chair, writing desk, and perhaps some other living room furniture. Floors of all rooms throughout the home should be level, with no thresholds at doors. Rooms should have plastered walls and ceilings and rubber tiled floor and base. There should be individual clothes closets in each room which may be locked. Doors to rooms may be locked if desired.

Infirmary and chronic sick section. This part of the building should house the temporarily ill and the chronic sick residents and should be designed to include some single rooms, two-bed rooms, and four-bed wards, each with its own or adjacent toilet facilities and closet space for each resident. This section of the building should also have one or two isolation rooms. There should be well-located bathrooms on the floor. There should be a nurse's call system at each bed and in the bath and toilet rooms. Nurses' stations should be conveniently located on the floor. This section of the building should also have the following rooms:

1. Dining room and serving kitchen for those residents who, though not bedridden, are not sufficiently well to use the main dining room.

2. Medical department, including doctor's office, examining room, treatment room, dentist's office, X-ray and dark room, physiotherapy department, pharmacy, utility rooms, laboratory where routine tests may be made and some research carried on, wheel chair storage room, and other auxiliary rooms as may be required.

Physical features. The building should be of fireproof construction and conform to all local building fire prevention and health department ordinances. The building should be oriented wherever possible so that all rooms shall have sunshine during some part of the day. If more than one story in height, the building should have modern electric hospital-size elevators. The number of elevators is dependent on the size of the building. Enclosed stairways should be well located for proper ingress and egress. Corridors should be seven to eight feet wide, be well lighted and mechanically ventilated. Corridors should have rubber tiled floors and base. There should be a slightly projected handrail in corridors for convenience of the residents. It is also desirable to install a sprinkler system for the corridors, stair halls, elevator shafts, storerooms, clothes chutes, kitchen, and boiler room. This gives added protection against the spread of fire if it should occur.

The doors to rooms should be 42 to 44 inches wide, easy to open and close. Windows should be double, hung with full-length screen and ventilator section at bottom. Each section of the building should have a solarium and an open porch for use of the residents.

There should be a public speaking system whereby services in the chapel or programs generally may be broadcast to the various areas where people are bedfast. There should be drinking fountains well located in each area, also telephone booths; and there should be telephone connection at hospital beds.

Generally, all rooms throughout should be painted in different color schemes, depending on their orientation. Furniture should be comfortable; beds, chairs, tables, and lamps adjustable as to height and light; and residents should be given an opportunity to keep their own special articles of furniture in their own rooms. The designer should attempt to create the atmosphere of a home rather than that of an institution.

DETACHED

DWELLINGS *Chapter VII*

BY JAMES F. PEACOCK

> *James F. Peacock is president of the Place Realty Company of South Bend, Indiana. He is one of the nation's out-standing operative builders and understands the important social implications of the private builder's role in American life. He has been a member of many important commit-tees of the National Association of Home Builders.*

As a BUILDER my concern with houses for the aged is that they are a commodity to sell—but a builder also has obligations. The obligation of the builder to satisfy needs of homes for this group is just as great as his obligation to satisfy the housing needs of veterans, of the growing family, or of the needy and oppressed. There is a growing feeling among builders that we render a service. Just as the doctor cures the sick, so the builder cures the demand for housing. Also, just as when a doctor knows he cannot completely cure some cases, the builder acknowledges some limitations to procure housing for certain types of demands.

In line with this attitude of service, however, since the war the builders have scratched their heads and worked out schemes for modernization: they expanded towns and cities by developing improved properties; they used better and newer materials; they evolved systems of heating that are revolutionary compared to the systems of the midtwenties and thirties; they devised better financing arrangements for the purchasers of homes; and they ultimately built millions of houses to take care of the demand.

How has this been accomplished? By newspaper and editorial promotion. By the acts of the government in goading, urging, and encouraging construction of houses. By the banding to-gether of builders into the National Association of Home Builders where problems, ideas, materials, finances, and any allied research materials are discussed and encouraged. You see, builders have their own clinics—of a sort. During the war it was the defense worker who had priority. After the war, it became the veteran. And now, we are getting down to the case of the real veteran—those who have labored through this "vale of tears" so that they may finally relax in their own homes.

The builders have unified in their business, or service, of building homes to meet the needs of the moment. Until recently everyone forgot the oldster who refuses, and rightly so, to be treated as the Eskimo ancients who were put on an ice floe to die. Until recently, the retirement age was the time when Americans could live on their salted savings, build the large homes of ornate design and extensive upkeep—homes which were the mirrors of their frugal and successful past.

Today's market from that level of society has been modified by taxes. Modified? The word is "liquidated." How does the builder react to this? Naturally, there is a still existent group of older people who can afford anything. They have no money worries. Situations of this kind are taken care of by the persons concerned. Magazines like *House Beautiful* provide the elegant models for this group and for the group who still have enough of a cash balance to build for income purposes. Our company builds and sells many homes to this fortunate group of people. The builder's reaction may be summarized by saying that he works on the potential services he can accomplish by educating the public in housing trends and that he takes responsibility in building homes that are suitable for the comfort and financial status of the aged.

Important Features of Homes for Older People

The ideal home for the aged will be described in other chapters of this book but there are several features which I would also like to discuss. We have found it to be true that older people want fewer rooms than the growing family. The square foot area of a home for the aged is less than the area of a home for the average family. The size of the lot the older individual desires is less than that wanted by younger families. The desire to "cut down on space" is the cry of the oldster. Men who are in the prime of life, who are making money, can pay more for a house than a retired oldster, widow, or infirm person can pay.

There is one thing on which both groups, the young and the old, agree. That is convenience. And from this consideration of convenience, our company has built a business that last year netted over three hundred new homes. The price range was from a lowly $7,200 to $35,000. These homes were built on property which we fully developed. Many of these homes, in all price ranges, were sold to oldsters. Perhaps we would sell to even more oldsters if we had some way of teaching old dogs new tricks, that is, if we could convince more old people of a need for a smaller and more convenient home for the later years.

Present-day Trends

This year, our plans have progressed upward in price and our houses start at $10,000 instead of $7,200. Remember, we are interested in a product to sell. I will tell you the reasons that have shaped our program for this year:

1. We are building no two-bedroom houses. These two-bedroom houses are a glut on the market. Older people we talk to who insist their needs require one or two bedrooms only, are informed of this. We stress the responsibility of everyone to purchase a home that has resale value, and it behooves older people especially to invest wisely in order to protect their return of money in case of resale. It is often our answer to the woman who still insists she wants only a two-bedroom house, "Here we are, two bedrooms and a sewing room." Or a dining room, or a den, whichever suits the purchaser. This is done in sincerity as we are anxious to have a satisfied home owner who realizes the most for his investment. In some cases we will convert a three-bedroom home into a two-bedroom home by removing a wall between two rooms to produce either a larger living room, or a larger bedroom. Always, however, we insist this be done in such a way that the house could be reconverted for future resale as a three-bedroom house.

2. Our homes are larger than we have built in previous years. Larger kitchens still seem to be popular with older people. Also, when there is no dining room in a house, a kitchen must have enough elbowroom in it for family eating. Closets are larger than they were years ago. When a couple bought a house several years ago after the man of the house returned from service, houses were small and closets were not too big because the young couples were just getting started and hadn't yet acquired many belongings. Now, however, we must build larger closets because families have stocked up on clothes and many other items. Oldsters always say, "Where am I going to put all the things I want to keep?" Letters, pictures, mementos—bridges with the past.

3. Prices are uniformly higher than last year.

Aside from this, there are new ideas and materials, this year, which form a part of our plans in homes for the aged who can afford our homes. First of all, we build no houses with basements. We have not built a basement in six years.

All windows of our new homes now have thermopane inserts. No storm windows are necessary. No stoop, no squat, no strain. Not only is this feature easy for maintenance, it is a quality item that guarantees complete insulation of windows both in winter and in summer. Screens are aluminum and fitted on the windows from the inside, and may be left in place the year around.

Heating is automatic gas-forced air. The heat travels through the floor in ducts that emanate from a centrally located furnace. These ducts fan out from the furnace to the outside walls, through the floors, and are connected around the perimeter of the entire house by an insulated pipe which promotes heated "cold" walls, makes warm floors, and produces draftless, healthful, hot-air heat. A trick we have worked out as part of the heating system is popular with young and old. We heat our bathtubs by one of the heat ducts.

The furnace is almost silent, and completely automatic. Although there is one thermostat, each room's temperature can be controlled by the vents in the floor heat registers.

There are no stairs to climb. A drop-down stairway in the hall of the house however, allows access to the attic for storage of trunks, suitcases, Christmas tree ornaments, and treasured "junk." This storage space could easily be provided on the first floor simply by converting one of the excess bedrooms for storage. This plan would not affect the convenience of the house, and would not lower the resale value of the house.

At least one bedroom will take twin beds, as well as a chair, dresser, and so forth. We cannot squeeze room for a chaise lounge into a bedroom of a house in this price range.

Each bath is equipped with a dressing table, and a clothes hamper which can be used as a seat at the dressing table or at the tub for soaking feet and resting after getting out of the bathtub.

There is a separate "mud-room" next to the kitchen where the rear entrance is. This provides space for a washer and a dryer as well as storage space for laundry equipment, and a place for rubbers and galoshes, and for hanging up outdoor clothes.

Some of the homes have carports and porches which provide a place where people like to sit and relax as well as a place for the car. In every case, the homes without garages have plenty of room on each lot for the addition of one.

In planning out present low-cost development we have the assurance from the bus company that after so many families are in, buses will run on a regular schedule. Older people have to travel too, and bus lines must be convenient. In addition to this, we are planning a good shopping center which will be within walking distance of every home owner in the district. Does this sound as if we were approaching an answer to the problem of homes for the aged?

I believe it does—at least for those oldsters who can afford one of our homes. Among other things, we feel that a home should be a place to putter around. Geriatricians will agree that well oldsters need small time-consuming interests, whether it is gardening, washing dishes, or writing a letter. Also, we have been firmly convinced for years that one-floor living is safer and easier than living on two or more floors. We feel that homes should be flexible enough to suit old and young, able to be expanded or made more compact. We believe that homes should be designed for furniture as well as people. When we plan our homes we use furniture templates which represent sofas, chairs, tables, beds, dressers, stoves, and the like. We work out our plans so that there are as many furniture arrangements as possible. A woman's foible, whether she be young or old, attests the value of this.

But what are we doing to provide homes for those oldsters who cannot afford the ones we build? We are at work now on a a larger four-bedroom house for around $8,000 for those families who can afford less, but need more bedrooms. This is a house that could serve as an ideal home for oldsters who want large rooms but few, by compacting the interior. But a one-bedroom house?

Probably the answer to the lower-priced house for old people is a dream-like situation where a builder could acquire some centrally located, improved property which he could develop for a community of old folks only. If he revamped the lots so that they would be one-third normal size, which would be less for a person to maintain or to pay for, or built a house of low maintenance material that would consist of one large bedroom, a bath, and a large kitchen; or made no provision for expansion and built a 20 by 28 foot house that would cost about $5,000, would one of these be the answer? Would older people resist a compromise of this sort? It would be far better than a trailer camp. Would a section given only to older people be practical for a builder or an investor to attempt? Financing would be the first problem.

The Problem of Financing

In South Bend, our largest employer is Studebaker Corporation. The pension plan there is exemplary. But will it take care of those who have become sick in their old age? Their plan, roughly, is this: The hourly wage earners receive a pension which can not exceed $45.00 a month after twenty-five years of service. This is the laborers' situation. Couple this with the Social Security maximum draw of $150 a month for an individual with dependents, and it presents not too bad a picture. But these examples are the maximum, not the average. The salaried employees of Studebaker have an even better arrangement. They contribute to their pension fund out of each paycheck; in addition, Studebaker makes the same pension arrangement with them as with their hourly workers.

As I have said, this is exemplary. And this is not the rule for other industries in our town. There are too many people who must depend completely upon Social Security. How many there are who have no savings we all know. How many there are who have been frugal enough to save some money, only to have it eaten away by sickness, lingering ailments, and constant medical bills. How many there are who are left to shuffle about as best they can. Our baby sitters are chiefly widows who are completely respectable, but who have had to work after their money and investments have gone down the drain. Even if there were mortgages—which there are not for older people—how many of the aging could become eligible for acceptance? The rule is that a monthly payment must not be larger than one sixtieth of an annual income.

If this sounds hopeless, it is the way I, as a builder, feel about it, in respect to the poor as well as the old. Perhaps there is already an answer to this problem. If not, I prescribe that the problem be posed to the National Association of Home Builders. Builders are accustomed to a challenge. And this certainly is a challenge. But homes for the aged also mean a market that our product and service have not reached. To treat the problem on the level of business, we are looking for any new market.

In Conclusion

I have written largely of the individual company's approach to individual homes for the well aged. My attitude is much removed from that of the entire industry. Let me summarize:

1. To date, builders have taken care of a certain class of older people, those who can afford to buy our houses, those who are educated along the lines of a "retirement" house as a marketable product which will be resalable. This resolves into a matter of design and location.

2. We have not taken care of those who can afford homes which cost $5,000 or under. We can not until some forces

arrange financing which will aid both the oldster and the builder. The answer to this problem would solve the entire situation.

3. Costs have risen to a point where older people's savings represent less than an amount which would have cushioned their retirement comfort. We, as builders, cannot combat this inflation.

4. Builders are doing a good job in meeting the needs of all, with the exception of this group of poor aged. Builders have progressed in design and materials. Builders have exerted every effort to induce better financing. Finance is therefore the fly in the ointment. But the situation is not hopeless. I suggest that this problem be turned over to the NAHB for active resolve.

COMMUNAL ARRANGEMENTS
FOR OLDER CITIZENS *Chapter VIII*

BY ERNEST W. BURGESS

Ernest W. Burgess, Ph.D., is professor emeritus of sociology, Department of Sociology, University of Chicago. He was formerly chairman of the Department. His bibliography is extensive and includes authorship of The Family, *Predicting Success and Failure in Marriage, and coauthorship of* Personal Adjustment in Old Age *and* Introduction to the Science of Sociology. *He is editor of the January, 1954, issue of* The American Journal of Sociology *which is devoted to aging and retirement. Dr. Burgess has been president of the American Sociological Society, the Society for Family Living, and the Gerontological Society, Inc. Currently, he is studying the sociological aspects of the trailer camp retirement villages in Florida.*

THE UNITED STATES is becoming housing-conscious. The public, as well as experts, realize the existence of a housing problem of magnitude that imperils the health, welfare, and happiness of millions of people.

The problem has several aspects. First of all, there are too few houses. Between 1940 and the present time, families increased faster than dwelling units. Second, much of the existing housing is below the minimum standard of health and safety. Third, housing is frequently poorly adapted to meet the needs of families and individuals. Fourth, the cost of housing is beyond the means of the lower income groups.

The problem of housing for persons sixty-five years of age and more has these characteristics intensified. First, the shortage of houses forces doubling up of families. This means that young couples are often compelled to live with in-laws in this age bracket.

Or an aged person with income too low to live alone must seek refuge with a married son or daughter.

Second, older people, on the average, are more likely to live in residences in need of major repairs. Third, new housing is constructed for young and middle-aged couples with children. Seldom, or never, is it specifically designed to meets the needs of older couples and individuals. Fourth, persons of sixty-five and over have low and often diminishing incomes, insufficient to provide the housing to fit their needs. Evidently the problem of housing for the older person is most serious and difficult.

This problem of housing for older people has no pat and easy solution. Facts are needed before it is feasible to plan for the adequate housing of the aging members of our society.

At a recent conference on aging it was agreed that we lacked adequate knowledge on the following points:

1. What is the present housing of older people?
2. What kind of housing do older people want?
3. What types of housing should they have?
4. How can older people be induced to want the kind of housing they should have?

These questions will be taken as guiding points for discussing the problem of housing for the aged.

How Are Older Persons Housed?

Until recently very little information was available about the housing of persons sixty-five years and over. A special census tabulation was prepared in July, 1951, of one-in-a-thousand nonfarm dwelling units. This was made at the request and the expense of the Division of Housing Research of the Housing and Home Finance Agency.

The following conclusions can be drawn from this tabulation about the housing of older persons as compared with that of the general population.

1. There are between five and six million households with the head sixty-five years and over. These constitute 15.4 per cent of all households in the United States. Persons sixty-five and over are about half this number (8.2 per cent).

2.   One-person households in which the persons are sixty-five and over are more than twice as frequent (39.0 per cent) as in those in which they are younger.

3.   Two-person households occur 50 per cent oftener with the head over, rather than under, sixty-five years of age.

4.   Households with heads sixty-five years old, or more, are less overcrowded than those of the remaining population.

5.   Two-thirds (67.2 per cent) of older household heads own their own homes. Home ownership is about 20 per cent higher in this group than in that of the remaining population.

6.   The percentage of owner-occupied dwellings valued at less than $2,000 is nearly double (27.7 per cent) that for all households in the United States.

7.   The proportion of older heads of households paying less than $20.00 a month for rent is 50 per cent higher than for all households.

8.   Older heads of households live in a somewhat higher per cent (18.3) of dilapidated houses.

9.   Nearly two-thirds (64.4 per cent) of all aged household heads have annual incomes of less than $2,000. This is double (32.2 per cent) the proportion of all household heads receiving less than $2,000.

In short, older persons, as represented by household heads, are more likely than the average household head to live in one-person and two-person households, to be less overcrowded, to live in dilapidated dwellings, to own their own homes, to own a higher proportion of homes of low value, to have lower incomes, and to pay less rent.

Other facts available from the census provide us information upon the marital status and household arrangements of persons sixty-five years of age and older. This information has a bearing upon their housing.

1.   Two thirds (66.3 per cent) of men but only one third (36.6 per cent) of the women of this age group are married.

2.   One fourth (23.8 per cent) of men and over one half (54.4 per cent) of women of this age are widowed.

3. The per cent reporting themselves single and divorced is almost the same for men and women (10.0 and 9.1).

4. Only a small per cent (men 6.0, and women 2.8) are living in institutions such as homes for the aged, mental hospitals, prisons, transient hotels, labor or trailer camps.

5. Living in households, but either alone or with nonrelated persons, are 12.5 per cent of men and 21.5 per cent of women who are sixty-five years or older.

6. Husband and wife living together but with no other household member include 35.1 per cent of men and 18.3 per cent of women.

7. Husband, wife, and other relatives living together comprise one third (32.4 per cent) of men and one sixth (16.9 per cent) of women.

8. Not living with a spouse but with other relatives account for a little over one eighth (13.9 per cent) of men and two fifths (40.5 per cent) of women.

The above facts highlight the conclusion that in terms of numbers the widow presents a central problem in the housing of aging persons. She is undoubtedly a very high proportion of those living with relatives (40.5 per cent) and of those living alone or with nonrelatives (21.5 per cent).

What Housing Do Older People Want?

Not enough is known about the attitudes of older persons to their housing problems. No large-scale study of their wishes and preferences has been made. Those who are closest to aging persons, however, tend to agree upon the following points:

1. Older persons, in general, prefer living in family households to residing in institutions.

2. They have a strong desire to remain in the home of their middle years even though they are alone and it is difficult physically and financially to maintain it.

3. Those who are willing to change to another type of living arrangement—boarding house, hotel, small apartment, congregate living—wish to remain in the same neighborhood or local com-

munity to be near relatives, friends, and organizations of which they are members.

4. Much of the present housing arrangements of older persons does not represent free choice. In other words, it is a result of necessity or at least of a mixture of necessity and choice.

5. Doubling up with a married son or daughter works out satisfactorily in some instances, in others it brings frustration to some, if not to all, members of the household.

6. Households composed of friends or other relatives than parents and children are not infrequent. They appear to operate satisfactorily where relations are congenial and the arrangement is one of choice of the participants.

7. Guest homes, boarding homes, and residential hotels provide housing for an unknown but large number of older persons who prefer this type of independent congregate living to institutional homes. At present little is known of the advantages and disadvantages of these living arrangements.

8. Large numbers of older persons reside alone in rooming houses. Very often they live an isolated and lonely existence, cut off from contacts with relatives and old-time friends. They may compensate by casual contacts of the rooming house, of the tavern, of the street, or the like.

9. Persons who are residents of institutional homes are frequently dissatisfied by the loss of their independence and the breaking of contacts with friends and relatives. They tend to resent the regimentation that characterized the old-time home for the aged. They respond favorably to recreational programs, particularly when they participate in the planning, and to the increase of freedom encouraged by progressive policies of administration.[1] They want their privacy respected and the opportunity to suggest better care or to suggest the care given.

There is need of more exact knowledge of the attitudes and preferences of older persons. Certainly, they will have to be taken into account in planning for better housing for the aging.

[1] *Man and His Years,* Rept. First Nat. Conf. on Aging (Raleigh, N.C.: Health Publications Institute, Inc., 1951), p. 172.

What Housing Should Older People Have?

As yet we do not know how to plan for the housing of aging persons. Even the experts are not agreed. The Committee on the Family, Living Arrangements and Housing of the First National Conference on Aging came to the following among other conclusions and recommendations:[2]

1. The majority of people in the older age group prefer to live in some kind of family household, if possible.

2. Congregate accommodations are certainly required for those who feel unequal to looking after their own households and for others who fear they will not be taken care of in time of illness, or who for other reasons need or prefer group living arrangements.

3. A significant fraction of nondependent older people are overhoused and underserviced and are not aware that various other ways of living are open to them. They think in terms of "independent" versus "institutional" living as the only possible alternatives. Some of the problems of older people would be lessened if they were aware of these alternatives and if homemaker and casework services were readily available.

4. The decreasing size of dwelling units currently being built produces a problem for aging people who might otherwise share housing with their married children.

5. The average size of families is decreasing and the number of families is increasing. As a result of this and other factors, there is an acute shortage of dwelling units for aging couples and single persons. In fact, there is a lack almost everywhere of desirable living accommodations of all types, independent and congregate, for aging people. They are apparently not wanted even in rooming houses and apartments, especially if unemployed.

6. Ultimately some of the one-bedroom dwellings currently being built in certain of the large cities, as well as living arrangements in family hotels, would become available for aging people, if they could pay the prices. For the most part, however, they are serving the newlywed or single men or women in the prime

[2]*Ibid.*, pp. 165-73.

of life. Moreover, the aging require services not ordinarily provided in the new so-called efficiency apartments.

7. There is need of special design and planning. With very few exceptions, aged couples and aged single persons in America are today living in dwelling units which were not designed to meet the needs of aged people. Even in public housing projects where two-person older families have been accepted, they have almost invariably been housed in the same type of dwelling unit to which a two-person younger family would ordinarily be assigned.

8. Private enterprise to the largest extent possible should provide dwellings for the aging just as for other groups of the population. Promotors and builders of large-scale housing, whether commercial, co-operative, or public, should all be urged to make provision for the aging, both single persons and couples.

Investors and builders operating on a commercial basis and without public aid are providing only for the relatively small sector of the well-to-do. Even then the dwellings are not actually designed to meet the special needs of/aging. Every proper inducement should be given to these operators to enable them to meet a larger proportion of the need of lower income persons. Without special assistance, it appears unlikely that private operators can produce satisfactory housing at prices which the average older person can afford to pay.

To stimulate home building for aging people of moderate income, special aid needs to be given to agencies whose primary motive is not maximum profit, such as large insurance companies which have a double incentive in prolonging the lives of policyholders, limited dividend companies, co-operatives and mutual housing groups, and philanthropic agencies. Such agencies might be assisted by government insurance and by government loans, although such loans should bear sufficient interest to protect the government against loss. Housing actually designed to meet the needs of older persons can be expected to be less expensive than dwelling units currently being built to house small families. Even so, satisfactory housing for older people in the low income group, including those living on benefits, will not be sufficient because these people cannot pay an economic rent. For them, public housing seems to be the only answer. National, state, and local public housing agencies, therefore, should give attention to the provision of housing for the aging, including single persons as well as married couples.

9. A congregate or group living arrangement in "a home for the aged" is only one of the housing resources that communities should make available to persons who need or choose this type of living arrangement as they grow older. An isolated home for the aged that is not actively related to the social program of the community is no longer acceptable as a place where the aged can live comfortably and carry on their contacts with their families and the community. Every home should maintain its unique place in the pattern of community services, associating closely with other agencies in the community to achieve the best standards of constructive services.

10. These major types of community services, regarded as desirable aids in establishing satisfactory relationships between aging persons and their families, were identified as: (1) informational, (2) counseling, and (3) homemaker. It was agreed that in providing these services, needs of persons with substantial incomes, as well as people in the lower income brackets, should be taken into account.

Evidently, there is no single best living arrangement for older people. The age group from sixty to one hundred years comprises four decades. With advancing years needs of persons change. Family relations and situations are different. Preferences as to housing arrangements vary.

At the present time, it is highly desirable to encourage diversity in plans for the housing of aging persons. Progress will come out of demonstrations of differing housing designs. Therefore, a few housing plans will be presented as somewhat representative of current developments.

Institutional Homes

The traditional pattern of housing for the aged is that of institutional homes. "In the Chicago area," Breckinridge reports, "over half of the homes are under religious auspices, and about one fifth are sponsored by nationality groups."[3] Others are maintained to serve members of fraternal orders, "retired business or professional men, unmarried women of 'culture and refinement,' former railroad employees, soldiers' widows, and the 'destitute.'"

There are fifty-nine institutional homes for the aged in the Chicago area. Almost half of these accommodate between fifty and 100 persons. The next largest group provides for 150 to 200 aged persons. Only five homes serve less than twenty-five residents and eight homes accommodate 200 or more.

Mather House, recently opened in Evanston, Illinois, is presented to illustrate the characteristic newer type of institutional home:[4]

The Mather Home provides accommodations for 103 women. The structure and its equipment cost $2 million. The building was provided for in the will of the late Alonzo C. Mather, president of the Mather Stock Car Co., railway freight car firm. He died in 1941 at the age of 92. Mather decided after an investigation of social needs that a great service could be done by setting up a home for "aged ladies of refinement from good families who are unable to procure for themselves a home of their own." The industrialist left the bulk of his estate of more than $5 million for the project.

The home has about 1,600 inquiries and applications for admission and currently 10 to 20 telephone calls and six to seven letters are received daily. "Every letter is filed," said W. C. Jackman, executive director of the Home. "We have a staff of trained social workers who go over each one of them carefully. Women are not accepted until a thorough, scientific study has been made." Jackman said that about 10 or 12 "guests" will be admitted to the luxurious home monthly until it is filled. "Primarily, the guest will be selected to help make a home," he added. A nine-man board of trustees has formulated several specific requirements on eligibility. They include: (1) the applicant must have reached 65 and not have passed 85; (2) she must be a citizen and have lived for at least 15 of the last 20 years in Cook, Lake, Du Page, or Will Counties.

An admission fee, varying with the assets of the individual, is determined after a formal application is filed. Approved applicants

[3] Elizabeth Breckinridge, *Community Services for Older People; the Chicago Plan* (Chicago: Wilcox and Follett Co., 1952), p. 77.
[4] *Chicago Sun-Times*, June 10, 1952, p. 30.

must, on entering the home, assign to it all property, cash and other assets. In referring to religious requirements, Jackson said that the home "is maintained as a Christian Protestant community." Many of the ladies are college-trained. "Loneliness, a feeling of insecurity and the fear that some illness may overtake them—these are the primary reasons in back of the desire of aged women to come here," Jackman declared. In recognition of these and similar problems, the home has set up a counseling service under the direction of Mrs. Lois G. Slonaker. "Our guests can come and go as they wish—we believe in permitting freedom of action," the executive director said.

The women have individual, well-outfitted rooms. They add their own personal touches to them, if they so desire. Sitting rooms and lounges are provided with television sets. Highly functional equipment of the latest design is chosen for the buildings, which has a completely equipped medical and dental department. Recreation rooms are set aside for handicraft work, art, music, and sewing. A kitchen in which the women can make cookies or candy likewise is provided. The home has a library. It also has a beauty parlor which has become a highly popular spot with the women as a morale builder.

Noninstitutional Housing Project

Another type of planned congregate housing for older persons may be called noninstitutional. The building provides a relatively large number of dwelling units which are rented to individuals and couples. Additional facilities are available but additional extra charges are made for these. The plans for a pilot project of the noninstitutional type has been launched in Boston under the sponsorship of the Commonwealth Housing Foundation, a newly organized charitable trust.[5] A description of the project follows:

The initial project, for which two sites in Boston are now being studied, will cost between $1,500,000 and $2,000,000 and will include between 100 and 200 dwelling units of one or two rooms each. The project will have the following features:

Common rooms in which ordinary social activities, lectures, concerts and the like may be carried on for the group and for their friends from the neighborhood. Workshops, such as tool shops and rooms for the study and pursuit of useful hobbies and work, either to produce new skills or to carry on part time paying activities. A physical recreation area, such as a simple gymnasium, bowling alleys, or game rooms

[5] *Boston Sunday Herald,* Oct. 7, 1951, p. 14.

where the tenants and their friends and neighbors may keep themselves physically fit.

A cafeteria, or some similar dining room, where good meals at low cost with social associations can be served to such tenants as wish them. An infirmary where ordinary illness can be cared for by the physician of the tenant's choice and from which nurses, physiotherapists and others can give necessary service to tenants temporarily ill in their apartments. A group of stores carrying groceries, drugs, stationery and so on where the tenants can do all ordinary shopping without encountering the hazards of the streets or "toddling two blocks to get a loaf of bread." In addition, the designers are studying interior appointments with a view to making the apartments safer and more convenient for the elderly.

Equity and working capital for this program came from the home for Aged Colored Women which, like other homes for the aged, had lost its function in an era of social legislation, but still had a large sum of money in its treasury. Henry Wise, Boston lawyer, who is chairman of the Housing Association of Metropolitan Boston, a Red Feather service, and W. C. Loring, Jr., executive director of that organization, brought about the organization of the Commonwealth Housing Foundation, and the trustees of the Home for Aged Colored Women obtained from the Supreme Court authority to transfer $250,000 of its funds to the newly-formed trust. Additional funds are now being sought.

"We think we can provide rent low enough to be able to take care of a considerable proportion of the tenants on funds guaranteed by Old Age Assistance," Dr. Monroe said. "But the majority of the apartments will be above that figure and, frankly, we are looking for aging people who now pay higher rents in Boston and are still independent by reason of working or of income from other rather than charitable sources." Loring explained that under the Old Age Assistance program the government will pay only $16 a month for a room, but $36.75 for rent and utilities for a proper dwelling unit. "That would not meet our costs, of course," he said. "But if we can obtain a desirable location, where tenants will not object to their friends visiting them, we can charge those having incomes $50, and even things up." The trust, he said, would be able to pay off the capital cost of the project because the 1950 amendments to the FHA Act permit of amortization over a period of 40 years for certain well built types of housing "thus reducing payments to a point where we can swing them."

Dr. Monroe said there would be no compulsion on the tenants to use the special facilities in the project. The services would be hired by the tenants as they wished. "One definite, but very important element in this situation," he said, "is to tie these aging people into the normal community life. It is my impression that old people do not now have an incitement in this area to make them behave as good neighbors,—or make the community behave as good neighbors to them. We can see arguments for keeping old people in homes, but we can also see a lot of arguments on the other side. What we do see clearly is the need of a place where those who wish may be guaranteed relief from the normal distractions of young people, and vice versa."

The trustees of the Foundation expect that a demonstration of the success of the pilot project will result in the establishment of other projects of this type. They hope that this kind of housing will prove a sound investment so that private capital can be attracted into this field.

Converting Dwellings into Communal Homes

In England, where new building is severely limited, there is now a considerable body of experience in adapting large single buildings into housing for older people. In his book, *Adding Life to Years,* Lord Amulree[6] states the principles to be followed in converting dwellings into communal homes:

Generally speaking, such Homes should be in towns. The average old person is a town dweller, and a town dweller cannot bear to be removed from familiar sights, from friends, and from all the bustle of town life, even to the most beautiful country house.

From the residents' point of view there is an advantage in taking a former dwelling house for a Home. For one thing, it will continue to look like a dwelling house, and not in any way like an Institution. It must, however, fulfill certain requirements. It must, in the first place, be near some form of public transport, whether it be a bus or tram route, or in London, an Underground railway station. This is essential, not only so that visitors can come to the Home, but so that such residents as are able to go out can visit their friends, go to shops, churches, public houses or cinemas. The absence of convenient transport facilities not only complicates the visit of friends and relatives but,

[6]Lord Amulree, *Adding Life to Years* (London: Baniston Press, 1951), pp. 71-78.

what is more important, makes it difficult to obtain the services of non-resident domestic staff.

The size of the house deserves consideration, for it must be neither too large, nor too small to be economically run. If the number of residents is too large, it becomes difficult to maintain the personal and friendly atmosphere which is essential to success. As the Ministry of Health has suggested in Circular 49/47 and again in Circular 87/48, the ideal number of residents is in the neighborhood of thirty-five. A Home for less than twenty residents is uneconomic unless a substantial charge for maintenance is made.

Obviously any house that is taken over for a Home should be in good structural condition and should, if possible, have plenty of accommodation on the ground and first floors; and, as old people find difficulty in going up and down stairs, the fewer the stairs the better. The gradient of the stairs should be easy, with a low rise to each stair and no winding stairs.

Accommodation in a Home can be for men or women only, but it makes for a more normal community if both sexes are allowed to live in the same Home. Such a rule makes it possible for married couples to be admitted, and also makes it possible for residents to marry. This is not a common experience, but several marriages have taken place in Homes that cater for both sexes.

As it is so important that a Home for the elderly should as nearly as possible resemble in its atmosphere the sort of home from which most of the residents will have come, all that can be done to encourage the growth of this home-like atmosphere must be done. There should not, therefore, be too much insistence on a scrupulous tidiness. The Home is to be a "home" and not a hospital, where rigid cleanliness and tidiness are essential to the health of the patients. Too often the well-meaning efforts of local authorities and voluntary societies are frustrated by the maintenance of a degree of neatness and tidiness that would do credit to a barrack dormitory.

Every Home should have an adequate number of sitting-rooms or lounges. In a mixed Home, it is desirable to set aside one room, no matter how small, for the men; for men enjoy being able to get away from the women from time to time, to smoke their pipes in peace, or to play darts, dominoes or draughts.

The dining-room should be furnished with small tables, rather than with one or more large tables. By the use of bright table-cloths and the provision of flowers an atmosphere can be created which, if it is less intimate than that of a private house, is as agreeable and friendly as that of the better type of hotel. The main meals are usually eaten in common in the dining-room. This suggestion has two advantages. It not only insures each resident having the benefit of an adequate diet, but it is also a useful check upon illness. If a resident does not appear for a meal, an enquiry can be made in his room, which will save the necessity for an official daily round of all rooms by the warden. Each resident should have some means of boiling a kettle so that he can entertain a friend to tea if he so wishes.

It is not always possible to find a house with enough small bedrooms to ensure that each resident can have a room of his own, but by judicious use of partitioning, even with so light a material as three-ply wood, a large bedroom can often be transformed into two or more small ones. It is often maintained that old people prefer to share a bedroom with one or two others, but this is rarely true. Even when an old person has been forced throughout his life to share a bedroom with other members of his family (an evil all too prevalent both before the war and now), he welcomes with avidity the opportunity of having a room of his own, no matter how small. The rooms should not be too small, however; a minimum of 100 square feet for a single or 160 square feet for a double room is a reasonable size.

A Mixed Home may well have a few double rooms for married people, or even for sisters who wish to sleep together, but they should be in a minority. The idea that the majority of elderly people like to share a room because they are afraid of being alone, or of being taken ill, is widely held, but experience shows that it has little foundation in fact. If it is impossible to divide large rooms into several small ones, it is always possible to curtain off each bed in such a way as to provide each resident with a certain amount of privacy.

Wherever possible, residents should be allowed to bring some of their own furniture into the Home. They find great comfort in being able to live with some of their cherished possessions around them. Unfortunately, the limits of space make it necessary for the authorities to have the final word on what furniture is suitable. Old-fashioned beds, for example, are frequently too big for the small bedroom space available. And as many residents often have no furniture in fit condition to be brought, a reserve of furniture, belonging to the Home is necessary.

There should be a minimum of rules governing a Home, and the residents should be free to come and go and to receive visitors when they wish, with the reservation that they should all be in the Home at a reasonable hour, especially in the winter. They should be allowed to leave the Home for week-ends or for holidays, although they should, of course, tell the warden when they wish to go away and when they propose to return. It is a mistake to molly-coddle the residents too much, and the warden will be well advised to exercise a wise discretion in allowing the residents to leave the Home. It is better to let them take the risks they would normally take if they were living at home, than to make their lives uncomfortable by well-meant but burdensome restrictions.

The presence of a garden will go a long way to satisfy the desire for freedom of movement that most old people possess. Any awkward steps on the garden walks should be changed into ramps, and because many old people have an unreasoning fear that grass may be wet, and will not sit in chairs upon it, part of the space available should be paved, or have a gravel surface.

The staff of a Home for the able-bodied need not be large, for most of the residents will be able to keep their own rooms clean and tidy, and may even be able to help with some of the general work of the household and grounds. Among the necessary resident staff will be the warden who may, but need not necessarily, be a trained nurse. It would be an advantage for the warden to know something about nursing, but the supply of State Registered Nurses is limited and they can better be employed in hospitals or Homes for the infirm or frail ambulants.

The warden will need someone to deputize for her when she is out, on holiday or ill, and this should also be a person with some nursing experience. It is an advantage if the cook or other domestic resident is married, for the presence of a man who is willing and able to stoke boilers, look after the garden and do odd household jobs is a very great help. The remaining staff are usually non-resident: a kitchen-maid and two or three cleaners are all that are needed for a Home of 30-35 residents.

If a large house, with several stories, is taken for such a Home, it is sometimes an advantage to let rooms on the top one or two floors to single women who are still in employment. They often have great difficulty in finding suitable accommodation, and their presence helps to counteract the feeling of segregation that the old people might otherwise feel. Such younger women are prepared to pay rents, which will help to pay for the running of the Home.

Under the National Health Service each resident in a Home will have his own doctor, whom he can visit or call in if he is ill, but it is useful if a local practitioner can be on call in case a sudden emergency arises. Where the residents each have their own room there is no need for a sick bay. For minor illnesses the residents can remain in their own rooms as they would at home. There is always the danger that the Home may wish to retain patients who should be in hospital, for the desire to nurse is widespread among the types of person who apply for the post of warden especially if they have some nursing training and experience, and some hospitals are only too anxious to take advantage of this willingness.

Home Services

The large proportion of old persons who now live and desire to live in their own homes highlight, under certain circumstances, the need for home services. Particularly necessary is the provision for domestic help and marketing services when the aging couple or individual is no longer physically able to perform these activities. These are now often undertaken on a voluntary basis by relatives, friends, and neighbors. But such assistance is not always forthcoming. Breckinridge[7] reports a project—partly survey, partly demonstration—undertaken by the Chicago Housing Authority of the older residents of the Ida B. Wells housing project in Chicago:

(The investigators) found 137 old persons living at the project, most of whom received Old Age Pensions. The remainder had incomes equally limited, from private pensions or other sources. One-fourth were visited and interviewed. In the group surveyed there were some elderly couples and some widowed persons living alone following the death of the spouse. In the latter situations, efforts were made to help the aged person find a relative who could share the apartment and who would be acceptable to the tenant. In some instances, this was another elderly person.

Among the group visited, most of them needed help in the home either occasionally or regularly. A few had help from interested neighbors or relatives. Several had no help at all. Needs varied from those who required the help of someone to run errands when they were ill to those who needed someone to keep the house clean, to do the marketing, or prepare at least one meal a day. One elderly couple, both too ill to do much for themselves or each other, refused to discuss any change to a nursing home or other protected arrangement even if it could be arranged.

[7]*Op. cit.*, pp. 96-98.

There were no organized services in the community available to these people. From a conference with Cook County Bureau of Public Welfare, it was learned that in some situations the cost of home services might be included in the Old Age Pension grant. If an OAP recipient was ill and the attending physician recommended that he needed certain personal services, consideration could be given to including in the grant an amount to pay for these services. First, the ill person or his relatives or friends must find someone who would give the service recommended by the physician, and secure approval of the agency for employing the person for a specified number of hours. The employed person submitted a bill after the services had been performed. An amount to cover this cost was included in the recipient's next check.

The welfare agency, which had not up to this time been authorized to develop a housekeeper or homemaker service, pointed out several problems. The client must find the person to do the work. The hourly wage was small. The person employed must wait for two or three weeks for her money. The money was paid to the client and if, through misunderstanding or because of unexpected expenses, the money was used for other purposes, the person who performed the services had no recourse. This system has worked best where there is a continuing need for service since, after the initial waiting period, the employed person can be paid regularly. The running of errands, such as marketing, could not be included for those on Old Age Pensions, but could be provided for persons receiving help under the Blind Assistance Program.

In an effort to develop a pool of persons interested in participating in a home-service program, it was decided to ask a nonsectarian private agency which had an organized housekeeping service to provide a training course for persons recruited by the Housing Project staff. Recruitment would be chiefly within the Housing Project, from women who had a few extra hours a day and who could earn a few dollars without traveling far. Although this suggestion did not receive the full approval of the private agency, some progress has been made in recruiting and training women for this service.

The Housing Project in the meantime secured the cooperation of the Girl Scouts to run errands for the older people. Cards were given old people who required help. When they needed an errand run, the card was put in a window and any Girl Scout who passed was to stop and do the errand.

Presently, an effort is being made to develop a volunteer domestic service program through the Housing Project's Women's Service

Club. Agencies which have housekeeper services, the Volunteer Bureau, and the American Red Cross will be requested to cooperate in providing training. Supervision will be given by the Housing Project Staff. This effort was approved by a committee representing several of the agencies to be involved.

The survey at the Ida B. Wells Project serves as an example (1) that needed services are not available to older people; (2) that urgent need exists; and (3) that services must be developed even if they do not meet recognized standards.

It is our conviction that there are many older people who need help with housework marketing, or other errands who are themselves capable of supervising the work of the person who helps; that such help would enable them to remain independent; that such help can be provided without expensive training and supervision; and that, at least until such time as the community develops sufficient organized and supervised housekeeper services, every effort should be made to develop some of the needed domestic aids.

Consideration should be given as to how and under what auspices either volunteer or paid services can be developed. Volunteer efforts by women's church groups to serve their own members should be initiated. Community councils might consider this as a project for improving the conditions of old people in their own neighborhoods. The Chicago Housing Authority should use the knowledge gained at Ida B. Wells to extend this kind of planning to other projects. Older peoples' groups or clubs might organize such a program in their own neighborhoods. Neighborhood houses and community centers might provide leadership for such efforts.

How to Change Attitudes Toward Housing

Older persons, as we have seen, have definite attitudes toward housing. These preferences stress one's own home, love of privacy, independence, and freedom of movement and choice in decisions upon housing arrangements.

Yet continuing to live in one's own home is often against the public as well as against the person's interest. This situation is most dramatically illustrated when giving up a dwelling of large size by its owner would release housing accommodations for from five to twenty or more individuals. Remaining in one's home is against the owner's interest when he is no longer physically or financially able to maintain housekeeping. It is against his interest if he can live more happily and fully under another household arrangement.

Social security legislation has now given nearly all older persons a certain minimum of financial independence. It has increased their freedom of choice and action. It has made it possible for agencies—public, charitable, and commercial—to plan housing and other services for older persons with more assurance for the future than formerly.

At present the greatest need is for demonstrations of housing designs and community services for the aging that embody the best thinking of those working in this field.

Once these pilot projects are in operation they can be evaluated so as to reject those that are not satisfactory and to make recommended improvements and modifications in the most satisfactory. When a project has been validated by experience, it should then be widely publicized.

A campaign of education is necessary to bring successful housing designs to the attention of the public. Special efforts should be made to acquaint persons in their fifties and early sixties with the developments in housing for persons in their later decades with the advantages of congregate living and with the facilities and services for the aging available to those living in their homes.

The attitudes of older persons must be taken into account in all planning for their housing. Congregate living should, for example, provide to the fullest possible degree for their love of privacy, freedom of movement, and social participation.

Older persons are likely, more and more, to take the lead in programs for their benefit as they become better acquainted with the newer designs for housing and the advantages of community services. They will not only accept them, but will demand their adoption and expansion.

IMPROVISATIONS IN
RURAL IOWA[1] *Chapter IX*

BY RAPHAEL GINZBERG, WILLARD C. BRINEGAR,
FRANK K. DUNN, AND VILMA OLSVARY

> *Raphael Ginzberg, M.D., is senior physician, Veterans
> Administration Hospital, Tomah, Wisconsin. He was for-
> merly director of the Gerontological Unit, Mental Health
> Institute, Cherokee, Iowa.*
> *Willard C. Brinegar, M.D., is superintendent of the Men-
> tal Health Institute, Cherokee, Iowa.*
> *Frank K. Dunn, M.A., is director of the Social Service
> Department, Mental Health Institute, Cherokee, Iowa.*
> *Vilma Olsvary, B.S., was formerly ward therapist, Mental
> Health Institute, Cherokee, Iowa.*

THE PURPOSE of this chapter is to call attention to the aging who
are living on their children's property, or near by, in former
garages, former one-room schoolhouses, trailer homes, or specially
built one- or two-room cottages. Arrangements of these types were
studied in Iowa in rural districts, and in small and medium-sized
towns.

Little is known and almost nothing is published concerning
housing of elderly people in rural and rural-farm districts in the
Middle West. As elsewhere, different types of housing can be
found in this region. The spectrum is wide and varied. On one
end are excellent one-family houses or cottages with three or more
rooms in which one elderly person or a couple lives alone or with
children. On the other hand, are shacks and slumlike dwellings
in which the aged live under the most unsanitary conditions.

[1]Special acknowledgment is given to Mr. Harry Fuhrman, Mrs. Willa B.
Reiniger, and Mr. Ed. Wieland for their assistance in the project.

Many more live in boarding homes or small-town hotels where, occasionally, one can find the elderly person living on the same floor on which one or more of his children live with their families.

Two Groups of Retired Aged

In rural and in rural-farm areas at least two major groups of retired aged can be distinguished: farm owners, and former farm or nonfarm laborers. Many of the farm owners retire on the farm; some of them, however, especially in northwestern Iowa, where most of the field work for this study was done, are well-to-do people who usually retire from the farm to a small or medium-sized town where they buy a house in which to live the rest of their lives. There are a minority of former farm owners who lost their property either during the years of economic crisis or through such mishaps as illness of spouse or of self; these share the destiny of those who have no money and no property. They join the ranks of the former farmhands and laborers, the bulk of the Old Age Assistance recipients. Some of the latter find their way back to one of the members of their families, and often live with a daughter or a son.

We observed that at first the mother or father was taken into the home of one of the children. In none of the known cases was the construction of a cottage planned in advance, but was rather a solution resorted to later under pressure of circumstances, when life became difficult. Most of the difficulties were of a psychological nature, although some of them originate in other causes. Frequently, the cause was a physical one, the elderly person's illness necessitating the building of a cottage where stairs and other obstacles could be overcome. Overcrowding was another reason for building a separate dwelling for the elderly member of the family.

The cost of these dwellings varied, depending on whether the son or son-in-law used his own or hired labor, on the cost of sanitary facilities, on the size of the cottage, and on whether it was a new or remodeled structure. None of the observed cottages, however, exceeded a cost of $2,000, the majority of them being built at costs from $500 to $1,000. In some instances in which hired labor was used and plans were made to have a bathroom and toilet facilities connected with the sewer system, estimates ran as high as $3,000.

Quantity of This Type of Housing

The Gerontological Unit of the Cherokee Mental Health Institute made a sample study of this type of housing arrangement for elderly people in Sioux and Clay counties. From information obtained from the social welfare directors of an additional twenty counties in the northwestern part of Iowa, it was estimated that in twenty-two northwestern Iowa counties more than five hundred arrangements of this type were in existence. It is felt that the 532 cottages recorded in Table I are under, rather than over, estimations, because in several counties only cottages of known Old Age Assistance recipients were stated. Probably in these counties, as in others which were investigated, the OAA group forms only the minority of the total arrangements of this type.

Random investigation of other parts of the state of Iowa disclosed approximately the same frequency of these arrangements. It was estimated, for example, that in Polk County there are about sixty-five cottages of this type. It was therefore not unreasonable to conclude that the number of cottages on or near the property of the aging person's children is not less than two thousand in the state of Iowa. This was also the opinion of responsible officials of the State Welfare Department.

Nature of the Housing Pattern

The size of the cottages is rather small, the smallest, 8 by 10 feet, the largest, 18 by 24 feet. As a rule they are constructed for one person. In Clay County, of the estimated forty cottages of this type, not one was known to house more than one person. All cases in this study were either widows or widowers. They moved in near their children either immediately after the death of their spouse, or later when they were in need of help because of sickness or lack of earnings.

As can easily be recognized, these housing arrangements were not the result of the spirit of a stem-family pattern. No "stem"

Table I

County	Number of Dwellings	Remarks
Calhoun	12	
Cherokee	20	10 are OAA recipients
Clay	40	18 are OAA recipients
Crawford	25	Only OAA recipients recorded
Dickinson	55	
Emmet	75	
Hamilton	6	Only OAA recipients recorded
Humboldt	25	16 are OAA recipients
Ida	50	
Kossuth	7	
Lyon	6	
Monona	20	
O'Brien	6	
Plymouth	10	
Pocahontas	25	
Sac	6	
Sioux	70	10 are OAA recipients
Webster	23	
Winnebago	25	12 are OAA recipients
Woodbury	23	Only OAA recipients recorded
Worth	1	
Wright	2	
Total	532	

NUMBER OF DWELLINGS (NEWLY-BUILT COTTAGES, REMODELED GARAGES, SCHOOLHOUSES, AND TRAILERS) ON CHILDREN'S PROPERTY, ON FARMS, AND IN SMALL AND MEDIUM-SIZED TOWNS ESTIMATED BY COUNTY SOCIAL WELFARE DIRECTORS IN TWENTY-TWO COUNTIES IN NORTHWEST IOWA.

of the family was in existence, since the family had long before dissolved and the two-generation family pattern was established. Neither do the arrangements described resemble other European patterns, frequent among farmers, such as seen in Germany when the farmer retires to "Altenteil" ("the old people's deal"), or observed in Austria when he retires to the "Auszughäuschen," or in Switzerland to the "Stöckli."[2] It also does not resemble the British custom of a small "dowerage" on the estate to which a widowed mother retires. The described pattern encountered in Iowa is rather a reunion of the elderly person with members of his family who have meanwhile become the nuclei of new families. It is in some way a correction or reversal of the two-generation family pattern.

An attempt was made by the Gerontological Unit to obtain information from other parts of the United States. Answers to inquiries were received from New England, New York State, California, and Florida. No housing arrangements of this type were known to the informants. No inquiries were made in, or no satisfactory answers were received from, the neighboring states. Since, however, there is a great similarity in the socio-economic and cultural patterns of all Midwestern states, it must be assumed that developments such as those found in Iowa likewise exist in the other states.

Case Histories

As in any spontaneously arising developments, many positive as well as negative characteristics can be seen. The nine samples which follow are cited to give a cross-section of the housing conditions investigated. Newly-built cottages, trailer houses, and remodeled garages were seen. The investigators had no opportunity to see reconstructed former one-room schoolhouses, although they were known to exist. Both psychological factors and housing arrangements are considered in the following descriptions:

Case 1: Age 81. Retired farm-worker. Born in Holland. Widower. Unemployed since age 66. Moved into son's small,

[2]Dr. Hertha Kraus of Bryn Mawr was kind enough to discuss some aspects of this problem in private correspondence.

crowded farmhouse. Soon friction and tension developed, especially between subject and his grandchildren. Son built a cottage with his own labor.

Cottage: 20 x 8, consisting of bedroom and living-room-kitchen. Well-installed and equipped oil-heating unit. Kitchen corner has 2 small kerosene cooking-stoves, several kettles, dish cupboards, radio. Electricity. No running water. Outside toilet facilities situated 75 feet from the cottage.

Subject has been living there for the past 5 years and likes the arrangement. Enjoys his privacy. Feels free to do as he wishes; for instance, goes to bed at 8 P.M., gets up at 2 or 3 A.M., has a cup or two of hot tea, and turns on his radio. If weather conditions permit, goes for a short walk, returns to the cottage, and falls asleep again for another 2 or 3 hours. Gets up at 8 A.M. He takes care of himself, works in and around the cottage, and cooks his meals. Relationship with other family members improved considerably. In fact, subject changed some of his rigid principles; had been opposed to his grandchildren's going to movie theater. Not only did he give up his resistance, but began to attend movies himself, admittedly enjoying it.

The next two samples illustrate similar conditions, but also show how chronically ill persons could be appropriately managed in a cottage. In addition, Case 2 shows that a retired elderly person can be useful to the entire family for a considerable length of time—more than ten years in this instance:

Case 2: Age 78. Born in Germany. Widow. Moved in with her daughter after the loss of her second husband. Within a short time, for the subject's convenience, son-in-law built a cottage with his own labors. Subject has lived in this cottage for the past 11 years.

Cottage: 28 x 10, consisting of bedroom and living-room, situated 25 feet from the main building, with which it is connected by a paved path. For emergency there are two means of communication: (1) electric light outside of cottage which can be turned on from either building, serving to illuminate the pathway as well as for signalization, and (2) two-way house telephone which is in reach of subject's bed. Oil-heater, icebox in living-room; large bed, wardrobe, and radio in bedroom. Beside the bed is a commode camouflaged as a seat. No running water.

For 10 consecutive years, subject kept house for the whole family, relieving the daughter who worked on the farm instead. She suffered a stroke a half a year ago. Is being treated by a local doctor. Is up and around, but needs help which is given by daughter. Is still partly able to take care of herself. Is on OAA. She volunteered to say that if not for her health she would be completely satisfied. Likes her cottage.

Case 3: Age 75. Widow. Hemiplegic. The cottage was built for subject by her son on his farm.

Cottage: Comfortable 3-room cottage, situated between the homes of her son and daughter, at about equal distance (300-400 yards) from each. Two-way telephone connects her with both children.

Is in treatment of local physician. Although handicapped, she is capable of doing about 25 per cent of her work. Both her daughter and her son asked her to move in with them, but she refused, stating that she likes this arrangement and prefers her privacy.

All cottages described in the first three samples are sufficiently insulated, are protected by trees from excessive heat in summer and from snowstorms in winter. Toilet facilities are primitive and largely unsuitable for elderly persons. The psychological condition is, in all three cases, satisfactory. The elderly have justifiable complaints regarding their health, but there were no complaints about their housing arrangements.

The next two samples show that there are cottages which are less appropriately built:

Case 4: Age 78. Widower. Lost his wife 6 years ago. Lives on the farm of his son in a one-car garage remodeled to living quarters by his son.

Cottage: 12 x 16, consisting of 1 room. It is 50 feet from the main building and 30 feet from the outdoor toilet. No insulation and no shade trees. Is uncomfortably hot on sunny summer days and cold in winter. Large oil-heater inconveniently occupies the middle of the room. There is electricity but no running water; it is poorly furnished, and no cooking facilities are provided.

Subject spends most of his time in a small community cafe where he gets his meals. He does not particularly like his housing arrangement, and wishes he had a "real home" of his own. He realizes, however, that this solution is better than any other one possible.

He especially enjoys his privacy. He ties himself to his bed by wrist-cuff every night because once, when he thought he saw someone in the room, he jumped up and hurt himself on the heater.

We call attention to the self-prescribed restraint in Case 4, which the subject devised for his own protection. It is not excluded that he had a transient psychotic incident or a delusional reaction. The main danger, however, was not his mental condition, but hazards originating in the poorly-planned room.

Case 5: Age 74. Widow. She is in ill health suffering from pernicious anemia and urinary infection. Had been a resident of a nursing home, but since she was unhappy there, she was taken out and given a bedroom on the second floor in the home of one of her four daughters. Because the subject had difficulty in climbing stairs, a cottage was built for her on the grounds of a family settlement in a residential district of a small town. (2500 pop.).

Cottage: 8 x 10, consisting of one neatly furnished room. Conveniences include an oil-heater, a double-burner hot-plate, cooking utensils, and a radio. Electricity, no running water. Uses bathroom facilities in the main house which is only a few feet away. No insulation, but is protected from summer heat by shade trees. Subject complains of excessive cold on winter mornings.

The cottage is located between the 6-room house of subject's daughter and the rather large comfortable home of the son-in-law's parents. Near the cottage is a garage almost twice as large. Subject has lived there for 3 years. She feels isolated, complains that no one understands her. She feels rejected, and is bitter. States that even her little grandson does not respect her. She accuses her son-in-law of treating her badly; she has to leave the main building when he comes home. Subject is on OAA. Would prefer to live elsewhere.

Case 5 shows how such small cottages should not be built. There were obviously deeply-rooted conflicts within the family. The psychological situation also seems to be responsible for the inadequate planning and arrangement of the cottage. This, in turn, adds a new source of humiliation, demonstrating to the subject her inferior social position, which contributes to an aggravation rather than to an amelioration of the existing tensions.

The following is the largest cottage which was observed by the Unit. It was well insulated and expediently built:

Case 6: Age 65. Divorced. Born in Norway. The cottage was built for her on the daughter's property in the residential district of a town of 7,500 population. In spite of some zoning regulations, permission was obtained to build the cottage.

Cottage: 18 x 24, consisting of kitchen, bedroom, living-room, and a fourth room which serves as a large closet but which is planned to be made into a bathroom. Installation of bathroom facilities was postponed for financial reasons. Conveniences include electricity, running water, a party-line telephone, oil-heater, and a completely equipped kitchen. The dwelling is insulated. It is neatly and individually furnished.

The subject is on Old Age Assistance.

The following two cases illustrate arrangements utilizing trailers or trailer homes. One is permanently established in a definite location, the other moves seasonally from one child to another:

Case 7: Age 70. Widow. Victim of poliomyelitis and invalided since younger years. She can walk only with a walker. Subject had her own 3-room house from which she was forced to move because of unsanitary conditions created by her handicap which kept her from keeping house adequately. Her children wanted to take her in, but she refused, preferring to live alone. The trailer-house was therefore bought for her and established near her son's farm-house. The subject can take care of most of her own needs in the more compact home. She is on Old Age Assistance.

Case 8: Age 70. Widower. Born in Denmark. Former farm-owner who retired 8 years ago because of his wife's illness. She died two years ago. He spent all accumulated funds ($11,000) during her illness, and is now on Old Age Assistance. His children bought him a house in town but he was restless and unhappy there. This house was therefore sold and a trailer 8 x 30 was bought. He drives, and moves the trailer alternately from the son's to the daughter's farm homes every three months. In the hayfever season he drives the trailer a few hundred miles north and does fishing which he enjoys very much.

Although the subject in Case 8 appears to be content with his arrangement, it is doubtful that this was the best solution possible for him. He apparently suffers from depressive reactions and restlessness which are channeled in his constant moving about with his trailer.

In striking contrast with the majority of other cases is, in many respects, the last sample:

Case 9:   Age 86.   Widower.   Born in Holland.   Has four children.   Has lived for the past 10 years in an old, run-down trailer. There is one small window.   The door, an old and decrepit mass of loosely-hung boards, is propped open with a shovel.   The dwelling is dark and uncomfortable inside.   In the middle of the room is a rusty iron wood-stove.   Furnishings include a cot, 2 large wardrobes, and a chair.   There is electricity, but no running water and no toilet facilities.   The structure is within 2 blocks of a son's business establishment in a small town (2500 pop.).

Two years ago the subject suffered a right side stroke; his speech is still impaired and understanding is difficult but possible.   He is easily irritated, monosyllabic, and only partly oriented.   He walks with a cane.   Because of lack of judgment or for other reasons, he uses any place around his home for urination and defecation.   There is often a considerable odor which disturbs the neighbors.

He was removed from Old Age Assistance rolls because it was found that he was not eligible.   One of his sons has a more than comfortable income, and is legally responsible for his support.   The aid he receives from his children consists of a visit once a day from one or another of them to bring him a meal and carry water; otherwise he takes care of himself.

Case 9 is one of the most depressing the Unit encountered during the survey.   The only encouraging aspect of the case was that this physically and mentally handicapped person managed to care for most of his own needs.   It was obvious, however, that the cooking and heating arrangements, as well as the unsanitary conditions, constituted a potential danger to the subject and to the neighborhood.

Discussion

Housing practices which emerge in rural districts appear to be rather primitive.   Although the idea of adjusting former garages, one-room schoolhouses, or trailers to living quarters seems to be inconsistent with modern views, it is still a reality in rural areas in Iowa today. Such remodeling, or even building of small new cottages, has served to solve or to help alleviate disadvantageous housing circumstances for a number of elderly persons. It is most often a comparatively inexpensive solution, especially in cases where one or more persons of the family contribute their own labor. In some instances, the planning and construction of the cottages was not expedient. In others, however, originality and understanding of the aging person's needs created housing conditions which, though primitive, were both suitable under existing circumstances and acceptable to the elderly person.

Once the cottage is built, its maintenance is rarely an additional financial problem as long as the elderly person is able to take care of it himself. And since the houses are small one-story dwellings, their up-keep is usually within the scope of a physically well elderly person's abilities, except for rare occasions when a younger person's help might be needed.

Certainly one of the main disadvantages of many of these arrangements is the substandard sanitary facilities. In several instances, however, it was found that there is no awareness that it is a problem; in fact, on the farms the aging are living in this regard under conditions no different from those of their children in the main house. More than one-third of the farms in some regions still have unsatisfactory sewerage installations. It is possible that awareness of the needs of older persons for improved sanitary facilities may stimulate appropriate developments among the general population.

A source of potential danger to the individual and to the community in some instances was the unsuitable heating and cooking arrangements. Kerosene stoves are fire hazards, and wood and coal stoves, in addition to being hazardous, are difficult for the elderly to manage. In several cases where oil heaters were installed, the heating problem seemed to have been solved satisfactorily. Although electricity was found in every cottage, electric cooking units were observed very rarely.

Insulation was also found to be inadequate in several instances, with the result that sunny summer days found the cottages to be intolerably hot, while in winter the occupants suffered from the cold. Sometimes an attempt was made to solve the problem by installing numerous windows, thereby bringing some relief from heat in summer but contributing to cold in winter.

Some other specific conveniences necessary for the safety of the elderly were also often neglected or overlooked. For example, cupboards were out of arm's reach, throw rugs created hazards in walking, and often no communication system was installed. In three instances, however, very expediently arranged private or public telephone connections were observed.

With the exception of the lack of toilet facilities and water supply, all the above-mentioned disadvantages could be eliminated with a minimum of expense. Sanitation improvements would require some economic planning and financing which would not, however, create any particular difficulties in Old Age Assistance cases nor in the less needy ones.

In spite of the fact that these disadvantages, which are not insurmountable, continue to exist, the advantages of such an arrangement outweigh the unfavorable factors. Wherever there were no discernible, deeply-rooted psychological conflicts, and where the living arrangements were reasonably adequate, the aging seen in this survey stated that they were satisfied with the solution and liked their cottages. They felt greater security in the knowledge that their children were nearby in time of need or emergency, yet they were largely independent of their children financially, and maintained their independence and privacy as far as their pattern of living and personal habits were concerned. It was observed that in such cases there was also less mutual interference between the generations than is ordinarily found when the elderly person lives under the same roof with the children. In fact, they sometimes show a greater flexibility in adjusting to newer cultural patterns. In addition, the very fact that having their own dwellings gives them an opportunity to take care of themselves and decreases their feelings of being a burden to family and community.

There is another important aspect to this type of housing arrangement. These cottages are not only suitable for the healthy or almost healthy aging, but are also practical for those who suffer from chronic illnesses which can be managed outside of a hospital, as, for example, after effects of stroke, arthritis, crippled limbs, diabetes, and the like. Certainly, the chronic diseases observed by the Unit in the subjects of this survey could be treated adequately there. Of course, dietary therapy, and especially physio- and rehabilitation therapy, could and should be applied to these cases to a greater extent than they are now. But these lacks do not result from the housing condition as much as from the present stage of rehabilitation therapy. New trends in this important field of medicine and social welfare for the aging will have to take into consideration rural conditions and make all necessary adjustments.

The Gerontological Unit felt that these cottages were suitable for not only chronic medical and neurological cases, but also for certain types of psychotic aging, especially for mild mental cases. Admittedly, psychotic and even mildly psychotic elderly persons can be the source of great inconvenience for the family and there are always some risks created by hazards. But very often the environment, rather than the psychotic elderly person himself, is the cause of any dangerous reaction. Appropriate psychiatric and psychological counseling can help overcome these exogenic obstacles and help keep the elderly in their homes and out of the overcrowded institutions.

The Gerontological Unit believes that the development of housekeeping and nursing services and psychological counseling, which have already begun in larger cities, will find a place in rural life. These services, in conjunction with the housing arrangement described, would give many elderly people the opportunity to spend the last years of their lives under better, safer, and more satisfying conditions.

The positive aspects of the type of housing arrangement disclosed by the present study warrant further investigation of its financial possibilities, its place in community planning, its psychological and social implications, and its role in the management of mild psychiatric and chronic medical cases. The Unit feels strongly that this spontaneous beginning can be the starting point for further developments in housing of the aging in accordance with modern trends in gerontology.

Housing Older People Requiring Sheltered Care and Medical Supervision

PART III

NEEDS AND
PROBLEMS *Chapter* X

BY ROBERT T. MONROE

> Robert T. Monroe, M.D., is associate in clinical medicine,
> Harvard Medical School, and senior associate in medicine,
> Peter Bent Brigham Hospital. He is the author of Diseases
> in Old Age (1951) and editor of Medical Papers dedicated
> to Henry A. Christian. Dr. Monroe is a member of the
> American Medical Association and of the Gerontological
> Society.

The Need for a New Approach

THE NEEDS and the problems of housing older people requiring
sheltered care and medical supervision are such as to frighten
and repel us if we are not careful. We have a tendency to
categorize groups of people rather arbitrarily in order to focus more
distinctly upon their problems, and in so doing the pictures we,
ourselves, create are sometimes frightening. The alarm words in
this instance are "older," "sheltered," and "supervision." They seem
to suggest that deterioration and dependency inevitably increase
with age, and since old people are increasing rapidly in numbers
and in proportion, there is, perhaps, a certain justification for
alarm.

Discussions of the problems of aging by experts, and also by lay
people, seem to be based on a feeling that younger old people
are different from older old people. In the younger group, diseases
and disabilities of all kinds are held to be of primary importance;
attempts to cure them may be very rewarding. But in the older
group, roughly those over seventy-five years of age, age itself
comes, somehow, to be of greater significance than disease, "At
your age, what can you expect?" is a common statement of this

attitude. It can lead to a quality of care that has no expectation of reward in cure or in improved performance. It can sentence people with minor ailments to death or to a living death. It sees euthanasia as sometimes justified, and it argues that the Maker of the Universe is mistaken in allowing life to linger so. It is an abandonment of the central democratic principle of the worth of every individual under all circumstances.

We can be practical and admit the greater difficulty in studying and altering older bodies and older attitudes. But we can also admit that we have not yet tried very hard to find the skills and tools and services that are needed to do the job. When we see some very old people living to a great age, in good mental and physical health and performing useful functions, we can assume that vigorous efforts with others might be expected to swell their numbers. The facts are that older people are still people and they all have areas of normality left in them.

Sheltered Care

What is meant by "sheltered care?" Undoubtedly, it refers to institutional situations—mental hospitals, chronic disease hospitals, nursing homes, convalescent homes, public and private homes for the aged. Statistics on mental and chronic disease can be built up to a particularly frightening picture: half of all hospital beds in the country are occupied by patients with mental disease; millions of people have persistent diseases and disabilities. All of them need "medical care and supervision." We cannot challenge the statistics, but at least we might interpret them correctly, particularly as they concern the aging. For one thing, every one at every age needs medical care and supervision. We devote a great deal of care to children; we should not be disturbed to consider as much of it for old people.

A second fact is that scarcely 4 per cent of people over the age of sixty-five are in institutions. A rather superficial survey in Massachusetts a year ago showed that the patients in mental hospitals, chronic hospitals, nursing homes, almshouses, and private homes for the aged came to about that. A report from the 1950 United States Census stated that 96 per cent of old people live in their own homes, or what pass for homes; and the situation is the same in England, according to the information in *Social Medicine of Old Age*.[1]

But the burden of mental disease is greater than 4 per cent of old people. My study, *Diseases in Old Age*, published by the Harvard University Press in 1951, showed that about 15 per cent of the persons over sixty-five years of age have cerebral arteriosclerosis and about half of them have psychosis; about 2 per cent of the aged have senile dementia, these cases coming largely from public and private old age homes. It was also determined that the most common causes of mental deterioration in old people are diseases outside of the central nervous system, such as heart disease and malnutrition. Very few of the cases in my series were committed to institutions, either because they were not gravely disorganized or because relatives preferred to assume their care. Mental health officials are, quite properly, concerned over the increasing commitments to institutions of patients over sixty-five, but the over-all view is that more than 96 per cent of old people stay out of them.

A critical study of papers on chronic disease makes one question whether it is helpful in research to group together diseases whose only similarity is persistence in time. Thus, in the National Health Survey of 1935-36, one finds hernia, hemorrhoids, hay fever, sinusitis, varicose veins, chronic tonsillitis, chronic appendicitis, and other diagnoses of doubtful authenticity added to cases of heart disease and rheumatism. If the sum of patients with chronic disease is the point to be determined, it could be settled confidently by simply selecting some number greater than the total population beyond the age of forty-five, because every one in middle age has some structural defect and not even all younger people are perfect. If the questions are such as: what persistent diseases are progressive, which of them interfere with general health and performance, and when do they interfere, they are better questions, but we do not have satisfactory answers. Diseases, people, and circumstances vary so greatly that the care of all

[1] Joseph H. Sheldon, *Social Medicine of Old Age* (London: Oxford Univ. Press, 1948).

illness is best when it is based on general hospital experience, and only occasionally is it helpful to isolate particular groups for treatment or research.

Health Characteristics of the Aged

In his old age every one accumulates a number of chronic diseases. Everyone has hypertrophic arthritis, hard arteries, and sclerotic patches in the spinal cord and brain. The majority have heart disease and high blood pressure. Many have peptic ulcers and gall stones. Yet old people usually get along very well most of the time in spite of them. Their geriatricians are impressed with two facts. One is that some of the diseases activate others in times of crisis, so that it is essential that their presence be known and plans be ready for action in crisis. For example, a coronary artery occlusion may precipitate hemorrhage from a peptic ulcer, or the other way around; a surgical operation may activate diabetes.

The second and really impressive fact to the geriatrician is the influence that general living forces have upon diseases, not merely upon morale. Everyone knows how often heart disease strikes down men who are facing the retirement crisis; the disease was already established, but the shock of lost place, lost usefulness, and changed program activated it. Living on the side lines promotes malnutrition and brings old symptoms into prominence. Loss of family and friends creates sadness and apprehension and makes continued performance less meaningful; thus bodies and minds are used less, and minor losses in muscles, joints, and nerve pathways appear and invite further deterioration. Changes in living because of loss of spouse or other living companions, or to the children moving away or back again, or to restricted income on retirement cause important medical states: weariness in the attempt to continue housekeeping without help, isolation in undesired surroundings, lack of good nutrition and good social and physical outlets. These again magnify minor heart disease and mental depressions, minor psychoses and diabetes. The care of the aged is then not just the prescription of pills for symptoms; it is the search for and control of all disabilities that can be found. But most of all, it is the care of the old person as a whole person.

no matter what his state and status. What the geriatrician needs are physical and mental rehabilitation centers, occupational services leading to jobs, housing developments, and social outlets.

In describing medical care in sheltered situations we must insist that physical and mental and social fitness be promoted. If we do, these situations can be powerful centers for all possible convalescence and for influencing the lives of the 96 per cent of old people that are not in them. If we do not, if we describe custodial care only, we shall ruin the rest of the lives of the inmates and confirm the gloomy views of all who struggle to keep out of them.

Mental Treatment

Mental health officials have made known the needs of psychopathic hospitals for the services of psychiatrists, psychologists, nurses, and social workers. They know how much can be done with adequate facilities for many patients with cerebral arteriosclerosis and psychosis. They have not had enough opportunity to work with physical rehabilitation techniques to know how much can be done to restore function in hemiplegia, to lessen speech defects, and to improve performance in paralysis agitans. These services are just now being created in a few centers in the country. Mental health officials should be granted opportunities to encourage their patients to develop hobbies and some useful occupation, activities which have proved to be great therapeutic agents in mental disease. Strenuous efforts should be made to tie in with other medical centers and all other community activities the work in psychopathic hospitals, so that we may know and share in their work as an exciting and rewarding adventure. They should be encouraged in their establishment of outpatient clinics and the granting of vacations to improved patients.

Good mental nursing homes should be developed to supplement the work of the psychopathic hospitals. At present they appear to serve best the very seriously deteriorated old people. The homes do not have the workers and the money to do an intensive job on those who are less disturbed. They are costly in comparison to public institutions, but they can produce simpler and more acceptable custodial care.

Treatment of Chronic Disease

Chronic disease hospitals are being developed in many areas. They will meet an important need, but their separation from general hospitals must be deplored. Tuberculosis hospitals, for example, which have contributed so much to our knowledge of tuberculosis, have taken the disease so completely out of the area of the teaching hospitals and of general practice that only specialists are competent to deal with it. The English system of long-term annexes to general hospitals seems far better for administration, teaching, research, and the care of patients as members of their communities. However the patients are quartered, it is necessary to develop new services in the hospitals for rehabilitation of minds and bodies. Old people cannot safely be left idle in bed in the intervals between meals, pills, and X-ray studies. They must be incited to be active and to lead as normal lives as possible while their illness compels them to remain in the hospital. The ambulatory can eat together, they can assist with ward tasks, they can play and work together. Space must be provided for personal belongings and some privacy. All this will require more physiotherapists, social workers, teachers, and a considerable increase in human understanding on the part of harassed house officers and nurses, but the cost per capita may not be as great as it is now in acute hospitals, and the results can be extraordinary. The work of Dr. Marjorie Warren in England testifies to this.

Nursing Homes

Nursing homes are growing in number with the demand for long-term medical care situations. They are inhabited largely by old people. Most of them are criticized severely by physicians, but they seem to be necessary. How can they be improved? By providing medical supervision, in the first place. At present, many of the patients have no physicians, those who have are seldom visited by them, and the proprietors use their judgment as to when professional advice is desirable and whom to ask. This neglect is due only in part to poor financial reward and lack of interest in long-term illness; I think the real reason for it is the impossibility of good professional study and care in the homes as they now are. Few of the homes have graduate nurses, few of them have enough practical nurses or partly trained women. Housecleaning workers are few. Dietitians are scarce. Physiotherapists, occupational therapists, and physical rehabilitation workers are absent. Usually there is no provision for laboratory work or room for sociability between patients or with visitors. Once in a while a little diversion is provided, but the few social workers for the great load of old people on assistance can seldom check up on their charges. What can be done to raise the quality of care? The association of proprietors of nursing homes will stabilize some practices at least. Can neighborhood hospitals extend the services of their staffs to them?

Old Age Homes

Privately run homes for the aged should, theoretically, not be bothered much by medical care needs because most of them still insist that their inmates be free from organic disease when they enter. Such a provision is an impossibility, of course, but it acts to select a group that have been defeated more by life than by disease. Several Jewish old age homes are models in the quality of medical care that they give and in their generous attempts to reconstruct a new home life. The great majority of the rest are outmoded and inadequate, to put it mildly. The things done, and the things not done, by good people acting as agents for churches, fraternal organizations, and trusts are astonishing. There is little evidence to warrant hope that they will improve. Perhaps they should not be encouraged to do so, for institutional life limited to one sect or sex is not what normal Americans crave.

The almshouses of Massachusetts, or the public infirmaries, have largely become, through various circumstances, places of custodial care for old people with chronic nonmental diseases. The same tendencies appear to operate elsewhere. These infirmaries compare favorably in quality of living with the private homes, but the resources which are granted them do not permit medical care any better than that in the average nursing home. Where study and care are not given it is comfortable to assume that the condition of the patients is due to their diseases and is irremediable. In Pittsburgh, Dr. Murray B. Ferderber and Dr. Alfred C. Kraft showed what a belief in the value of the individual plus a little common-sense encouragement of personal hygiene can do for repulsive old people far gone in squalid senility. As a result of their work, a new county infirmary is to be built in which patients can have good care and have many opportunities to improve and to share in life again. There are other infirmaries where teaching hospitals or groups of physicians have done valuable work. It may well be that these public institutions will tend to become the chronic hospitals or long-term annexes that we need.

Home Care

What kind of shelter and medical care are required by the 96 per cent of old people that maintain their own homes? The small proportion that are financially well provided for deserve attention because they have found that money cannot buy friends or occupation or goals. They are as vulnerable as others to physical and mental unfitness, and to malnutrition with disease. The struggles of the great majority of independent old people to pay their bills in times of inflation, to keep house with less help and failing strength, to find new friends and tasks and interests when old ones are gone, have only to be suggested to make us realize why fear and fatigue and frustration are the chief precipitating causes of active organic disease in them. What can we do to help?

Home medical care programs have been successful in New York City, started first by the Montefiore Hospital group. They are being copied elsewhere. They may serve a very useful role with old people. One can hope that the medical workers on the teams will realize that defense of a patient's independent status is of fundamental importance in any treatment program. Geriatric clinics should be established in all teaching hospitals so that ways of handling old people can be discovered and taught. The care of sickness is best in the hands of physicians who are chosen freely by the patients, and certainly physicians have much to learn in this growing field.

We must experiment with new kinds of homes, too. We need to develop homes which old people can call their own because they pay rent; homes where household tasks and shopping can be lightened by the kindness of neighbors or by fees for such services; homes where there are opportunities for physical play, for seeing friends, for exploring hobbies and jobs, for continuing to play a part in community life. We need a new type of nursing home where the aging can go, at small cost, for minor or short-lasting illnesses, and where they can be taught to overcome handicaps such as paralysis. It is gratifying to report that such experiments are already under way in several places. Old people used to retire to the country or small towns expecting to find simple living at less expense. They now tend to stay in the cities where their working lives were spent, for urban tastes are not lost easily. Therefore, the new style homes will be multidwelling apartment houses—congregate living without institutionitis.

These are the needs of older people requiring sheltered care and medical supervision. They will cost much in money, in workers, and in services. None of these are available in adequate amounts today. But as the results of caring well for old people, now sensed by only a few, become known to more, we can confidently expect that the needs will be met. Then a new chapter in the democratic way of life will commence.

NURSING AND CONVALESCENT
HOMES   *Chapter XI*

BY EDNA NICHOLSON

> *Edna Nicholson, M.S., is director of The Central Service for the Chronically Ill of the Institute of Medicine of Chicago. She is also special lecturer, Program in Hospital Administration, Northwestern University. From 1942 to 1944 she was consultant on medical assistance of the Bureau of Public Assistance, Social Security Board, Washington, D.C.; from 1938 to 1942 she was director of the Medical Relief Service, Chicago Relief Administration. She is the author of* Tuberculosis Mortality Among Young Women, National Tuberculosis Association, Social Research Series No. 1, 1931, *and* Tuberculosis Among Young Women in New York City, No. 4 *of the same series,* 1933. *She has also written* Surveying Community Needs and Resources for Care of the Chronically Ill, 1950, *and* Terminal Care for Cancer Patients, 1950, *as well as numerous articles in various professional journals. She is a member of the American Public Health Association of Medical Social Workers.*

As a basis for considering the place of nursing homes among community provisions for meeting the needs of older people, it seems important to clarify, if possible, what types of facilities are included in this category. Although nursing homes rapidly are becoming familiar sights in every community, there remains considerable confusion regarding their nature, their functions, and the characteristics—if any—which distinguish them from other facilities also offering shelter and care for older people.

Complete and accurate figures are not available, but we know that there are at least fourteen or fifteen thousand homes and institutions in the United States offering long-term care for elderly infirm, and chronically ill people. These places are operating under many different names. They are described variously as convalescent homes, rest homes, nursing homes, boarding homes, homes for incurables, "geriatric" or "chronic" units in general hospitals, infirmaries, sanitariums, health resorts, guest homes, and homes for the aged. Some of them are privately owned and operated. Some operate under the ownership of church groups, fraternal orders, and other not-for-profit corporations. Others are owned and administered by cities, counties, and other governmental units. Some of them are large. Others are very small.

What is a Nursing Home?

Even a brief review of the nature of these variously named places makes it obvious that, regardless of the names under which they operate, many of them are housing essentially the same kinds of people. The services they are providing, or should be providing, are approximately the same, and differences in the names under which they operate show little or no correlation with differences in the needs of their residents or in the services required to meet them.

Since the names under which they operate do not provide a valid basis for distinguishing one type of facility from another, one may ask just what basis should be used in attempting to classify the various facilities and to define the part which each should play in meeting the total need for special housing and care of older people. It is possible to classify these facilities on the basis of:

1. Their size.

2. The types of buildings in which they operate; whether they are housed in converted family residences or in institutional types of buildings.

3. Their ownership; whether they are privately owned, are operated as not-for-profit enterprises by churches, fraternal orders, or similar groups; or are owned and operated by cities, counties, or other governmental units.

4. The age of the persons accepted for care; whether only persons sixty-five years of age or over are admitted or persons sixty or fifty or forty years of age also are accepted.

5. The services provided; whether a place is a nursing home, if it has nurses on its staff, and not a nursing home if it has not.

6. The kinds of services needed for the proper care of persons housed in the home; whether the patients are physically and/or mentally ill to the extent that they require some degree of nursing care, or whether they are able to care for themselves and are thus self-sufficient.

It may be noted here that, at the present stage of development of homes and institutions for the care of older people, there is a real difference between classifying them on the basis of the services which they are providing and on the basis of the services which should be provided. In a high proportion of such homes and institutions there is a wide gap between the services which should be available and those which actually are being provided. Incidentally, this gap is at least as wide in the homes and institutions operated by voluntary not-for-profit corporations and by governmental units as it is in the small, privately owned homes.

Each of these possible points of distinction may be a valid basis for classifying homes and institutions for a specific purpose and at a specific time. Obviously, there are occasions when it is important to know what proportions of the total services are being provided under private ownership, under nonprofit auspices, and by government; or what proportions are available in facilities of twenty-five beds or under, fifty beds, one hundred beds, one thousand beds, or other sizes; or it may be important, for a particular purpose, to know what parts of the total services in a community are being offered in old residence buildings, old institutional buildings, or buildings constructed particularly for this use. There are times when it is significant to know what age groups are accepted in the various homes and, often, it is important to know what services are being provided. In my opinion, however, our first concern should be with the needs of the people in the homes, and the nursing home should be distinguished from other facilities in the community primarily on the basis of whether it accepts responsibility for providing a home for people who need nursing supervision or care.

Having defined a nursing home in this way, subclassifications for other purposes may be made on the basis of size, type of building, ownership, age group served, or other factors. It seems important to recognize, however, that these factors are of secondary importance. They do not change the basic character of the place.

Need for a Comprehensive Approach Toward Homes and Institutions

Such a definition of a nursing home includes many places not now calling themselves nursing homes and not currently providing nursing services. From the point of view of the welfare of the elderly people who need nursing supervision and care, however, it is important that all places accepting responsibility for their housing and care be included in the category of nursing home and be expected to meet the same standards with respect to the adequacy with which they meet the needs of their residents.

This is important for a number of reasons. It is essential if we are to have equitable treatment for people with similar needs. It is necessary if all of the various places now operating, and all of the persons operating them, are to receive fair treatment under licensing laws and standard-setting programs. And it is fundamental to any successful efforts to plan and develop good new services in our communities for the many elderly people who now need more and better services, and need them desperately.

Equitable Treatment of Residents

All persons who seek and need the protection of sheltered living arrangements in any type of congregate home have some things in common. They have reached a point where they no longer are fully able to live independently in the community and no longer have the protection of living with their own families who, otherwise, would assume the responsibilities which they no longer can carry independently. Because they do not have the normal protection of personal independence and family responsibility, society accepts an obligation for general supervision of the care provided to them. This obligation usually is expressed through standard-setting and licensing programs.

The wide-spread confusion as to how to classify sheltered-care facilities operating under various names is being reflected in the confusion and inconsistencies in the application of standards and licensing requirements. As a result, we see one set of standards being applied to the care provided for a group of elderly people living in a place calling itself a nursing home and a totally different set or—a more frequent and hazardous occurrence—no standards at all being applied to the care of another group whose needs may be identical but live in a place calling itself a "boarding home" or home for "well old people."

The elderly lady, living in a so-called "boarding home" or "home for well old people," who is in need of a controlled diabetic diet and is not receiving it, may go into coma or develop a gangrenous extremity just as quickly as the one who is living in a place described as a "nursing home." She will suffer just as much as a result of the inadequate care she is receiving, and the ultimate cost to the community in prolonged invalidism will be just as great. If the community has a responsibility to protect elderly people who need sheltered care, it seems important that this protection be extended equally to all persons in need of it, regardless of the name that is given to the homes where they are attended.

At the present time, blind, crippled, disoriented, and sick old people are often huddled in so-called boarding homes, where no pretense is made to meet their needs for medical attention and nursing care, and where they have no protection from licensing authorities or standard-setting bodies, and this because the name of the place in which they are living is assumed to indicate that no protection is needed. Even government institutions and voluntary philanthropic homes are guilty of this offense.

Equitable Treatment of Home Operators

Nor is this erratic form of licensing fair to the persons and organizations operating the homes and institutions. Where a home need only call itself a "boarding home" or a "home for the aged" to evade completely any supervision by licensing authorities, there is a real justification in the protests of the orthodox nursing homes who feel that they are subjected to supervision and licensing requirements which are not applied to other places housing persons with similar needs. It seems important, in justice to the homes and institutions as well as for protection of the elderly people, that in formulating and applying standards of care the standards be based upon the needs of the people requiring the care and that the same standards be applied to all places housing persons whose needs are similar.

Need for a Comprehensive Approach in Planning and Developing Community Resources

There are few, if any, communities where present resources for protection and care of elderly people are sufficient to meet the need. In most places there is urgent need for the development of substantial numbers of new facilities and services. If this need is to be met, some very practical steps must be taken. It is not enough to know that there are many elderly people who are not receiving adequate care. There must be factual information, also, with respect to how many people there are, specifically what kinds of care they need, how much of it already is available in the community, how much is in process of development, what additional facilities are needed, where they should be developed, who should own and operate them, how much they will cost, and how they can be financed.

Today, with the pressure to develop more facilities for older people, there is danger of superficial thinking, inadequate planning, and of developing facilities which, too late, may be found inadequate to meet the real need. When the pressure of unmet need is great, there is also danger that the need may overshadow the resources already in operation to a point where their present and potential contribution toward meeting the problem is seriously underestimated. This is especially true when the nature of some of the facilities is not clearly defined and understood.

The problem of planning and developing more institutional facilities for the aging is complicated further by the fact that it currently is being approached by two groups which, I believe, should be integrating their planning more closely than has been done in the past. One group concerns itself with the development of adequate services for promoting health, preventing infirmities, providing housing and long-term care for the chronically ill; and all this includes a substantial amount of service to persons in the older age groups. The second group characterizes its efforts specifically as "work for the aged," yet the needs of older people that it meets are similar to those of the first group. Differences in terminology not only confuse thinking but lead to duplication in the development of good services.

As an illustration, figures recently assembled in my own community indicate that the people who frequently are described as "well old people in need of institutional care" are, in reality, the same people who simultaneously are described as "ambulant persons with chronic disabilities or diseases." If subsequent figures are consistent with the fairly substantial amount of data so far assembled, it will be evident that these supposedly different groups actually are the same people and that there has been an overlapping of between two and three thousand beds in the estimates of the total number of additional facilities needed in our community. At current costs, this amounts to nearly $50 million in construction expense alone.

Obviously, it is important in planning and developing the additional facilities needed, that we clarify our thinking; base our plans on factual and comprehensive information about the people to be served and the needs which they present; recognize clearly all of the facilities already available and the ways in which they can be used more effectively regardless of the names under which they may be operating; and do our best to avoid the gaps and duplications in services and the unnecessary expense, which are the inevitable results of segmented planning.

Nursing Homes and Homes for the Aged

Defined as any place which undertakes to provide a home for persons requiring nursing care, the term "nursing home" covers many places not now using this title, including most of those now classified as homes for the aged. There are many people who will disagree with the use of the term in connection with such places. There are good reasons for this disagreement, and there would seem to be little to be gained by all such facilities forth-with labeling themselves "nursing homes." Particularly from the point of view of their residents, a name with more attractive connotations may seem preferable, and there is probably no reason why the homes should not continue to operate under what-ever particular individual names they prefer, provided that every-one concerned, the home operators, the persons responsible for licensing and standard-setting, and those concerned with com-munity planning and organization, recognize their basic character.

Increasing Need for Health Services and Medical Care in Homes for the Aged

The past half century has brought far-reaching changes in social organization, economics, and medical care. These changes have greatly altered the kinds of persons seeking and needing care in homes for the aged, and have changed the types of care required.

Most of the older homes for the aged were established originally to provide shelter for needy old people who were in good health but had no money to live elsewhere. At that time, there were very few pension or old age insurance provisions. There were no cash assistance programs, and practically no sources of any kind from which needy elderly people could obtain an income to enable them to remain in homes of their own. Their only recourse was to enter an institution where food and shelter were provided in kind. At the same time, pneumonia, dysentery, typhoid fever, and other acute diseases were prevalent and were responsible for the deaths of many older people. These illnesses tended to strike suddenly and to terminate rapidly. Since more people died from these rapidly fatal illnesses, fewer lived to suffer lingering disabilities.

For a number of years there was a significant need and de-mand for homes for the aged offering food and shelter for older people who were in good health but were without funds. The homes, in fact, were homes for elderly people in good health.

In more recent years, however, there has been almost phenomenal growth in pension and insurance systems. Cash assistance programs have been widely established. As a result, many older people now have access to cash incomes which make it possible for them to remain in their own homes so long as they are physically and mentally able to care for themselves. There is no longer any need for them to seek care in a home for the aged solely because they have no money to live elsewhere. Simultaneously, advances in medicine have almost eliminated the diseases which strike quickly and terminate rapidly. As fewer deaths are caused by these diseases, steadily increasing numbers of people are left to wear out with slowly increasing disabilities caused by the so-called chronic diseases.

As a result of these and other factors, the number of older people seeking and needing institutional care while they are still in good health has been decreasing almost to the vanishing point, while there has been a steady increase in the number of older people in the population suffering from chronic infirmities and illness in varying degrees of intensity. Even a brief review of the health status of the persons now living in homes for the aged, and of those seeking admission to them, gives striking evidence of the extent of this change in the need for institutional care of older people in good health. Even in those homes which limit their admissions to persons who are up and about and in what they describe as "good health for their age," records show that from 85 to 100 per cent of their residents have some degree of disease of the heart, arteriosclerosis, hypertension, diabetes, arthritis, kidney disorders, neurological conditions, disturbances of hearing and vision, or other infirmities. Thus it becomes necessary that the residents of these homes have good medical and nursing supervision to protect the degree of health they still have, and to provide the added amounts of care they require as their disabilities gradually but steadily increase.

It is doubtful that anything of value necessarily would be gained by insisting that these elderly people in the early stages of their chronic diseases, while they are still comparatively self-sufficient, be labeled chronically ill. Probably there is nothing inherently dangerous in describing them as "well old people in need of institutional care." There is serious danger, however, in the tragic extent to which the health of these older people has been neglected during these early stages of their illnesses. Because they have been considered to be "well" people, their need for medical guidance and nursing supervision has been almost completely ignored until their diseases have progressed to a point where they are bedridden and almost totally disabled, and where there is no longer anything to be done but to let them lie helplessly in their beds while someone provides constant nursing care.

There is urgent need for a new understanding of health as a matter of degree, and for a far more constructive use of medical and nursing care in homes for the aged and elsewhere to maintain the best possible degree of health and physical and mental well-being in the early phases of chronic illness among older people.

Importance of Continuity in Care

Almost all of the older people seeking and receiving care in homes and institutions are suffering from conditions which call for some degree of protection immediately, and which can be expected to progress gradually, causing them to require slowly but steadily increasing amounts of care. For most of these people there is no dramatic break between the time when they need minor care and when they need extensive care. Consequently, it is extremely difficult to draw a sharp line between the time when "ambulant" or "boarding" care is needed and the time when "nursing" or "nursing home care" is needed. There is no way of differentiating clearly, therefore, the point at which an individual should be removed from the "boarding home" or "home for well old people" and placed in the "nursing home" or "infirmary." There are, of course, instances in which a dramatic break occurs. These are in the minority, however. In most cases it is impossible to identify any definite point at which the need for one type of care ends and the other begins. Because there is no clear line of demarcation in the needs of the people being served, it is important that the facilities providing the service be so organized and administered that there need be no sharp break in the provision of care for the individual.

There are other reasons, also, why there should be no sharp divisions between the facilities providing care for persons who are still up and about and fairly self-sufficient and those providing the care needed after the individual has become bedridden or otherwise in need of fairly constant nursing care. One of these lies in the emotional adjustment required of the individual. Among the most difficult adjustments required in human life is that which must be faced by the older person who reaches the point where he is no longer able to maintain his own home under his own control. At this point, he loses not only the freedom to live his own life just as he chooses to live it, but he must make the difficult, emotional adjustment inherent in facing the fact that he is no longer an independent, producing member of society, and is entering upon the declining years of his life in which he is progressing toward helplessness and death. As he leaves his own home to enter the boarding home, the old people's home, or any other type of protected living arrangement, this whole situation confronts the individual. He is surrendering the security which comes from full capacity to take care of himself and full control of his own life, and is forced to entrust this control in greater or less degree to other hands. Usually, he does not know to what extent he can trust these others to know his wants. He is not even sure that they care what happens to him. It is small wonder that so many elderly people present emotional difficulties and behavior problems in making this adjustment. There is every reason to feel insecure and frightened as we face the final stage of life, recognizing that death lies at the end and that from this point on our daily lives will be controlled by others. There is no way in which this adjustment can be avoided. It is possible to do many things to make it easier or more difficult for the individual but, in the end, it is one which every human being who lives that long must make.

If, when he leaves his own home, the individual enters a good home or institution, he gradually finds that life has not yet ended and that the people who have the power to control his daily life are sincerely interested in his welfare and can be trusted. Gradually, he begins to regain some feeling of security and to relax. He is rarely entirely free of some fear, however, about what will happen as he grows older and more helpless. If he is in an institution offering care only for persons who are up and about, and providing no care for them after they have become more helpless, his panic may return as he realizes that he is growing less and less able to care for himself. At the time when he has become sick and helpless and is frightened by approaching death and what may lie ahead of him, the individual has another difficult adjustment to face. If, at this point, he must also lose the security of the only home he has and once more entrust his life and care to strangers, in strange surroundings, he is facing tragedy. Viewed with an understanding of these facts, the difficult behavior presented by many individuals at this stage in their care is easily understood.

For humanitarian reasons, therefore, as well as for efficiency in administration, it should not be necessary to admit an elderly person to one home where he can remain only so long as he needs some care but not very much, and then to discharge him from that home and admit him to another when his needs increase. Instead, every home which admits elderly people should provide at least enough "nursing home" or "infirmary" beds to meet the requirements of all the persons for whose care the home accepts responsibility. I do not believe that there should be any homes for "well old people" which do not include in their facilities and programs "nursing home" services. In one sense, it might be said that every old people's home should either be a nursing home, or should operate a nursing home unit as an integral part of its facilities and program. The institution may choose to call its nursing home division an "infirmary," a "hospital section," a "geriatric unit," or some other term. The important point is that home-like surroundings with security and good nursing care be available.

Relationship to Hospitals

It is my belief that older people are an integral part of the community and that they should not be segregated from the rest of the population for medical care or in other ways. I do not believe that older people want to be segregated, and I do not think that community money should be wasted in setting up duplicate sets of facilities, one to serve people through their sixty-fourth birthdays, and another to which they must be transferred on their sixty-fifth.

Elderly people who require specialized diagnostic and treatment services should receive these services side-by-side with others in the population in the general hospital. Just as he does at the age of sixty-four or fifty-four or twenty-four, the patient of sixty-five or over should remain in the hospital so long as he needs these specialized facilities and services and should be discharged to his home at the point where they no longer are needed.

A high proportion of older persons, like other people, have homes of their own to which they return when hospital care no longer is needed. For those persons who do not have families and homes of their own to which they can return, adequate substitutes for their own homes must be provided. These may be found in homes for the aged, nursing homes, special units attached to general hospitals, or in other facilities. Essentially, however, these facilities should be homes. They should provide the individual with the best possible substitute for a good home of his own. They should not attempt to become diagnostic or treatment centers or to duplicate the facilities of good general hospitals. Doing so may result in the loss of the home-like values of the institution and, in addition, will necessitate needless duplication of facilities, and waste of money.

Characteristics of a Good Nursing Home

Time does not permit detailed consideration of the characteristics of a good nursing home. Some brief comments may be made, however.

Location. In general, nursing homes should be located in centers of population; easily accessible to the persons they are serving and to their families and friends; close to sources of good medical care; and in places where competent staff can be attracted and held.

Size. With a high quality of administration, good staff, and well-planned physical facilities, it is possible to provide pleasant, home-like surroundings and good care in homes as large as three or four hundred beds. It is doubtful that such homes ever should be more than five hundred beds in size. A home of twenty to thirty beds can be an efficient operating unit. The most efficient sizes for operating purposes are in multiples of about twenty-five beds, anywhere between twenty-five and three hundred bed total capacities. In sizes much beyond three hundred beds operating efficiency decreases with increases in the size of the institution.

Services. The services provided in the home should be adequate to meet all the needs of the residents. Physical care is highly important. It is not all that is needed, however. Good provisions for wholesome activity, emotional satisfactions, recreation, and companionship may be as important to the individual as his shelter, food, medical attention, and nursing care.

Ratio of staff to patients. The amount of service needed in a home, and the facilities and staff necessary to provide it, will vary with the types of persons accepted for care. This is especially true of nursing care, the service of dietitians, occupational therapists, physical therapists, and of some other specialized personnel. On an average, from two to four hours of nursing staff time per patient per day will be needed for adequate nursing care of disabled, infirm, and chronically sick people. A substantial part of it can be given by well-qualified practical nurses, nurse aides, and attendants, provided there is good professional nurse supervision. Total staff required in the institution to maintain good service approaches a ratio of one staff member to one patient. In homes having a heavy predominance of persons who require comparatively little personal care and nursing service, adequate standards can be maintained with a ratio of about one staff member to two patients. In homes filled with patients requiring large amounts of care the staff required to provide adequate services may be as high as 1.5 or 1.8 staff members per patient.

The building. The amount of space required and the quality of construction needed are about the same in good units for long-term care as in general hospitals. The space used in general hospitals for nurseries, operating rooms, and other services not required in the nursing home, is needed in the nursing home for dining rooms, occupational therapy, recreation, and other activities not required in the general hospital, or not needed in the same amounts. Because the amount of space needed and the quality of construction are about the same in a good nursing home and a general hospital the cost of constructing adequate buildings is about the same.

Operating expense. Operating costs in nursing homes vary directly with the quality and amount of service provided. Salaries for staff services account for between 60 and 80 per cent of the total operating cost in good nursing homes. Operating costs are greatly affected, therefore, by wage and salary scales. In general, total operating costs in good nursing homes in any given area are about two thirds to three fourths of the operating expense of general hospitals in the same area.

Need for Community Participation

Comparatively few nursing homes today are providing good care. Almost all of them are attempting to improve their services and are making substantial progress in doing so. Further progress, however, will be dependent almost as much upon others in the community as upon the people operating the nursing homes. There is urgent need for more adequate financing of care, particularly for better standards of payment in public assistance agencies. There is need, also, for more knowledge and new attitudes on the part of the public toward nursing homes and the services they provide.

Summary

Very significant progress has been made during the past ten years in clarifying the problems related to the care of infirm and chronically sick older people. More progress is greatly needed, however, in identifying the needs of these elderly people and planning and developing good services to meet them. There is still wide-spread confusion with respect to the character and appropriate functions of the variously named places now offering services to these persons. Differences in the terminology used to describe the people and their needs, and differences in the names applied to the places offering care, add to the confusion.

It is important for purposes of standard-setting and of equitable treatment of the various homes and institutions, and for purposes of planning and developing good community services, that the needs of the people being served be clearly understood and be the primary point of concern. Standards should be formulated on the basis of the requirements of the persons to be served and should be the same for all places serving persons with similar needs, regardless of the names under which the places operate, their ownership, their size, or other similar factors.

HOSPITALIZATION
FOR THE AGING *Chapter XII*

BY RAY E. BROWN

Ray E. Brown, M.A., is superintendent of the University of Chicago Clinic and director of the Graduate Program in Hospital Administration, University of Chicago. He was superintendent of the North Carolina Baptist Hospital from 1942 to 1945. He is author of Hospitals Visualized, *1952. Mr. Brown is a Fellow of the American College of Hospital Administrators and a Fellow of the American Public Health Association.*

HOSPITAL facilities for the aging is a topic that, to the average hospital administrator, has a good deal in common with Mark Twain's comment on the weather, "everyone talks about it but no one does anything about it." To extend the analogy I might state that the problem has another similarity to the weather— like the winters to the aging man, the problem becomes worse by the year. Unfortunately, for the community at large, as well as for the hospital administrator, the problem of hospitalization for the aging cannot be shrugged off with the comforting knowledge that a seasonal change is just around the corner.

The extent of the problem is growing rapidly. The dramatic victories of medicine over bacteria-related diseases has in a single century increased the average life expectancy at birth from about thirty-eight years to about sixty-six years. The increase was from forty-nine to sixty-eight years between 1901 and 1950. Already one out of each dozen of our population has reached sixty-five years of age and the total is increasing at the rate of 400,000 a year. The country's population sixty-five or older went up 36 per cent between 1940 and 1950. By having eliminated most of the environmental disease hazards, medicine has accentuated the much more difficult problems of degenerative diseases, both organic and functional. No group knows better than the medical group itself, the difficulties presented by the degenerative diseases. The medical advances in this field have been relatively slight. Actually, the life expectancy of those reaching age sixty-five is not significantly longer today than was that of the sixty-five-year-olds in the time of Napoleon, or even of those in the time of Caesar.

Problems of Old Age Hospitalization

There are many factors that complicate the hospitalization of the aging. Most of their illnesses are associated with the degenerative diseases and consequently most are chronic and long term. Because the duration is long the financial burden is great. The chronic nature of the illness means, in most instances, a complete loss of earning power to individuals who were already at a serious competitive disadvantage because of age. More than 32 per cent of those persons over sixty-five years of age in this country live in households with a total annual income of less than $2,000. In 1950, 43 per cent of the families headed by a person sixty-five years of age or older had a cash income of less than $1,500. At the end of 1951, fewer than one in every three persons sixty-five years and older was receiving income from employment either as an earner or spouse of an earner.

Modern habits of living have further complicated the illness problems of the aging. The size of houses and apartments today provides no extra room in which a person can be sick at home. The small size of modern families does not provide the extra pair of hands for home nursing that existed in most households a few generations ago. The odds are not too unequal that any able-bodied younger woman in the home will be busy at a job away from home. This same factor of job opportunities for women in industry has almost eliminated the supply of domestic help, while pricing those still available out of reach of most families struck by chronic illness. It is within the framework of these complications that the patient, the doctor, and the hospital must attempt to meet the hospitalization needs of the aging.

Hospitalization Needs of the Aging

The hospitalization needs of the aging can be classified into three types. The first is the need for acute, definitive treatment; the second is the need for continuing definitive treatment but of a rehabilitative and convalescent nature; and the third need is for custodial care of those patients whose condition has reached a static stage and who are largely bedfast.

It is the first group which under our existing organization of medical facilities is the primary concern of hospitals. The care of the second and third groups is at present considered by most hospitals as the function of nursing homes. There is no medical reason why this has been true. General hospitals have separated the care of the short-term patient from the care of the long-term patient, and while moving heaven and earth to meet fully the needs of the short-term patient, have moved about the same amount of real estate in order to remain aloof from the needs of the long-term patient. We shall examine later in this paper the reasons general hospitals have been so reluctant to take on the problem of the long-term patient.

The hospitalization of those individuals over sixty-five years of age requiring acute treatment does not present a special problem to the doctor and the hospital. The same facilities of the general hospital are required as are needed in the case of other adults suffering from acute illnesses. It is my firm conviction that the aging patient should be admitted to the same nursing units as are other adults undergoing similar treatment. Nothing is gained for either the hospital or the patients by segregating the aging during the period of acute treatment. I also question the current movement toward developing geriatrics as a specialized branch of medicine. The enormous complexity of modern medicine forced the specialization of medicine by system and structure of the body. The degenerative diseases emphasize that need for specialized knowledge. The creation of a horizontal and generalized branch of medicine cutting across the several medical specialties is a contradiction of the way medicine is taught and practiced. While I do share to some extent the concern currently being expressed over the fragmentation of medical practice, I am reluctant to believe that the remedy lies in slicing horizontally instead of vertically.

The hospitalization of the aging person during the period of acute treatment does require one important component of hospital care that many of our general hospitals lack entirely, the medical social worker. The medical social worker best demonstrates her role as a member of the medical team in the treatment of the aging. The success of the medical treatment of the aging patient depends a great deal upon the proper interpretation of the diagnosis to the patient and his family, to secure their understanding and acceptance of the prognosis, and to help them and the doctor plan for the subsequent care of the patient. Here is the value of the medical social worker. Her work must be done during the period of diagnosis and acute treatment, if it is to be done properly. It must also be done for all patients, irrespective of their financial situation. Medical social work is not a service specifically for the indigent; it is a part of the medical service and should be utilized according to the medical need rather than the financial need. Our general hospitals cannot adequately meet their full responsibilities to the aging patient and to his physician without providing medical social service as an extension of the medical service.

In the main we can say that the acute illnesses of the aging can be adequately treated in our general hospitals. The unsolved problem is the provision of adequate facilities for long-term care. In my earlier classification I separated the long-term patient into the group requiring continued medical attention because their condition indicates further progress may be obtained; and the group whose condition have reached a static stage and who are largely bedfast. I am convinced that the first of these two groups should be the responsibility of the general hospital. I am not at all certain about the second group. If we use the simple principle that hospitals are medical institutions it would seem that the second group are not the responsibility of the general hosptial.

Long-term Hospitalization

There are many obvious reasons why general hospitals should accept the responsibility for hospitalization of the long-term patient requiring continuing medical and nursing care. Almost all the diagnostic and therapeutic equipment is already congregated in the general hospital. It would be wasteful for the community to attempt to duplicate that equipment. The combined utilization would lower the cost per unit through better utilization of highly trained and expensive technical personnel. Most important, general hospitals have medical staffs organized to provide medical care and to maintain the quality of that care. One can offer no better assurance of gaining, for the long-term patients, the best professional care a community has to offer than to bring those patients within the orbit of the general hospital. Nor can one provide any better plan for assuring the maximum interest in research and education related to long-term illnesses.

The location of the long-term patient in the same building in which the doctor makes his daily rounds would represent a great convenience to the doctor. It would also provide for integration and continuity of treatment through transfer of patients between the acute section and the long-term section of the hospital. The fact that the long-term patient was in the hospital environment where positive treatment is stressed would have a wholesome effect on the morale of the patient and his family.

If the advantages of providing care for the long-term patient in the general hospital are so great, then why have most general hospitals so carefully avoided such arrangements? There are several important factors that have inhibited such a development. To begin with, the medical staffs of hospitals have not demanded that hospitals furnish facilities for the long-term patient. Some of this reluctance on the part of the doctors can be explained by their sympathy for the financial problems already faced by hospitals. Also doctors have not, until recently, appreciated the additional margin of salvage possible by continuing the care of the patient through the period of long-term illnesses. Nor have they been fully aware of the net profit to the patient, in terms of reduction of the disability resulting from degenerative disease, that can be obtained through medical care aimed at rehabilitation and preservation. For much the same reasons the public has shown scant interest in demanding equal facilities for the long-term patient. The accomplishments in the treatment of the acute illnesses have been so rapid and dramatic that they have overshadowed the more difficult and less certain gains to be obtained from adequate treatment of the long-term patient.

Hospital trustees and administrators have doubtless been the most backward influence in the entire situation. Their coolness toward the idea of involving the general hospital in the problems of the long-term patient has not been due to their failure to recognize the problem. Every general hospital is faced daily with the problem of persuading relatives to remove such patients from the hospital. Despite these efforts, long-term patients occupy more than 15 per cent of the bed capacity staffed for acute patients.

Financial Problems in Long-term Hospitalization

General hospital trustees and administrators have shied away from the responsibility of providing care for the long-term patient because of the very difficult financial problem involved. I mentioned earlier the bleak financial situation that characterizes the aging persons in our population. The financial situation is infinitely worse when that person is felled by long-term illness. Whatever employment he might have had is now terminated. He enters the long-term stage of his illness in most instances after a financially exhausting siege of acute illness. Very rarely will he have hospitalization insurance. This is true because the manner in which such insurance is marketed has stacked the cards against him. Most of the acceptable hospitalization insurance available in this country is sold on a group basis and on a payroll deduction plan. The aging person is least likely to have a job and a pay check from which to deduct. Much of the insurance written automatically bars those persons over sixty-five years of age, even though they have funds to carry the cost of coverage; or else they discourage individual payments by imposing on those who retire from the employed group a differential in rates that is prohibitive. Almost universally, the number of days of hospitalization benefits provided in insurance contracts is so set as to cover only the period of treatment usually required for acute illnesses. Such discrimination by Blue Cross and commercial hospitalization insurance underwriters is regrettable, but necessary if they are to remain solvent. My small knowledge of arithmetic forces me to agree with the opinion evidenced by them in their contracts, that the prohibitive costs involved precludes the underwriting of the expense of long-term illness by voluntary insurance programs.

The general hospital, however, cannot afford to undertake the care of the long-term patient without full assurances of reimbursement. Our voluntary hospital system is almost entirely supported by patient income, including payments by third parties who pay in the patient's stead. Who is to do the paying is fairly obvious. If the patient cannot pay, either directly or from prepayments made to insurance programs, society in general must pay. Donations by society in any amount consequential to the problem are out of the question. The answer lies in taxation in some form and at some level of government competent to produce the funds necessary to cover full costs of care for the long-term patient. It should be pointed out here that such payments will have to cover a reasonable professional fee for the doctor, as well as the payment of the hospital bill. The medical staffs of hospitals simply cannot be expected to add the burden of free medical care for the long-term patient to their existing load of charity work for the acutely ill in the hospital.

Some of the failure of general hospitals to undertake the care of the long-term patient has been due to the fiction of average costs per patient-day. Administrators have inaccurately based estimates of cost per patient-day for long-term care on their actual costs per patient-day for short-term care. This manner of thinking denies the concept of avoidable costs while at the same time ignoring the principle of marginal costs in connection with nonavoidable costs. There is no reason why any segment of the cost of long-term care should be higher when given contiguous to a general hospital than the costs of the same quality of care would be if given in a similarly designed unit remote from a general hospital. There is reason why certain segments of the cost of both types of care would be lower because of the advantages of increased spread of overhead and many other items of nonavoidable costs.

The confusion about costs of long-term care if provided in a general hospital, comes about by our failure to recognize that one institution under the same roof can render two different types of service. This can of course be done only if the facilities are designed and staffed for a different type of care.

General hospitals would make a grave mistake to attempt the care of long-term patients in facilities planned to meet the problems peculiar to short-term patients. This would result in decreasing the total of beds available for short-term patients, in inefficient and expensive care, and in inadequate care for the long-term patient. The plant layout for long-term patients should be designed to meet the special needs of those patients, while at the same time taking advantage of the fact that they do not have many of the special needs of the short-term patient. The task of such planning requires the best knowledge of all those familiar with the care of the long-term patient and it would be presumptuous for me to attempt to enumerate the details to be observed. An important consideration that must be kept in mind, however, is that the auxiliary and service areas to be used in common in the care of short- and long-term patients must also be carefully evaluated and brought into balance with the needs of both types of care.

The Hill-Burton Program
The provision of the needed hospital facilities for long-term care will require tremendous capital funds. The facilities simply cannot be inferior to those of the modern general hospital. Thus far, little interest has been demonstrated in the provisions of these funds. The usual sources of capital funds for the general hospitals have been weakened by the heavy taxation policies of the past two decades, and there is serious doubt that they can

maintain the flow of capital funds necessary to meet the replacement needs of the existing general hospitals. Hill-Burton programs offer our greatest hope. To date, however, most states have given little Hill-Burton support to long-term facilities. They have largely concentrated their attention on the smaller rural hospitals for acute care. If any sizable part of the construction funds needed for adding long-term beds to the general hospital plants are to be secured through the Hill-Burton program, it will be necessary that the pattern be changed. If this is to be the channel through which the funds are to be obtained, it is important also that all those interested in the problem of hospitalization for the aging give the strongest possible support to continuing and increasing the appropriations for the Hill-Burton program.

The problem of hospitalization for the long-term patient is no new problem. We have hesitated to come to grips with it because we could hide it in worn-out, oversize dwellings in deteriorating neighborhoods. The swelling increase in the number of aging persons is increasing the problem beyond our ability for calculated unconcern. The question now facing the doctors and hospitals of this country is the best method of handling the problem. Many will argue that the general hospital should not shoulder this responsibility. At the same time there are strong voices from within, and without, the hospital field that are urging general hospitals to take over the functions of public health agencies, and also to extend their responsibilities to include the care of the patient in his home. The only answer that makes sense is one that has the general hospital accept fully, and accept only, those responsibilities that the general hospital is more uniquely qualified to handle than any other agency within the community. The general hospital is the depository of the medical skills and equipment for the community. Because those resources are congregated in the general hospital it is logical for the community to expect that the general hospital will make those resources available to all who need congregated medical care. The indications of need for such care are medical, and the use of any other criteria, such as the length of stay or age of the patient, represent a failure in the general hospital's responsibility to its community.

THE COUNTY INFIRMARY ROLE
IN LONG-TERM ILLNESS AND
DISABILITY *Chapter XIII*

BY ALFRED C. KRAFT AND GERARD P. HAMMILL

> *Alfred C. Kraft, M.D., is physician-in-charge of the Department of Physical Rehabilitation and superintendent of the Mayview Division, Allegheny County Institution District, Mayview, Pennsylvania. He is coauthor of* Physical Restoration of the Chronically Ill and Aged, *presented at the International Gerontological Congress, 1951. Dr. Kraft is a member of the Medical Society of the State of Pennsylvania, the American Medical Association, the American Geriatrics Society, and the Pennsylvania Association of County Home Superintendents.*
> *Gerard P. Hammill, M.D., is director of the Allegheny County Institution District, Pennsylvania. He is a specialist in hospital administration.*

LONG-TERM illness has always been present in our society, but its current increase, and the statistical prospect of greater increases in the future has created a separate and distinct problem. Longer life expectancy, with a population shift toward older age, is necessarily followed by more long-term illness, for it is in the older group that serious protracted illnesses are common, permanent disabilities are most incapacitating, and medical response is slowest. The challenge of this increased life expectancy is to ensure that time gained in years of life is not lost in long illness. While much is already being done to provide for adequate management of the problem, both on medical and social levels, the approach is not yet well organized on a widespread basis and in many phases represents more compromise than solution.

In all planning, there is a need to provide long-term patients with competent care at reasonable cost. For those who are severely ill, less resourceful, or totally disabled, there appears to remain a permanent need in all population centers for an efficiently operated institution specifically qualified to render care to the long-term ill.

Among existing facilities, this institution is represented in most communities by the county home or infirmary. The large number of such units spread across the nation collectively constitutes a vast national resource for alleviation of the long-term illness problem. Unfortunately, their full value as a public asset lies dormant because of antiquated philosophy, economic barriers, and public apathy. Rather than cast the county infirmary aside as a disreputable relic of older days, it is worthwhile to reconsider its potential usefulness and to determine methods by which it can be redeveloped to meet the needs of long-term patients.

Infirmary's Place in the Community

The most favorable position for the county infirmary in the medical structure of the community appears to lie as an annex and close ally of the general hospitals. Functionally, it must be equipped to treat patients for whom prolonged general hospital care is economically unsound, yet for whom home care plans of any type are inadequate. This, of course, embraces a sizable number of the aged sick population. Use of the county infirmary, with physical and technical expansion to meet the needs, seems far more reasonable than attempting to assess general hospitals with this type of care.

The tempo of the general hospital is geared to the care of short-term illness, and its usefulness to the community depends upon constantly maintaining bed space by rapid turnover. This, however, does not exclude the possibility of operating a chronic illness department, providing there is vent to facilities which will permit turnover in this department as well. Such a unit can become the very keystone of the community's approach to a chronic illness program. Utilizing the facilities at hand, the general hospital can ascertain complete and accurate diagnosis, evaluate the severity of disease, and prescribe a long-range plan of treatment. Unless, however, the patient can be transferred to a competent facility for follow-up study and continuation of intensive treatment, any ground gained by a period of admission is quickly lost. This, perhaps more than any other factor, is the background for the reluctance of the average general hospital to accept a long-term case. As all hospital authorities realize, the most difficult phase in the care of chronic illness is proper disposal after the usefulness of the general hospital is exhausted.

Need for High Turnover

In order to function efficiently in the system, the infirmary, too, must have a fluid population with high turnover. This is why the philosophy of "cure, not confine" is so essential to its operation. Not only must it be possible to return patients to the general hospital when the need for special care arises, but there must be a workable system for the return of patients to the community. The social caseworker who has labored to guide the patient to this stage may find this a most difficult hurdle. For the patient who no longer needs intensive care, yet is handicapped and must remain dependent, adequate home care must be provided. For the patient who has recovered well enough to live independently, there may be problems of housing, family adjustment, and either job placement or charitable support. Operating under this concept, the infirmary would devoid itself of much stagnation, contributing its greatest service by shortening the stay of those who would ordinarily form its longest term residents.

Current Defects

There are certain generalized attitudes about county infirmaries that have prevented orderly evolution into highly efficient public service units. The resultant defects that have arisen cannot be rectified until the community understands the proper function of the county infirmary.

One of the defects of the institutional system in the past has been the custom of pooling county home residents from a wide variety of categories. The old-style poorhouse was a catch-all for the homeless, the indigent sick, the disabled, and social misfits, all of whom were thrown together under one roof to thrive as best they could. Often without full qualification or ability to render valid service, some county infirmaries even assumed responsibility for mental disease and tuberculosis. The existence of such a system was a true oversight of community planning, and resulted in substandard dumping grounds where people suffered only for the fault of illness and poverty.

Fortunately, our governmental and voluntary agencies have done much to make it unnecessary for many people to spend their last years in the county home. In Pennsylvania, for instance, most county home admissions have been limited to the indigent sick since 1937, on the basis that other agencies are now responsible for many former types of institutional inmates. This permits the abolishment of the county poorhouse system, and creates the county infirmary. With this new-founded purpose, it is possible to serve a more homogeneous classification of patients and to devise more applicable standards of care.

The most unsuitable feature of the Pennsylvania law is the designation of indigency as a criterion for admission. While it gives preference to the most needy, it fails to serve the middle-income patient who, although technically resourceful, is unable to finance long-term care. If his term of illness exceeds his ability to pay for private services, he is eventually forced to succumb to public care through sheer financial exhaustion. We recognize this as a serious fault, because, if we are eventually able to bring about recovery, the patient may be left too destitute to re-establish his station in life. Until the public establishes more appropriate limitations, the infirmary can best serve only by defining indigency in broad and liberal terms.

It has also been a fault of many communities to regard the county infirmary as a permanent refuge for "chronics" and "incurables." As every institutional administrator knows, this is an incorrect concept. It implies to the community that its county home need be maintained only to meet the needs of people for whom little or nothing can be done, and for whom only minimal medical and nursing services need be provided. The error in this thought is demonstrated by the fact that many county infirmary patients actually require care equaling or surpassing that of the average general hospital. All but a few patients will remain static or decline if treated passively; but, with vigorous restorative techniques, a surprisingly high number can be returned to their former way of life in remarkably good condition.

In order to serve its public well, the county infirmary must take a more optimistic attitude toward its inmates. There have been amazing forward strides in medicine during the past decades, and most advances are applicable in the geriatric field. Older people are not prone to recover as quickly from illness as younger people, and need more care and guidance to ensure that their acute illness does not become long-term. As specific examples, certain types of disorder might be compared. Hip fractures once contributed to many deaths because forced bedfastness resulted in deterioration and pneumonia; today, modern surgical procedures allow weight-bearing in a week or less, permitting the patient to remain active. Stroke cases, formerly committed to bed because of fear of producing cerebral damage, are now placed on a rehabilitation regime as soon as consciousness returns. Amputees are now activated early to prevent loss of function, carefully fitted with good prosthetics, and thoroughly trained; this prevents the wheel chair habit, and permits the patient to return to normal life in a short time. In general, it might be stated that the treatment of illness in the older age group requires an all-out attack, aggressively applying every available development of the general and special medical fields. It does not suffice to let nature take its course with older people, for this is usually the road to disaster.

The greatest single enemy to the progress of long-term therapy is apathy. This is engendered by the extent of the task of recovery, the lack of dramatic and swift cures, the aura of hope-lessness of many cases, loss of patience, boredom, and disinterest. When this condition exists only in the mind of the patient, it is a serious problem; when it extends to staff, administration, and finally to the public, it is a psychological catastrophe. The fight against the development of this morbid state must be vigorous and unceasing. Results can be obtained only by a strong, positive approach to management of the institution and its patients.

The Cost of Infirmary Care

Assuming that the defects can be corrected by an enlightened administration, there remains the critical problem of cost of care. The plague of the county infirmary administrator is the task of maintaining high standards at a cost favorable to the taxpayer. The public must realize that the failure to provide good medical care for improvident sick people is the first inroad to socialism and a destruction of the American way of life, for man treasures health as his greatest asset and will sacrifice even freedom for its preservation. Furthermore, the public must recognize that good medicine pays high dividends. For instance, the cost of caring for a sixty-year-old diabetic amputee, in a good infirmary where excellent nursing supersedes all other functions, will be more than $30,000 if he lives twenty years. For an investment equal to less than a single year's care, he might be fitted with an artificial leg, physically rehabilitated, and returned to employment. In addition to saving the public an enormous sum for long-term care, he will contribute to the economy by becoming a productive taxpayer. This points up the fact that the communities must begin looking for medical bargains, and must abandon the philosophy that chronic illness is a hopeless problem worthy of only passive consideration. The time has long arrived to arouse public interest, and to demonstrate that development of the infirmary, even at high cost in many respects, will show a good return on the investment and will reward the community with a more independent, productive, citizenry.

Need for Community Interest

Perhaps the basic disadvantage of the public institution is its reason for existence: it represents the result of a pressing social problem. Its obligation has been to fill various gaps created in the evolution of our hospital systems, voluntary health agencies, and social services. Under such circumstances, the quality of the institution and the efficiency of its services is in direct proportion to civic pride and spirit. In areas where public interest is enthusiastic, the institutions are usually reputable and progressive; where the public is indifferent, there is always danger of incompetence and neglect. It must be recognized that some problems may reach beyond the limitations of the community, requiring intervention of higher governmental agencies. This has been especially true of mental disease, and, to a certain extent, tuberculosis. It must be strongly emphasized, however, that the most favorable site of responsibility is within the community itself, where the personal interest of every citizen can be maintained. There may be situations, particularly economic, requiring state or even federal assistance, but the intention of such aid should be to provide a suitable solution, and to devise means whereby the problem can be returned to the community level.

The Allegheny County Infirmary

Allegheny County, serving the Pittsburgh area, has maintained public institutions for a full century. During this period it has been required to alter its county home system many times to satisfy the needs of a growing community. In the beginning, simple almshouses were provided for the poor, the homeless, and the unemployed. After 1900 an infirmary was developed for the chronically ill, followed by a large mental disease unit and a tuberculosis sanatorium. By the midthirties, the county home was actually an independent community of almost 5,000 people. The task of managing the enormous physical plant and of providing a diversity of medical and social services became burdensome and impractical. It was timely, therefore, that the Institution District Act of 1937 severed some of its functions, limiting the county home obligation to the care of the indigent sick.

Since the act, the record of the infirmary has been characterized by steady achievement and determined progress. The medical and nursing staffs have been enlarged and improved. The critical shortage of registered nurses was compensated by an on-the-job training program for lay attendants, enabling these employees to perform the routine nursing chores. A consultant staff was procured, composed of recognized experts, most of whom are on the teaching staff of the University of Pittsburgh School of Medicine. Participation in well-supervised research programs is increasing. A new department of social service has been introduced, and a pathological department is in the formative stage.

The following commentary on some of the advances of the past decade in the Allegheny County infirmary is presented with the hope that it may serve as a guide to the improvement of standards in other institutions:

(1) Relations with other facilities: Full responsibility for a long-term illness program cannot be easily assumed by the average county infirmary. In order to remain effective, the infirmary must either duplicate general hospital services or devise agreements with the community hospitals for sharing their facilities. In Allegheny County, through arrangements with the Hospital Council, acute disorders occurring in patients for whom the institution is legally responsible are treated in private general hospitals. In return, the infirmary relieves the hospitals of their long-term indigent patients. Also, infirmary patients who require treatment beyond our scope are transferred to general hospitals for intensive care. This pact is a forerunner of our desire to have all infirmary patients treated first in the general hospital, a procedure now prevented only by the current demand for treatment by acutely ill persons.

In the relationship with other infirmaries, we steered the organization of the Pennsylvania Association of County Home Superintendents. This active group, with growing membership, provides liaison between all infirmaries of the State, and conducts regional and statewide conferences for the study of institutional functions.

(2) Rehabilitation: Many long-term patients are placed in the infirmary because of severe, intractible disability. However, we now recognize that most patients confined to bed or chair by common

disorders can derive considerable return of function through physical rehabilitation.

The infirmary has successfully operated a physical restoration service since 1946. The value of this project cannot be over-emphasized. Reference to our five-year report at the Second International Gerontological Congress should convince every infirmary administration that this is the most important development in the history of institutional care. It explores an almost unlimited field, and produces remarkable improvement in patients who were once our "hopeless incurables." Fortunately, the low cost with which this service can be initiated and maintained makes it available to even the smallest infirmaries.

(3) Teaching: The county infirmary is the greatest potential source of geriatric material in any community. For the medical student, it contains examples of the rare and unusual phenomena of nature, a concentration of degenerative diseases for observation and comparison, and a blend of medical and social problems defying solution. For the nurse, ordinarily best skilled in the care of acute disease, it is a resource in the study of concepts of care in old age and long-term illness. For the student of social sciences, there is a profound array of difficult situations, each of which is a challenge. In order to contribute to the education of interested groups, the infirmary prepares reports and documents for distribution, and arranges special programs and demonstrations for the benefit of students.

(4) Social service: In the past, almost all case-work has been relative to placement in the infirmary. To the social worker of the community, disposal of a patient to the institution was the ultimate end after all other efforts to help failed. Since the aspects of the case at this stage seemed dismal indeed, little was done to return the patient to his former way of life.

We have been gratified to note that the newer methods of care produce such excellent results that many patients, sent to us for permanent confinement, become well enough to return home. For this reason, we have introduced a new department of social service, the purpose of which will be to facilitate discharge. We intend that this service will become well founded, for, in the proper assumption of our responsibilities, we recognize the importance of returning patients to the community as well as the need for rapid turnover.

The major obstacle in the development of our infirmary has been the antiquity of the physical plant. The institution, divided into two groups five miles apart, is composed of seven major structures, only two of which are reasonably modern. These buildings were originally a part of the poor farm and were never intended for long-term care as it is visualized today. When it was deemed that the units were hopelessly beyond adequate renovation, the administration decided to abandon them and construct new facilities. From the very beginning, it was resolved that there would be no compromise on quality and that what we wanted was the finest institution of its kind anywhere.

After six years of intensive study and planning, we are prepared to begin construction of a 2,000-bed hospital-infirmary before spring, 1953. Its site, deliberately chosen after long and hard debate, is sixty acres of magnificent hilltop on the fringe of a suburban residential area, twenty minutes from downtown Pittsburgh. We feel very strongly that the cleanliness, fresh air, sunshine, quiet, and inspiring panorama will be the greatest single asset for the comfort of long-term patients. The opposition to this view is that the most favorable site is within or near the Medical Center, to permit close alliance with the Medical School, and use of Medical Center facilities. Our interpretation is that the Medical Center certainly requires a chronic disease unit, but that it should be a short-term hospital for intensive therapy working in co-operation with our long-term facility. Under this system, the Medical Center can operate a smaller unit with high turnover, and long-term patients will gain considerable comfort in their environment.

Structurally, the new hospital-infirmary will have four major sections. The hospital will be modern and complete in every detail, featuring a diagnostic center, an expansive rehabilitation department, and spacious lounges. Accommodations will be private, semiprivate, and ward, the use of which will depend only upon the patient's requirements. The semiambulant wings will serve patients who require close medical supervision, yet can enjoy greater freedom of movement and access to the grounds and to recreational facilities. The colonies, composed of small, integral units with homelike features will afford maximum freedom for ambulatory patients. The recreational area is spacious and complete enough to provide leisure and comfort during the seven months of adverse weather. Among its features are a multilevel auditorium for various types of entertainment, a chapel, patients' library and reading rooms, an occupational therapy suite, and a roof-top solarium.

Conclusion

There is little comfort in the heart of a patient facing long-term illness. The sole determinant of success in our time depends upon what we do with our hands and minds. In a competitive society, individual security depends upon productivity. While our station in life can be affected in many ways, nothing is so positively decisive as loss of health. It is dismal enough to suffer the discomfort of disease over months or years, but it is far more depressing to helplessly watch security crumble before our eyes. With the problem of long-term illness growing among us, there is a call in every community for intensified action to preserve the comfort and dignity of our friends and neighbors.

Financing Housing for the Aging

PART IV

FINANCING HOMES FOR
OWNER OCCUPANCY   *Chapter XIV*

BY NORMAN STRUNK

Norman Strunk, M.B.A., is executive vice-president of the United States Savings and Loan League, Chicago. He was formerly secretary of the Society of Residential Appraisers and chief of the Management Services of Trans World Airlines. He is author of Appraisal Guide, *a publication of the Society of Residential Appraisers, and of the chapter on "Urban Real Estate Finance" in* American Financial Institutions. *Mr. Strunk is a member of the Chicago Real Estate Board and vice-president of the American Finance Association.*

THE HOUSING OF OUR AGING FAMILIES is one of the important social problems in America today. It is, however, scarcely a new problem. What differences we have today largely result from the fact that the American family unit is not quite what it was fifty or one hundred years ago when families were larger and the responsibility of the children to "take care" of the old folks seemed to be felt more deeply. I will comment more extensively on this factor later. The fact that the proportion of our population over sixty and sixty-five years of age is larger today than at any previous time, and that this proportion promises to increase, of course, gives emphasis to the problem.

Statistics from the 1950 Census of Housing revealed that 68 per cent of all households headed by persons of sixty-five or older were in owner occupied units—this compares with an owner occupancy ratio of 53 per cent for the population as a whole. This is to be expected since the head of the family aged sixty-five has had substantially more years to save for a home than a family head aged thirty or forty. The same census indicated, as would be expected, that the residences owned by persons over sixty-five years of age had a lower average value than the average value of all owner occupied homes. This is expected, of course, because the older families have typically owned their houses longer, and older houses generally have a lower value.

Some older families, of course, live in houses which are unfit or unsatisfactory because of inadequate plumbing or because the property is so dilapidated as to be unsafe. Unless the property is completely beyond repair, the family living in it which has some equity in the property and some income should have no insurmountable problem in making the house habitable and sanitary. Home improvement loans are not hard to obtain by aged families who have reasonable credit. Frequently, a family will be able to finance home improvements with a mortgage loan or by securing an advance on an existing mortgage and, now that Regulation W is a thing of the past, can pay for the improvements over a period of five years or more. Families living in completely dilapidated properties on which any additional expenditure of money would be largely wasted have a different problem, of course. Frequently such properties can be sold for other uses and, if the aged family has any equity in the property, the family can get some money out of it to be used as a down payment on a more liveable place.

What constitutes a housing problem for many aging families is the fact that they are overhoused. In their peak productive years and while they were rearing a number of children, they acquired a large house. In these later years, their income—because of retirement, in most cases, diminished, and children left home to form homes of their own. The amount of housing needed by the remaining family is less and the ability of the family to run a large house is also diminished. Renting out a part of the home may be one answer to the changed circumstances. Renting out the whole home and buying a new one or renting an apartment for themselves is another. Or, the family may sell the home and buy or rent a smaller one, perhaps using the balance of cash thus acquired through the sale to supplement living income or to pay for needed housekeeping and maintenance services. One of the reasons for housing problems and other problems of some aging persons is that they are poor because they do not use the capital they have accumulated; for example, they may scrape along, barely making ends meet, then die, leaving a $25,000 house (less inheritance taxes) to heirs who may have no use for the house or little need, comparatively, for the money it will bring on sale.

I assume the major problem to consider under the topic of financing homes for owner occupancy deals with that part of the 32 per cent of all households headed by persons of sixty-five and older who do not now own their own homes and, for one reason or another, want to buy a home.

Basic Principles of Mortgages

I think it important, in connection with this subject, to understand some of the fundamental philosophies underlying the mortgage business. With the exception of the Federal National Mortgage Association, the Veterans Administration, the Home Owners Loan Corporation of depression days, and a few private lenders, the mortgage loans made in this country are made by men who are lending other people's money and not their own or the government's.

Savings and loan associations currently are making about 36 per cent of all the home mortgage loans in this country. Whose money is it that is being lent? It is not the money of a few wealthy individuals of the community, the money of big business corporations, nor the money of the men who manage the institutions; it is the money of others in the community—the savings of others, including many older families just like the ones we are talking about, who have saved through the years for their old age security. While the funds in most of our institutions are protected up to $10,000 by the Federal Savings and Loan Insurance Corporation, just as the Federal Deposit Insurance Corporation insures deposits in banks, the men who run the savings and loan associations, with very few possible exceptions, are honestly trying to manage them so that the funds of the Federal Savings and Loan Insurance Corporation will never have to be used to protect the safety of the funds entrusted to them. These institutions are managed so that the funds of the savers will be safe without the necessity of calling upon the funds of the Insurance Corporation; even if that were not true the examiners and supervisory authorities would insist upon it. The record also shows in the few cases on record, that usually when the Insurance Corporation must step in to protect the safety of the savers' funds in a financial institution a new management and board of directors emerges, indicating a supervisory expression of no confidence.

Some interesting psychology is involved when a person selects a place for his savings and the investment of the funds accumulated for his old age security and other purposes. While insurance of accounts is a factor in most instances, it is probably no more important than the confidence in the integrity and ability of the management of the institution. The management of our institutions are extremely conscious of their trustee responsibility and take pride in operating an institution in which the savers' funds are safe.

About 6 per cent of all the home loans are made by mutual savings banks, principally in the eastern states. These banks are roughly similar in character to the savings and loan associations except that, in addition to having authority to invest in home mortgage loans, they are permitted to invest in municipal and corporation bonds.

About 20 per cent of all mortgage loans are made by commercial banks. While there is in the banks some private capital in the nature of capital stock and surplus owned by the stockholders of the bank, over 90 per cent of the funds available to the bank belong to the people and businessmen of the community. Most of the funds for home mortgage loans made by the bank come from the savings deposits which are of essentially the same character as the funds in savings and loan associations. Again, there is the same management desire to operate the bank so that the funds of the depositors are safe without calling upon the Federal Deposit Insurance Corporation. I am sure this is as you would have it.

Another 20 per cent of the home mortgage loans are made directly or indirectly by the large insurance companies. Here again the money loaned is money belonging to other people. These institutions, like the banks and savings and loan associations, must be operated with an eye toward the permanent stability of the institution and the safety of the funds entrusted to them.

Thus, about 70 per cent of all the home mortgage lending in this country is conducted with funds of people other than those making the loans. The responsibility of trusteeship runs high. Mortgage lending institutions are not philanthropic organizations. They are in the lending business in order to be able to pay a reasonable incentive for thrift and an adequate return on accumulated funds, a return upon which many older families depend for income. Because they lend other people's money, it is sometimes said that the mortgage loan officer of any type of lending institution feels that there is only one thing more important than making a loan and that is making sure the loan is paid back. I am sure that if you were in the position of being responsible for the safety of other people's money and responsible for earning for them a return on their funds, you would have exactly the same idea.

There is another basic philosophy of lending institutions involved in this question. Mortgage loan officers feel they do a disservice to a family if they make a loan that cannot be paid off or make a loan on terms that are likely to involve substantial hardships or heartaches. Mortgage lending institutions do not like to make loans on which there is a reasonable chance they will have to foreclose in order to secure repayment of the money, if for no other reason than that foreclosures are burdensome, expensive, and tend to give the institution a bad name.

Thus in the case of loans to older families, lending institutions will hesitate to make a loan to an aged couple if it appears likely that, upon the death of the husband, the loan might have to be foreclosed in order to protect the institution's funds. The loan officers properly feel that loans made under such circumstances had better not be made—from the standpoint of all parties—even though there would be little chance, or none, of the lender losing any money in the transaction. Thus, lending institutions, selfishly and from the standpoint of the happiness of the borrowers, do not like to make loans unless there is a reasonable chance that the loan can be paid off either out of income or other funds without resorting to actions that would harm or cause unhappiness to the borrower.

Loan Policies and Practices in Financing Homes for Older People

Discovering at the outset a virtual absence of specific information on the policy and practices of lending institutions in financing homes for aged families, I used the resources of the United States Savings and Loan League and surveyed a number of our member savings and loan associations on this question. The results were somewhat surprising to me and should be heartening to all who are honestly concerned about the problem of housing of aged families. I also queried a number of insurance companies on the same question and found that their policies were roughly the same as those of savings and loan associations.

As to the more precise lending policies of savings and loan associations, we find that only about 5 per cent of our current lending volume is in loans to borrowers who are sixty years of age or more and only 2 or 3 per cent of loans being made to borrowers of sixty-five or over. Only 16 per cent of current lending is to borrowers fifty years of age or over. Thus, my survey dealt with policies in making loans to families whose head is age sixty or over rather than age sixty-five or over.

Only about one fourth of the institutions queried in my survey group indicated that they have detected any general tendency during the past decade or so for the typical age of their borrowers, other than G.I.'s, to be higher than formerly.

While my survey showed only about 5 per cent of our current lending volume is in loans to people sixty years of age and over, a number of our institutions have a much larger percentage of their business in loans to older families. This is particularly true of institutions in warmer climates such as Florida and California to which many families are moving to spend their old age. Many of these families, of course, have some capital and income and we are fortunate to have in this country lending institutions which specialize in conventional loans, that is loans not insured or guaranteed by any government agency, and which as a result can be completely flexible in their lending policies in order to be able to finance a home for these families if at all possible.

One fact I should like to emphasize is this: not one of the institutions I surveyed indicated that the borrowers in higher age classifications are automatically refused loans for the acquisition of homes by reason of their age.

Generalizations in Mortgage Lending

As to broad generalizations on the policies of mortgage lending institutions, and particularly savings and loan associations, in the making of loans to aged families, the following may be offered:

1. The lending institution will make the loan if they can see reasonable prospects of the loan being paid off (*a*) preferably by regular amortization out of the income of the borrower or his family or (*b*) by the pledge of life insurance or (*c*) the funds of someone else who might be willing to cosign the note.

2. Loans made to aged families are generally more conservative loans in terms of percentage of loan to value of the property and the percentage of the income of the borrower required to meet the loan payments. The percentage of the loan to value in the case of older families is typically lower because the physical security protecting the loan tends to be more important than the personal credit of the borrower. This does not tend to be true in the case of loans to young families. Lending institutions like to see a somewhat lower percentage of the borrower's total income pledged to the loan payment than in the case of younger families because there is greater possibility of sickness taking a substantial part of the family's income. And

there is, of course, less possibility of increases in the borrower's income than in the case of younger families.

3. While there is no hard and fast rule on the part of lending institutions, most of them generally like to have the loan payment schedules worked out so that the loan will be amortized or paid off by the time the head of the family reaches age seventy. If the loan payments must stretch beyond that age of the borrower, lenders will look for some other source of funds to retire the loan, either a pledge of life insurance or the signature of someone else on the note.

Further Observations

In addition to these generalizations, the following observations as to lending policies may be made:

Very few lending institutions have any firm requirements for the pledging of life insurance to secure a loan to the borrower of advanced age. This does not mean, of course, that life insurance for the borrower, whatever his age, is not regarded favorably by the lender. Depending upon circumstances, if life insurance is available, and it appears otherwise to be desirable, the lender may ask for an assignment of a life insurance policy to secure all or part of the loan. If life insurance is not available, lenders, of course, find it almost impossible to require borrowers to take it out. In many instances the borrowers are not acceptable insurance risks, and premium rates for people at age sixty or sixty-five tend to be prohibitive.

Savings and loan associations and other lending institutions are, it need hardly be said, in business to make loans and, except in those brief times when there may be a shortage of money, they will try very hard to work out a loan plan with a borrower. This is particularly true with local community institutions making conventional loans. Loan officers will explore all aspects in an effort to see if a loan cannot be handled in some way. In the case of older families they, of course, have a difficult problem at times. Often very personal considerations are involved, such as: what would the wife do and where would she live in the event the husband died; what problems would be involved if the property went into an estate; what is the financial ability of the children. It has been my observation that savings and loan people are very considerate of the housing problems of aged families and will do everything compatible, within their trusteeship obligation, to make home ownership possible.

Thirty-seven per cent of the savings and loan associations in my survey group indicated that it is not their ordinary practice to require some other member of the family to cosign the note in the case of borrowers age sixty or more, but consideration is given the age of the borrower on the date of final payment of the loan. If that age may extend beyond age seventy and in some cases sixty-five, they will ask another member of the family to become a cosigner. Lenders sometimes refer to the effective age of the borrower, as they do to the effective age of the house in making mortgages, although I know of none who requires medical examination prior to the making of a loan.

In the case of our savings and loan associations, slightly more than half of them report that they do not, as a general rule, require larger down payments in the case of older borrowers. One-fourth, however, say that as an established policy their terms for the older borrower are not essentially different than those for the younger applicants.

One in every seven reported that the practice was to limit loan terms to from ten to twelve years for borrowers over sixty; 20 per cent said that they try to keep the maximum loan term to ten years. On the other hand, several associations have a maximum loan term as high as fifteen years for borrowers of sixty years of age.

Some general comments reported to me on policies of making loans to older borrowers were as follows: "Our loans are made with terms to suit the needs of borrowers of whatever age." "Harsh terms made for borrowers of whatever age only handicap them in carrying out the provisions of the loan." "We check carefully the property securing the loan and the moral risk irrespective of the age of borrowers." "We make loan terms to suit the nature and extent of income." "We check the health especially of the older borrower." "We like to know that the borrower in advanced years has responsible grown children and to be assured that in case of difficulty a younger member of the family will 'take over.' "

I asked our members for their observations as to the success of families in their communities assuming home ownership at the age of sixty years or over. Less than 5 per cent indicated that these loans were not too favorable. The great majority replied that these loans turned out well or very well. Here are some of the comments received on this question: "Older folks are more concerned about keeping loans up to date than a good many of the younger ones." "The loans we have made to such applicants have excellent payment record." "We have more trouble with the young ones, but that may be due to more care in approving the older borrowers." "The older person is less apt to be impetuous and borrow beyond means to pay." "Payment in full by lump sum before maturity or sale of property in this age group is more likely, although it may seem otherwise." "They usually proceed with caution—do not purchase beyond their requirements or ability to pay." "More stable, and home comes first." "This group is among the earliest to pay each month." "These people make very desirable borrowers." "All in all, I am convinced that elderly persons represent a good market for savings and loan mortgages and every case should be screened very carefully and applications declined only if there is little or no hope of good, sound mortgages resulting."

Implications of the Survey Results

The results of this survey indicate rather clearly to me that if the older family has cash for a down payment on a house and has good credit and some income, it will have no difficulty in borrowing money to buy a house. Of course, for the family that does not have cash for a down payment the situation is difficult, but that is not unique with older families.

Families which have not saved enough for a down payment on a home by the time age sixty comes along evidence a lack of the frugality and thrift that savings and lending institutions like to see on the part of potential borrowers—or they have had more than their share of poor health and bad luck. Most families of the kind that represent a good credit risk at age sixty will have built a savings fund or acquired a home prior to reaching that age. If the home is unsatisfactory, they can sell and transfer their equity to a more suitable house.

Except for sickness or accidents or other unavoidable, unfortunate circumstances, if a family has not, by the time it reaches age sixty or sixty-five, acquired an equity in a home or accumulated sufficient funds for a down payment, it is difficult to see why society must help it buy a home. It has let the best years of its life pass without taking advantage of the abundant home ownership opportunities which exist in this country. For those who cannot buy, the great need is for rental housing, and with the termination of rent control certainly more new apartments will be built, and there will be a more equitable distribution of existing rental units.

At the outset, I mentioned that many American sons and daughters are not as prone today, as in by-gone years, to "take care" of their elders. On the other hand, it is true in many cases, I suppose, that younger people do not feel an obligation to provide such care. This attitude is indicative, of course, of the trends of the times which have seen the disintegration of many traditional close family ties and which have been nourished in part and probably inadvertently by such programs as Social Security, where the care of the aged is, in effect, transferred from the family to the government. My own view is that there is a deep moral obligation for the children to aid and assist their parents, particularly in their declining years, and I think every step we take in the opposite direction helps to shatter the moral fibre of our Christian society, which has its principal and firmest roots in the family.

We must recognize also that home ownership undertaken at older age, even when the family has adequate income, is not always feasible or necessarily desirable. A house does require care and maintenance, much of which can be done by the owner himself. If the health and strength of the owner is such that he cannot do the work around the place himself, he must hire others to do it, and that type of labor is scarce and expensive. In many cases the ideal situation for an older family after the children have grown up and have their own families is to move to a modest apartment where most of the normal house maintenance chores are done by the janitor.

Certainly it may be fairly said that rent control, because it has virtually eliminated the normal turnover in rental apartments, has aggravated the housing problems of many of our older families who would gladly move from their houses to some small apartment if one were available. I might say, parenthetically, that rent control has also caused a hardship on the older families, of whom there are thousands, who invested much of their life savings in small apartment buildings hoping to have adequate incomes from them for their old age, and now are denied this right.

Some families that presently own their own homes, of course, desire to move to other cities, move to another neighborhood, and, in many cases, to move to smaller homes. One problem that I have observed in connection with the new house requirements of older families of rather modest circumstances is that they find it difficult to reconcile themselves to the typical small house of today—a house of 8-foot 6-inch ceilings, without a basement, and with only three or four closets—such as I live in. Such houses are said by many aged couples to be too small for them and for all of their prized possessions. I have talked to a number of families living on the south side of Chicago, who, for a number of reasons, want to move out of the neighborhood in which they have lived the greater part of their lives. They point out that they have been unable to find a suitable house for less than $25,000.

This is surely illogical, unreasonable, inefficient—call it what you will—and it certainly makes up part of the housing problem of aging persons. But in a country like ours we do not and never would want to set down that a certain group of our population must give up its standards because somebody says that that is what is good for them. When the desires of older families clash head-on, however, with the economic facts of their own situations, some adjustment will have to be made on their part.

It is possible, of course, for families to buy inexpensive houses; they may not be the finest and may not be new. Most families live in houses which do not suit their needs perfectly and houses which do not represent their dreams. Even new houses are available at modest prices. A survey made by the Bureau of Labor Statistics and published in the *Monthly Labor Review* in 1952 indicates that even in some of the major cities in the north, it is possible to buy new houses for less than $10,000. In Chicago, for example, of all the new houses purchased in the first three months of 1951, 16 per cent were priced at less than $10,500. In Detroit, 62 per cent were priced at less than $10,500, and in New York, 35 per cent. New house prices have not advanced much, if any, since then. In the smaller cities, of course, a much higher percentage of all the houses built can be purchased for less than $10,000.

Summary

In summary, it might be said that the housing problem of the aged families which do not need special medical attention is no more difficult in its major aspects from the housing problems of families of any age. For any family, the purchase of a home requires money for a down payment which in turn requires either thrift and frugality on the part of the family or cash put up by someone else. It further requires an income sufficient to meet the mortgage payments and a good credit history. The older family has had a longer opportunity to save for a down payment. There is no problem in securing the credit history of an older family. They have either established good credit by the time they reach age sixty or sixty-five or they have established themselves as being poor credit risks. The major problem of the older family is in connection with the income; the annuities and pensions upon which so many have depended for their income during their twilight years have been severely cut by inflation. To the extent that the forces of inflation can be arrested and the stability brought to the dollar by wise federal fiscal policies, the housing problems of the older families in good health are in no way particularly difficult except for those who have a life history of carelessness in handling their own personal finances, those who have had exceptionally bad luck or those who, because of the infirmities of older age, do not have the strength to perform the domestic chores and who live in the many cities of the country where there has been an inadequate volume of construction of rental accommodations. For the aged family that has been in reasonably good health and that has been frugal and careful with its money, it is not very difficult to buy a home and secure a mortgage loan to pay for a substantial part of it, if that is the thing to do.

FINANCING SHELTERED CARE
AND MEDICAL FACILITIES
FOR OLDER PEOPLE   *Chapter XV*

BY JOHN R. MC GIBONY

John R. McGibony, M.D., is chief of the Division of Medical and Hospital Resources, Bureau of Medical Services, United States Public Health Service, Washington, D.C., Dr. McGibony began his public career in 1936 in the United States Public Health Service and became, in succession, hospital administrator (1938–41), director of health for the Bureau of Indian Affairs, and in 1945 became a member of the Public Health Service team which planned and developed the Hill-Burton National Hospital Survey and Construction Program and organized the Division of Hospital Facilities. He is the author of many published articles on hospital and medical subjects, and of the book, Principles of Hospital Administration, 1952. *He is a Fellow of the American Public Health Association and Diplomate of the American Board of Preventive Medicine and Public Health.*

I DO NOT PROFESS to be a medical economist, but I can readily visualize the frightening importance of the dollar sign in the organization and planning for medical and sheltered care of the aged. Would that I lived in an ivory tower! Would that I were able to close my eyes to the stark reality of trying to uncover the financial resources so essential to the answer to our problem. Cervantes, in telling the story of that brave knight, Don Quixote, spoke the truth when he said: "Upon a good foundation a good building may be raised, and the best foundation in the world is money."

Financial Obstacles

Lest I be accused of overemphasizing the need for the Midas touch in caring for the aged, however, let me point out three fundamental facts which continually thwart our efforts and which cannot be overlooked:

1. Older people have less money to buy medical care and fewer opportunities to obtain such care on a prepaid basis.

2. We cannot rely to any great extent on philanthropies or other charitable sources to take up much more of the load in caring for the aged. Private philanthropy, through innumerable social and religious agencies, has done a magnificent job. But the aging population is increasing, and it appears that the pressure in caring for them will be so great in future years that philanthropy will be able to cope with only a small segment of their numbers. As F. Emerson Andrews points out, less than 2 per cent of the funds of a typical community chest are allocated to the direct care and needs of our older citizens.[1]

3. Although the problems of the aged and those of chronic disease are not synonymous, they are so closely interrelated that they cannot be studied in separate parcels. Chronic disease is four times more prevalent in age groups over sixty-five than in groups under sixty-five. Therefore, our resources for handling chronic disease patients will be strained by large numbers of the aged. But who will pay for such care? This is the third fact that must be considered. Dr. E. M. Bluestone, who has done much to focus our attention on the needs of these unfortunate people, recently revealed that the total contribution of all patients toward their care at the Montefiore Hospital in New York is 24 per cent. In this same hospital, ward patients, as part of the total patient group, contribute only 6 per cent toward their maintenance.[2] And, remember, the situation is not static. As the patient's length of stay increases, the burden becomes greater. Today one does not have to remain in a hospital too long before one's life savings are depleted.

[1]F. Emerson Andrews, *Philanthropic Giving* (New York: Russell Sage Foundation, 1950), pp. 140-41.

[2]"A Program for Prolonged Illness," *Hosp. Mgmt.*, Nov. 1951, p. 46.

Categories of Older People

But, fortunately, there is a brighter side to this picture. Not every aged person requires institutional care or long-term medical help. From a medical point of view, the aged are often categorized into three broad groups: (1) able bodied; (2) infirm; and (3) sufferers from acute diseases, prolonged disabling illnesses, or other conditions requiring specialized medical or nursing care. None of these are water-tight compartments, however. A person may be able-bodied today and tomorrow be infirm—that is, he may require continuous care or supervision but not necessarily continuous medical or nursing care. Or he may contract an acute illness and be forced to seek temporary treatment in a general hospital. These "oscillating" cases complicate any planning or financial arrangements. Moreover, there is a real danger that the infirm, in particular, and the aged, in general, may find themselves in an administrative no-man's land with no resources to which to turn or with no hospital to welcome them. And, of course, there are always many able-bodied aged persons who have no financial resources, and who, having no home, require some form of simple domiciliary care.

Facilities Caring for the Aged

There is no doubt that at the present time there are many facilities caring for large numbers of the aged. Who are they and where do they get their funds? By and large, there are five principal types of institutions rendering sheltered or medical care to the aged: (1) homes for the aged, needy, or infirm; (2) nursing and convalescent homes; (3) chronic disease, cancer, orthopedic, and other special hospitals; (4) mental hospitals; (5) general hospitals.

The financial pattern varies in each of these five broad types of institutions.

1. *Homes for the aged, needy, or infirm.* Statistics on the number of such institutions in the United States are sketchy. A recent unpublished tabulation indicates that there were about 5,200 such homes operating in 1950.[3] About half of these (2,438)

[3]Unpublished data from the Division of Research and Statistics, Social Security Administration, Federal Security Agency.

were owned and operated by private commercial agencies. The other half were almost equally divided between public sponsored (for the most part, by counties or local communities) and those sponsored by voluntary nonprofit groups. Among the voluntary groups which have done much in this field are the various organized religious bodies and certain fraternal organizations and lodges. For example, the Board of Hospitals and Homes of the Methodist Church operated sixty-four such institutions in 1951.

Financial support for both construction and operation of these homes is from a multitude of sources in the case of the private (proprietary) group, from tax sources in the community or county sponsored homes, and from membership contribution in the case of fraternal and similar homes.

Governmental institutions usually restrict care to residents of the community who are completely indigent or who are otherwise regarded as a community responsibility. Sadly, the saying "over the hill to the poor house" carries with it a distinct social stigma and all too often care in such institutions signifies the "end of the line" for elderly people.

2. *Nursing homes, convalescent homes, and boarding homes,* of one sort or another, represent a heterogeneous grouping of all types of institutions, from the notoriously substandard to relatively deluxe accommodations charging corresponding rates. Of course, the number of aged persons who can afford the latter are so small that they can be immediately dropped from this discussion. The unpublished study previously cited lists about 6,400 nursing and convalescent homes in the United States, most of which are operated by private commercial agencies or individuals.

Figures which are available for a number of states show that the total number of nursing home beds is quite large in relation to the number of beds in general hospitals. For example, in Maryland, there is one nursing home bed for every three beds in non-federal general hospitals. In the state of Washington the number of nursing home beds is equal to nine tenths of the number of general hospital beds. In sixteen states for which we have figures, there is an average of 1.05 nursing home beds per 1,000 population—or about one third the number of nonfederal general hospital beds in those same states.

The line between nursing homes and general hospitals is drawn only with difficulty—the two types of facilities shade into one another—just as, on the other side, it is difficult to make a sharp line of demarcation between nursing homes and homes for the infirm and boarding homes.

The fact that nursing homes have developed on such a large scale indicates that they are meeting a real need. They constitute today our major type of facility for the care of chronic disease. Nevertheless, any real survey and appraisal of these homes would show, I am sure, that probably the great majority of these homes are, in the terms of the Hospital Survey and Construction Program, "unacceptable"; that they are not fireproof or fire-resistant; not adequately staffed; that there is insufficient medical supervision.

The great majority of the present homes have been built, or remodeled from former residences, with private capital. Their income comes largely from the payments made by patients, or relatives on their behalf, with probably a fair amount of the money coming from Old Age Assistance payments or Old Age Insurance benefits.

3. *Chronic disease hospitals* are another group of facilities which are important factors in rendering medical and sheltered care to the aged. In recent years increasing attention has been given to these institutions, due primarily to a long overdue recognition of the problems of chronic disease.

The plans submitted by the states under the program of federal aid for hospital construction show that we now have some 56,000 beds for chronic disease patients in this country—some of which are in general hospitals, the majority in hospitals established primarily to care for the chronically ill. Of these 56,000 beds, only about two thirds, 39,000, are considered acceptable. On the basis of currently accepted standards of two beds per thousand population for chronic disease, the states estimate that they need 250,000 additional beds in this category.

Of the four hundred or so nonfederal chronic disease hospitals in the country, over half are nonprofit; about a quarter are governmental (city, county, and state); and the rest are proprietary. The governmental hospitals, however, are larger in size and contain about two thirds of all the beds.

Income for the support of these hospitals comes partly from patient fees, but probably the majority comes from government, either in the form of direct appropriations for the support of these hospitals or payment for the care of indigent patients.

4. A considerable number of older people currently in need of sheltered and medical care are receiving this care in mental hospitals, mainly state owned and operated. At the moment, statistics on the number of persons sixty-five years and over in such institutions are sparse. We do know, however, that 24,660 such persons were admitted for the first time to state mental institutions in 1948, and 3,944 were admitted to private mental institutions during the same year. It is believed that many of these patients do not require care in such hospitals and consequently many of them are receiving a very unsatisfactory type of care.

5. Finally, we come to the general hospitals. There is little doubt—although there are no extensive figures available on this —that large numbers of the aged are receiving care and treatment in general hospitals. First let me say that there is a place for the aged in general hospitals. But to use the general hospital ward or bed as a custodial measure or for caring for prolonged illness is a waste which, I am afraid, is all too frequent, particularly in some county or city hospitals. This does not mean that there is not a place for such care in association with this type of hospital. It should be rendered in an annex or wing designed and operated to provide such care. Although this is an intriguing topic, there is no need to pursue it any further at this point. It has been discussed in a previous chapter, and a more detailed treatment may be found in Dr. Bluestone's compendium of articles and papers entitled, *Home Care*, available from the Montefiore Hospital in New York City.

General hospitals, like the special hospitals previously discussed, are sponsored by various voluntary, proprietary, and governmental groups. As a result, the economics of financing such care is complicated and varies with specific local situations. The financing presents endless difficulties, because older people have less money to buy such care and fewer opportunities to obtain it on a pre-paid basis.

These, then, are the facilities which are supplying sheltered and related medical care to the aged. Few would deny that they are a most heterogeneous, un-co-ordinated mass of buildings and programs. The two aspects of the problem of financing—for construction of facilities, and for care—cannot be completely separated. It is necessary that we marshall all our resources, voluntary and governmental, in an attempt to reach a solution.

Tentative Solutions

I have no panacea to offer for solution of the complex problems in this field. I would offer several suggestions, consideration of which might offer possibilities:

1. *Develop more adequate medical prepayment plans for aged persons.* As I have already indicated, aged persons face the same problems as the rest of the population in paying for medical care, only the problems are much more acute. As a group, the aged probably need more medical service than the average. This may not be true of physician's services, but figures from insurance programs show that they use from two to three times more hospital care than the general population. And on the average their incomes are lower. Finally, because they constitute "poor risks," they have less opportunity to enroll in the existing voluntary prepayment or insurance programs.

We are all aware of the debate about the adequacy of existing voluntary health insurance and the ability of this insurance to meet the health needs of the population. I have no desire to take part in that controversy. But I think we must recognize that the aged are at a special disadvantage in their ability to participate in these programs.

Specifically, most Blue Cross and Blue Shield plans will enroll persons over sixty-five under their group enrollment programs, but some plans have age limits of sixty-five or seventy-five for initial enrollment even on a group basis. Insurance companies selling hospital and medical care insurance on a group basis will generally accept aged persons as part of the group. Aged persons who retire from employment, however, lose their insurance under commercial hospital and medical insurance plans. The aged who are not now members of employed groups frequently cannot obtain hospital and medical insurance on any advantageous basis. Blue Cross and Blue Shield will not take them on an individual enrollment basis; and insurance companies will likewise refuse to accept them or will take them only at premiums which are 50 per cent or 100 per cent greater than that which people under sixty-five have to pay. Often the policies offered are so restricted and so costly that there is a real question as to whether it is worthwhile for an aged person to take out this insurance.

It is quite obvious that the aged are not being satisfactorily reached by present prepayment programs. For example, data recently compiled by a representative sample of Blue Cross plans showed that only 2.5 per cent of their enrollees were sixty-five and over; whereas in the general population 8.2 per cent are over sixty-five.

A large proportion of the aged are living on slender incomes. They cannot afford the cost of long-continued hospitalization or of care in adequately maintained nursing homes, when such care is necessary. We will not have adequate hospital facilities for the care of chronic patients including the aged, or adequate nursing home facilities, until we develop some better means of financing the patients who need this type of care.

I do not know what the solution to this problem is. One proposal that has been advanced is that of expanding the federal Old Age and Survivors Insurance program to include hospitalization benefits for persons sixty-five and over and for those drawing survivors' benefits. Undoubtedly, there are many other approaches to a solution of this problem. The point I wish to make is that somehow, some way, this problem must be solved. If we can find an adequate means of financing the care of the chronically ill aged, the question of how to finance the construction of the necessary facilities will pretty well solve itself.

2. *Promote more equitable payment by government for medical care of persons receiving Old Age Assistance.* One fifth of all

men and women over sixty-five now receive old age public assistance, which means that government has assumed some measure of responsibility for their maintenance and care. In some localities and states, the medical care furnished to Old Age Assistance recipients is adequate both in quality and quantity. In other areas, this is far from being a fact. In some states compensation to institutions is at a level which is commensurate with costs of services. In far too many, such payment is on a cut-rate basis.

From a federal standpoint, the 1950 amendments to the Social Security Act provided for federal matching of payments to vendors of medical services. With the development of pooled fund arrangements and with increasing co-operation among health and welfare departments, medical, hospital, and allied professions, the government—federal, state, and local—can make important contributions to the solution of the financing problem.

3. *Develop adequate facilities.* An example of a successful approach may be found in the hospital field, where voluntary groups and local, state, and federal governments united in their efforts to get the job done. This program, popularly known as the Hill-Burton Act, is one of the most successful in the health field. It is a local, state, and federal nonpartisan program with emphasis on local and state responsibility. Insofar as its funds permit, it is beginning to meet the need for general, acute hospital purposes, particularly in rural areas.

Relatively little money in this program has gone to chronic and mental disease and tuberculosis needs, because of a tremendous backlog, much better understanding, and public backing of the general hospital field.

With time and better knowledge of the problems of the aging, a similar pattern could work as well in that area. This does not mean that private and voluntary funds and efforts will not be needed. Indeed, they are absolutely necessary for total success, just as they are in the hospital program.

I am not proposing a Hill-Burton program for the aging, but that it be studied for possible applicable features. There are yet too many things we do not know.

Problems in the field of aging might be more difficult because of the lack of cohesiveness as existed in the hospital field. Too, the important role played by the proprietary group would require more consideration. Such a study might prove to be the rallying point for the many groups involved.

We must crystallize in our minds the major facets of these problems, drawn from facts and unemotional evaluations. With these must come suggestions for practical solutions, measured against the economic possibilities of the nation.

It was upon such a base that the Hill-Burton program was set. It was preceded by the Commission on Hospital Care, which gave long and serious study to national needs and possibilities of meeting those needs. An official agency was established and staffed in each of the fifty-three states and territories. That agency conducted an inventory of existing facilities and a survey of needs for furnishing "adequate hospital, clinic, and similar services to all their people." Under the guidance of the State Advisory Council, a state plan of co-ordinated facilities and services was set forth.

Federal, state, and local governmental and voluntary funds are used. Responsibility for operation and services is entirely local.

This latter I would emphasize, along with the basic pattern of united, co-operative effort and thorough study of the problem.

4. *Prevention and full utilization of resources.* Perhaps it is a blessing in disguise that we are presently unable to do too much building in this field. I am afraid that, had we the go-ahead signal to proceed in this direction, we might be tempted to build rather than to search for a more humanistic answer. By this I mean that we should devote our efforts to keeping the elderly out of institutions. This, I fully realize, is a tremendous and often impossible task—but it is a part of the solution worthy of our dedication.

Our present cultural pattern makes little or no provision for its senior members. Never have we had so many old people and never have we been so poorly equipped to care for them.

Even with adequate finances, sheltered care of the aged is not a problem in itself. Such care, from emergency and acute conditions to simple domiciliary and custodial attention, must be co-ordinated with other facilities and services. Only this will ensure safety, economy, efficiency, and a humanitarian approach.

We must be assured that the right patient is in the right bed at the right time. To detain a patient in a general hospital bed when all that is required is simple nursing care; to keep him in a nursing home when all he requires is simple domiciliary care under supervision; to keep him in a home for the aged without rehabilitative facilities when rehabilitation would be beneficial—all these represent a waste of dollars and an increased burden to the public. A great deal of our efforts to finance good domiciliary and medical care for the aged (or, for that matter, for anyone requiring such care) will be dissipated if such patients are permitted to linger in general hospital wards or in other specialized hospitals when such care is not necessary or even not desirable. To prevent such occurrences entails co-ordination and co-operation. No longer is it possible to operate all the various medical and hospital facilities as separate unrelated entities. Disease is much too complicated to permit such an outlook. And the oscillating nature of old age makes such co-ordination even more essential.

Conclusion

I have discussed at great length several approaches to the problem. All of them, it seems to me, are equally important; none of them can be accomplished by any one group. To summarize briefly:

1. As far as possible, keep the elderly out of institutions through a program of prevention and rehabilitation.

2. Co-ordinate existing resources to ensure "the right patient in the right bed at the right time."

3. Study the possibilities of a Hill-Burton type program for nursing homes, homes for the aged, and similar institutions. This would encourage local initiative in planning for adequate facilities and services where the need is acute.

4. Work for better prepayment hospitalization insurance coverage for the aged, and for more equitable payment by government.

I am convinced that there is a way out to the problem of financing sheltered care and medical facilities for the aging. I do not expect everyone to agree with the conclusions which I have presented. It is my sincere belief, however, that we must intensify our efforts to assure a more adequate role for our older citizens and to take every step possible to keep them out of institutions. We must ever remember that "economy is in itself a source of great revenue." Let us stop wasting the few dollars currently available for care of the aged and use them more effectively and at the same time more humanely. It is our duty and responsibility to make the winter of life a significant, worth-while experience.

"Give me but these, and though the darkness close
Even the night will blossom as the rose."

—John Masefield, *On Growing Old.*

PUBLIC SOURCES
OF CAPITAL   *Chapter XVI*

BY CLARENCE C. KLEIN

> *Clarence C. Klein, M.A., is administrator of the Housing
> Authority of the City of Pittsburgh. In 1938 he was sec-
> retary to the Unemployment Compensation Board of Re-
> view, Commonwealth of Pennsylvania, and from 1939 to
> 1944 was Director of Public Welfare in Pittsburgh. He
> has also held positions as president, Middle Atlantic Region
> of the National Association of Housing Officials, and mem-
> ber of the Advisory Board of the School of Social Work,
> University of Pittsburgh. Mr. Klein was national president
> of the National Association of Housing Officials in 1952,
> and during that year was author of monthly editorials in
> the* Journal of Housing.

PERHAPS a secondary school textbook is not sufficiently profound
to merit citation here, but in a book from which I once taught—
Problems in American Democracy, by Thames Ross Williamson—
I recall a quotation that made a profound impression upon me:
"Problems are the growing pains of civilization."

Static elements have no problems. Dictatorships and totalitarian
states are sometimes notoriously tranquil on the surface, even for
extended periods of time. The tomb presents no problems arising
from a necessity for constant adjustment to changing circumstances. But living organisms, like democracies, are alert, active,
and progressive, and by the very nature of their innate vitality are
dedicated to the successive creation of problems, to subsequent
solutions—and then still more problems.

Change is the lifeblood of any progressive civilization. Democracy, itself, is essentially evolutionary, as it struggles through con-

tinuous organizational changes to reflect more accurately in its institutional life the ideals of life, liberty, and the pursuit of happiness to which it is dedicated. Principles are permanent, but institutions are transitory and ephemeral. And it is as we struggle to realize more comprehensively the eternal principle of the democratic American way of life, that changes in administrative goals, operational techniques, and institutional procedures are necessary.

The very fact that we have a problem in housing the aged is in itself an indication of the ever-present vitality of democratic civilization. If we were coldly utilitarian like the Eskimos, we would have long since steeled ourselves to the precisely economical measure of killing off our no longer productive grandparents, a practice cited in Francis Stuart Chapin's *Introduction to the Study of Social Evolution.* If we were dedicated to the completely materialistic objectives of our twentieth century totalitarian societies, we would use the extermination furnaces of Dachau. On the contrary, the existence of our large, aged population testifies to the democratic triumph of a humane concept of preventive medicine and the science of public health. As medical and surgical science has developed, as preventive medicine has marched apace, as health resources have become more and more universally available, the percentage of the aged to the general population has grown proportionally. If, then, the very existence of the problem of the aged is a product of our democratic way of life, the problem itself becomes the proper concern of our democratic state. Triumphantly humane concepts manifest in our democratic way of life have created the problem. The democratic way of life must now aid in its solution.

Justification for Public Housing

The common weal, then, obligates the common machinery of the state—the public—to assist in the solution of a problem that its own benign level has helped to create. It is a problem that properly merits public concern. I am no proponent of the "welfare state" or of a benevolent despotism. I believe in the capitalist system of industry, in private property, in the profit motive, and in competition. But I know that democracy has long recognized that whenever an operation is essential to the common welfare, but cannot be handled by private endeavor alone, it must be subsidized by society either in part or as a whole. That principle is the essential justification of public education, public health, and even public highways. It certainly is the completely unanswerable argument on behalf of public housing, which exists, not as a substitute for, but only as an intelligent supplement to private building, to serve those income groups that private enterprise has demonstrated repeatedly that it cannot or will not serve. The elimination of slums and blighted areas is essential to the public welfare. Private enterprise is unable to accomplish the job alone. Hence, the *raison d'être* of public housing and, by the same logic, that of public responsibility for housing the aged. Democracy must solve the problem that its own philanthropic ideal has in part created.

But there are more practical reasons warranting the public interest in gerontology. If the aged are properly housed, if old folks are given opportunities for genuinely re-creative recreation, if their sense of dignity and worth is kept alive by intelligently planned opportunities, they represent a still available supply of economic productivity and socially creative endeavor, particularly in times of national emergency. If circumstances decree World War III, for example (and may God in His infinite mercy forbid it), the part that our older population can play in our geared-up productive operations is easily discernable. Then, too, they are valuable repositories of that public wisdom—practical, political, social, and even temperamental and psychological—that comes only from maturity and the painfully gleaned knowledge produced by experience. I am no advocate of gerontocracy but I do believe that the impetus given to human progress by "the bright young men" of the world is frequently improved if the cool reflective hand of age is available. All this is aside from the properly emotional responsibilities inherent in the biblical injunction: "Honor thy father and thy mother that thy days may be long upon the earth which the Lord thy God hath given thee."

Public Support Today

My specific topic is "Public Sources of Capital," which I take to mean official governmental sources—either federal, state, or local.

The story as of today can be told, unfortunately, in relatively few words. Practically no federal government funds have been specifically channeled for this highly worthwhile purpose. While some interest has been evidenced by state and local governments, and some initial legislation is being formulated, or is actually pending, very few steps in this direction have been taken by governmental agencies anywhere—except, of course, through the general provisions for old age relief grants and public institutional care.

In New York State, for example, Mr. Herman T. Stichman, State Commissioner of Housing, has ordered a minimum of 5 per cent of all units in future state-aided housing projects to be built with specially designed facilities for elderly couples and single persons. This is the first time a permanent and specific arrangement has been made for them in the state's $735 million public housing program. Massachusetts now is eying a program providing for a $5 million fund to subsidize about four hundred to five hundred units for the aged. And Michigan has established a study commission on problems of the aging in the state. In Florida, where they are faced with an unusual problem because of the huge inmigration of retired elderly people, the Florida State Improvement Commission is working on a plan that calls for the sponsoring of villages for such persons by large employers or unions. Hence, public capital is not involved there, although a public agency is concerning itself with the problem. In Detroit, the Corporation for Housing the Aged, under the leadership of the Reverend Thomas W. Murphy, is exploring financing methods—but is currently, I understand, reconciled to operating without public financing. Los Angeles County's Commission on the Aged and its Division on Housing have looked to public funds for help but, quite clearly, the lamentable outcome of the referendum on public housing in the city of Los Angeles in 1952 makes the possibility of official public support for such a measure exceedingly doubtful.

It seems to me, therefore, that the perfectly natural and most feasible channel for expressing the public's responsibility for housing the aged must come largely through the framework of current federal legislation, specifically through the public housing laws of 1937 and 1949, as supplemented by various state and local enactments. Here is a machinery already set up and in operation through which the public support of a housing-for-the-aged program may most reasonably and easily be channeled. True, it would mean a broader interpretation of the purposes of public housing and a revision of current management and administrative devices but, essentially, it remains the most practical solution.

Difficulties in Using Existing Machinery

I would not, of course, have you believe that, in the event the decision is made to use the established machinery of public housing for housing the aged, there are no practical difficulties in the road. In the first place, public housing authorities are properly limited by law to the housing of persons of low income—a fact that would not present many obstacles to housing the aged, because the great majority of elderly persons in the United States are either dependent or in definitely low income groups. In the second place, local housing authority personnel are generally not trained to supervise, nor can local housing authority equipment provide, institutional care. Public housing was established to provide "decent, safe and sanitary shelter" only for those families whose incomes preclude the provision of such shelter by private real estate interests. As a matter of fact, public housing has not yet clarified its own basic philosophy as to the extent to which it consists primarily of a real estate operation (however philanthropic and social in its implications) and the extent to which it involves those invisible and intangible purposes that would place it in the category of pure welfare or social work. Nevertheless, there is generally a decade between retirement from normal occupational activity and semi- or complete invalidism in which the problem of the aged remains primarily one of an intelligently designed physical shelter plus an equally intelligently developed community environment. Here, public housing, in its broader social implications, faces a challenge worthy of its mettle.

It seems to me natural and completely sensible that the already established channels of the federal government under the Housing and Home Finance Agency should be the best available for implementing society's share in the responsibility of housing the aged. Yet I would not have you believe that there are not other serious difficulties. They are difficulties, however, that can be conquered by determination and by an effective approach. I would be frank, for example, and point out that the public housing program itself is under vigorous attack from some of its enemies. We have been variously accused by our enemies of being politically dominated, administratively inept, and socialistically and even communistically inspired. While I for one know that these allegations are grossly unfair and know that the sane, practical integration of private capital supplemented by public agencies—such as the combination of this kind that is accomplishing the miracle of Pittsburgh's famed physical renaissance through the urban redevelopment authority and the public housing authority—while I know that such integration is neither wildly theoretical, nor "crack-pot," nor visionary, but an eminently down-to-earth, Yankee, common-sense defense against the normally inevitable decay of any physical organism, including a municipality, the fact remains that public housing is under attack. Hence, any effort on our part to widen our responsibilities and our usefulness— however patriotically inspired—may immediately be misinterpreted by some people to indicate a greedy desire to widen our prerogatives and to increase our powers.

Then, too, public housing is in its infancy and its management practices are still in their initial stages. Many authorities are, as mine is, I am proud to say, insistent upon college degrees or their equivalent as proper prerequisites for management employment, and some colleges are beginning to emphasize training in mass housing management on a professional level. But certainly, additional refinements will be essential in providing intelligent supervision for the housing of even noninstitutionalized old folks. Furthermore, many local authorities will be obliged to repeal their present regulations against housing the surviving spouse when death parts an aged couple; and, above all, provision will necessarily have to be made to integrate the aged into the general life of the community. Otherwise, the apartments designed for them will tend to take on the drab characteristics of an institutional environment.

In spite of all these difficulties, I still believe that the responsibility—financial and otherwise—that the public has for housing the aged in low income groups, can best be expressed through public housing and the other financing channels established by the federal housing legislation of 1937 and 1949. There are hopeful signs that the need for public responsibility is being recognized by the federal agencies created by those acts. Mr. Raymond M. Foley, Administrator of the Housing and Home Finance Agency, and Mr. John T. Egan, Commissioner of the Public Housing Administration, have attested to it. In Mr. Egan's own words: "We must . . . concern ourselves with the pressing housing needs of the aged.

The Awakening of Interest in Public Housing

For me, however, the really hopeful light in the darkness has been the murmurings of interest in cities, local housing authorities, and the housing profession itself. New York, Chicago, Baltimore, San Antonio, Cleveland, Tacoma, and Philadelphia all evidence a new-found interest in the problem. Harrison Courts in Chicago, a recently built city- and state-aided project, has been allocated largely to aged childless couples. And Hartford Park and Admiral Terrace in Providence, Rhode Island (federally-aided projects) have set aside some units exclusively for elderly couples who have no children. But most encouraging of all, in my judgment, is the fact that the profession of housing, itself, is becoming more alert to the whole problem through its professional organization—the National Association of Housing Officials. The Federal-Local Relations Committee of that organization (a committee dedicated primarily to a continuous review of the relationships between the Public Housing Administration and local housing authorities, particularly in the field of administrative policy) devoted a large part of its May 8 meeting, in 1952, with officials of the federal government, to the entire question of housing the aged. Not the least evidence of our interest in the whole problem is the June, 1952, issue of the *Journal of Housing* of the National

Association of Housing Officials with its heavy editorial emphasis on housing the aged and the Association's participation in the 1952 University of Michigan's conference on housing the aging, along with the Housing and Home Finance Agency. To me the Association's participation, and that of the Housing and Home Finance Agency, is especially significant because of my own, perhaps, peculiar belief that the best and most available means for the expression of the public's responsibility for housing the aged (and I include financial responsibility) is the already established machinery now operating under the Housing and Home Finance Agency and through the administrative apparatus of local housing and redevelopment authorities.

May I reiterate my earlier statement that there is little that has been done in the specific provision of funds by the federal government, and that the provision made by states and by local communities has been sporadic and insufficient. Nevertheless, it is not a picture that is completely negative or antagonistic in tone, but rather one of almost rudimentary circumstances relieved by evidences of genuine interest and concern. If the logical decision is made to use the machinery we now have for housing the great bulk of the aged who fall into the low-income groups, then I believe there are three things that yet remain to be done.

Considerations if Existing Machinery is to be Used

First, the need for the utilization of that machinery, or for any other machinery that may be devised, must be articulated intelligently, effectively, and consistently. In short, we must recognize that we are faced with a problem of competent public relations. Here it seems to me (or am I unduly pessimistic) that the elements of our social order that are protagonists of philanthropic and humane objectives have always been pathetically inept. Somehow, a better case seems always to be made in the public eye for profit than for sharing. The church has been less effective than the liquor interests in advertising, and narrow partisan loyalty seems to be evoked with more apt methods than the nobler loyalty to country and to principle. Public housing, for example, has done a remarkably poor job in the field of information. For if the public really comprehended our basic purposes: to supplement and not to substitute for private enterprise; to reclaim blighted areas; to provide homes, without which industry cannot house its workers, nor business have customers, nor society have taxpayers; to convert economically useless land into productive areas; the margin of our legislative victory in 1949 would have been much greater and the real estate lobby would have withdrawn its objections, or stood convicted as being inspired in its opposition by the most mercenary of reasons. If public opinion rightly comprehends the nature of the problem and the fact that intelligent housing for the aged is not only humane and democratic but contributory to the general, practical, welfare of the community, public support will be reflected in our legislative bodies. Whatever machinery is ultimately utilized for the public's share in housing the aged, the fact remains that the money must be appropriated by our legislative bodies and they, in turn, are responsive to effectively exercised pressure from enlightened public opinion.

Second, if public responsibility for housing the aged among low income groups—the problem is negligible where wealth can provide every physical device and comfort—is to be speedily assumed, the public must be made to realize that the apparatus of public housing is ready at hand, available to serve with but little, if any, change essential in its legislative mandate or its physical machinery. Public opinion, generally, is opposed to any further multiplication of public agencies. Of course, if overly meticulous cost limitations per dwelling unit hamstring the building of units especially designed for an abundant life for the senior citizen, the proposition will die "aborning."

Finally, public housing must clarify its own philosophy and readjust its mental binoculars to the higher concepts of its proper public responsibilities. Competent real estate and property management is, of course, indispensable to the operation of public housing. I have no more sympathy for slovenly, dilapidated public housing communities with sizable rental delinquencies— allegedly justified by the specious argument that our management interest is centered on "the higher goal of building a better community life"—than I have for the current philosophy of public education, with its little Latin, less Greek, and no accurate factual information of any type, on the grounds that we are building decent perspectives and worthy attitudes. The parable of the house built upon the sands is still valid today. But beyond property management lies the indisputable fact that an improved physical environment will encourage innately good qualities of citizenship, if supervised by a competent leadership that adroitly stimulates the growth of the human personality as well as the cleanliness of the garbage courts. In this area of a nobler endeavor and a higher professional perspective lies the problem of housing a great many of the aged who qualify by income for the facilities of public low rent housing. Certainly, the profession of public housing management will meet that challenge.

AVAILABILITY OF CAPITAL FOR
DIRECT INVESTMENT   *Chapter XVII*

BY HENRY W. STEINHAUS

> *Henry W. Steinhaus, Ph.D., is research assistant to the President of the Equitable Life Assurance Society of the United States. He was formerly lecturer at the University of Göttingen, and has been consulting actuary and economist to various public and private organizations. Dr. Steinhaus is the author of* Financing Old Age, Social Security Abroad, *and of numerous other articles on social insurance and financial problems of retirement.*

A University Retirement Housing Proposal

A LITTLE WHILE AGO one of the financial vice-presidents of the Equitable Life Assurance Society was approached by a friend of his with a proposal that the Equitable Society finance a housing development for retired members of the teaching and administrative staff of a large university. An ambitious layout had already been prepared, including bowling alleys, darkrooms, a community dining room, possibly a swimming pool, and sundecks. The university was thought to be favorably inclined toward creating, close by, a residence center like this for qualified specialists, who might serve as advisers, who might resume teaching in emergencies, and who would provide a center of interest for students, teachers, and alumni. It was even thought possible that the university might grant a suitable site located on the campus in order that the resulting lower rent might increase the effectiveness of the university's retirement plan.

The Equitable Society's Response

The proposal was studied carefully and made a favorable impression. Numerous changes were suggested, however. It might be interesting to follow in some detail how we at Equitable approached the various problems of the proposed development.

We operated on the principle that our primary responsibility to our policy holders is to safeguard their funds with respect to every single investment and to earn the interest rate guaranteed in our contracts, so that we will surely have available the funds necessary to meet our obligations. The President of the Equitable Society, Mr. Parkinson, said some five years ago: "When we invest other people's money, most often the hard-earned savings of the thrifty people in our population, we cannot take the responsibility of providing housing just because it is needed or just because politicians and government officials call for it. We must be sure that the investment of our funds is reasonably justified by present and probable future conditions." After the factors of safety and return are met, a mutual company is not under obligation to look for the greatest possible profit as would be an organization controlled by, and operating for the benefit of shareholders. Under current conditions, all we can do, as far as housing investment is concerned, is to use every possible precaution to ensure safety and adequate return.

Thus it was decided first, that construction and maintenance expenses must be minimized, naturally without sacrificing building values. For example, swimming pools have never been drawing cards for commercial ventures, with the exception of, perhaps, resorts. Bowling alleys would seem a type of recreational facility that a group of retired college professors would scarcely use extensively. Community dining rooms for a group of people with varying diets and perhaps finicky appetites would also seem a risky venture, involving a high expense of operation, so high that the occupants might not be willing to support such a venture when they found out the costs involved. In a similar development, actually in existence, at Penney Farms, Florida, where the Memorial Home Community houses retired church people and YMCA workers, most residents prefer two light meals a day in their rooms and dine out for their one substantial meal, frequently in the nonprofit cafeteria in operation there.

Of course, common social halls are desirable and can be reflected in decreased space for personal living quarters. Dark-rooms, sundecks, workshops can rather easily be worked into the plan, as a rule. So we suggested the elimination of the swimming pool, bowling alleys, and dining rooms. It was also felt that rental costs might be further reduced if construction were limited to two-story garden-type apartments. If land values are reasonable, as they often are in the country, and would be in this case if the university were to give the land, two-story construction is desired to avoid cost of elevators.

The subsidy element involved in the granting of the site, while reducing the original cost, is not of paramount consideration. In view of the long-term character of insurance company investments, amortization does not have to be rapid and it is therefore more important to maintain income and running expenses at an even keel. Moreover, subsidies are usually followed by regulations. Even in this case, to accept the gift of a site might mean that the university would restrict rental to members of the university staff with a certain standing as to tenure, etc., and this in turn might cause vacancies.

On the other hand, if there are tax advantages due to having the residence on the campus, then this would be a long-term expense advantage. So we expressed the desire to have the development on the campus, but without restrictions in case of vacancies, which might be filled by pre-established priorities, by professors still active on the payroll, by active members of the administrative staff, students, and finally, members of the general public. On that basis, our investment officers advised that the Equitable Society would be interested in financing the project on either a mortgage or leasehold basis, provided a reasonable part of the equity capital, say one third, was furnished by the members of the group interested in establishing such a residence center. The assumption was that these professors found them-selves in possession of houses too big for their current needs and would sell them, thereby obtaining the equity fund needed. In a sense, the original group would possess actual ownership rights, and any profits accruing would represent a return on their investments.

Of course, the higher the original equity arrangement could be made, in relation to total cost, the lower the rent could be. A rough estimate is that the kind of building one could construct to provide even one room which would rent for, say $25.00 a month, would be substandard housing unless there was equity money in it which would, in effect, at least match our mortgage money dollar for dollar.

Extending Retirement Housing Projects

This decision may give a clue as to the type of project that could be financed by an insurance company. Other universities might follow suit if this one project becomes a reality and proves to be successful. This could easily benefit all such establishments because qualified residents could exchange quarters all over the country and still remain with their academic groups. Residents of such a project in Ann Arbor might exchange quarters with someone in Florida or Southern California, and any such change would be in the nature of a vacation. Moreover, exchanges could even be arranged on the basis of health requirements.

There may be other homogeneous groups among churches or charitable organizations or professional employees of large corporations, which could work out similar group retirement plans. Fundamentally, there is no reason why such an arrangement could not work out for smaller communities, too, although two additional major problems arise, which are minimized in a special group such as that of university professors. These problems are concerned with management and ability to pay. To some extent they are related.

Problems of Management

In the case of the university group, the management would be handled either by the original group or by the university. The arrangement would, of course, be simplified if the university could assume the mortgage obligation, just as a university would, for example, if it were to build and manage dormitories, and finance them on a mortgage basis.

The administration in turn could, however, assure regular, permanent income, either by amendment of the retirement plan or by assignment of part of the pension. In Denmark, for instance, old age pensioners may move into such residence centers by surrendering half of their governmental pension. This tie-in between pensions and living quarters is worthy of further study.

Even though a group plans to give access only to ambulatory aged in fairly good health, serious management problems will arise, as individual health fails. In some community experiments, such as in Islington, England, an infirmary is added to a block of seventy-four apartments, so that the aged, in case of illness, can be transferred without losing contacts and the benefits of visits. Of course, if the illness is chronic, transfer must be made to suitable homes for the infirm, which do not need to be nearby. It seems to me that one of the basic requirements for success of a community project would be availability of suitable homes for chronic disabilities, regardless of ability to pay. There are long waiting lists for accommodations for the chronically ill, a clear sign of the deficiency of endowed beds.

You might note that in the case of the university, suitable facilities for temporary disabilities, at least, would be close by. Moreover, these research-minded academicians would be ideal material for geriatric studies, even in case of chronic illness. But you will, perhaps, visualize the management problem of an insurance company as owner, faced with the duty of evicting nonpaying disabled oldsters, or having to render numerous extracurricular services to bedridden aged. We might have to face a delicate public relations problem, quite apart from the financial one.

Problems of Finance

As far as finances are concerned, the retired professors have definite pension rights, in the future probably supplemented by Social Security benefits. Social Security payments are likely to be adjusted with increases in cost of living, teachers' pensions to some extent, too, either by university action, or by the operation of the newly created teachers' retirement equity fund, under which half of a teacher's annuity is invested in fixed dollar obligations, the other half in equities. Again, you might reflect that this particular project implied a good degree of financial security, not true at all for the general public.

As I have always stressed when discussing the financing of old age, we must take into account that living expenses have a tendency to rise, with occasional dips during deflationary periods, and with often inexcusable spurts during inflationary periods. It is difficult to accumulate funds for a minimum budget, practically impossible for a rising budget. Therefore we should anticipate as many cash expenses as possible.

One of the biggest items on the budget for the aged is the cost of living quarters. The average social insurance pensioner, even after taking into account the recently increased amounts, has a total monthly cash income from all sources of less than $100. Therefore, the rent problem is a real one for those who cannot live in their own homes. Only too often exorbitant rents eat up so much of the cash income that there is too little left for other vital expenditures. Rent is one expenditure that can be anticipated by home ownership. Ownership of living quarters not only provides an effective inflation-proof roof over the head, but, as European experience has eloquently demonstrated, may also serve as a source of income in various ways.

Some university professors may prefer a furnished room or apartment to housekeeping, because of the work involved in maintaining a house, such as tending the fire, mowing the lawn, painting, etc. Others may prefer a definite rent obligation to the indefinite expenses required to maintain their present residence, particularly if taxes and maintenance expenses are unusually high in their locality.

Buying the Retirement Home

We would like to help financially those who wish to own their homes. We have set up a large organization to accomplish this. We grant home ownership mortgages at 4 per cent in all states, practically in all counties of the United States. We insist on an insurance policy with the mortgage, which not only pays off the mortgage when the insured dies, but accumulates a cash loan fund which can be used in emergencies, or to reduce the mortgage period. This fund can also be converted at a later date to a retirement annuity and thereby furnish some income for payment of taxes and upkeep of the home. We have outstanding now about $500 million in mortgage money to some 90,000 home owners. While the average amount is slightly over $5,000, this represents the amortized value, not the original loan. Our rules provide that the mortgage must be paid up by the age of sixty-five when income is usually reduced, but we do make exceptions in the case of self-employed professionals or shopkeepers, whose incomes do not decline after age sixty-five as rapidly as that of·employed persons.

We prefer to make long-term loans, say twenty to twenty-five years, subject to that age limit rule. A person, aged forty, who gets a $10,000 loan, has carrying charges of $83.40 a month, inclusive of insurance. At age sixty-five the mortgage is paid up, and in addition, if the insurance with dividend additions is converted into an annuity, better than $600 a year is payable for life, enough to carry the house. Furthermore, during this period, that part of the payment representing interest is deductible from taxable income, whereas none of the rent is. Of course, in comparing rent with mortgage payments, one must take into account not only the original equity capital added to the mortgage, but also tax payments, fuel expenses, and other items not required in a rented dwelling. Nevertheless, the comparison over a long period of amortization should be favorable to a mortgage arrangement, particularly as one has something to show for the outlay when amortization is completed.

Formerly, people had to pay off a mortgage as soon as possible, perhaps because indebtedness was frowned upon, or because of fear of death or disability. Nowadays, it seems an advantage to have a mortgage on a house that one might want to sell; the insurance takes care of the contingency of death or total disability;

and the government helps pay the interest toward an inflation-proof investment.

Unfortunately, for millions of our citizens over fifty whose savings were first depleted during the depression, and then the remainder halved by inflation, home ownership is unattainable and rental the only alternative to living with children.

Community Considerations

The fact remains that a community housing development entirely limited to the aged will house a group of people whose purchasing power is declining and who may require an increasing volume of services. The burden of financing and of rendering services can obviously not fall on a private owner, but must be borne by the community, charity, or church with which such a project may be affiliated. I believe it follows that the primary management must be the permanent management, and the chance that the financing agency becomes owner by default must be minimized. It also follows that the safety factors must be of the same order all around.

While I am employed only in a research capacity, without authority for investment decisions, I do recommend that communities, wishing to tackle the problem of housing, consult with the appropriate investment officers of their local life insurance companies. I presume that the community would first have to study the matter thoroughly. I might mention again that this is not a subsidized, low-rent proposition, which can be combined, say, with a slum clearance project and produce housing for low income wage earners and the aged. Slum clearance, school buildings, and other municipal improvements call for separate considerations. Any community that wishes to assume the burden of management of a housing development for the aged, that assembles a group of citizens who will furnish (not necessarily without compensation but perhaps at cost) plans, layouts, and specifications, and is aware of the cost involved in providing municipal service for such a project without corresponding tax receipts, such a community ought to receive the support of private capital.

Sources of Capital for Housing Investment

There is a great deal of long-term capital formed every year, particularly savings for retirement, which should make an excellent source for housing investment. Insured pension plans alone have over $1 billion annual income now, informal or trusteed plans another billion, and municipal and state pension plans still another billion, or about $3 billion in total. An equal amount goes into federal trust funds for Civil Service, Railroad Retirement, Social Security, and similar reserves. But the spadework must be done locally, and it is for that reason that I would prefer local action to national action. Employer groups should be interested in having local retirement funds invested locally in housing for the retired groups, thereby helping to stabilize the purchasing power of the pensioners. The same is true for municipal funds, for teachers, or for policemen. Local funds have more likelihood of economy, of reasonable builder's profits, of municipal co-operation, and public acceptance.

As far as public funds are concerned, local or federal, the first call on such funds should probably be given to housing the indigent, infirm, and chronically ill aged. The more subsidized facilities exist for low income or indigent groups, the easier it will be to obtain private capital for direct investment in adequate housing for those aged able to finance themselves.

RENTAL HOUSING—SPECIAL
CAPITAL SOURCES *Chapter XVIII*

BY WILLIAM C. LORING, JR.

> *William Cushing Loring, Jr., Ph.D., is executive director of the Housing Association of Metropolitan Boston and executive director of the Commonwealth Housing Foundation, Boston. Formerly, he was instructor in sociology, Oklahoma A. and M. College, and field adviser of Defense Housing Co-ordination. He is a member of the American Sociological Society.*

THE FOUR special sources of capital for rental housing for the aging, which I wish to suggest, can offer to older people most of the advantages of control, and greater flexibility than ownership. They afford a sense of security from eviction and undue rent increase, which speculative rental housing cannot give. They are: (1) newly raised co-operative funds, (2) unused funds of old trusts and charities concerned with the aged, (3) guaranteed life rentals in place of cash annuities, (4) corporation, trade association, or labor union retirement housing for worker-members.

The Aging in Earlier Social Patterns

Before getting into my topic further, however, there is a fundamental point I think we need to get clear. Housing for the aging is not a new demand. The magnitude of the demand is new. New also with our culture is the fact that such housing is a problem. The aging in any culture are those who have established or reaffirmed the customs of their land during their active years. If they had foresight enough to care for their parents or to provide for themselves by this very affirmation of custom, they would be in a position to be the best housed of all their people. From Chinese villages to western Irish peasants' homes and across to our shores we find that the peoples of rural cultures provided well for themselves, if during their lifetime they had access to land. By their customs they historically required the heir to the farm to provide for them in ample quarters on the homeplace. As yet, however, no comparable pattern has grown out of the industrial years of the new urban world we now experience.

Need for a New Social Pattern

The old rural and early urban pattern of ownership today is all right for some; but the fact remains that a large number of aging owners are living in low-value, overlarge dwellings and cannot afford to buy any better or newer ones.

One of our present objectives is to help the present aging, and those who have yet to age, to establish for our new culture a customary pattern which will be found satisfactory in the years to come. With the advent of the high mobility of the urban industrial world, the old rural pattern of housing the aging is no longer suitable. When retirement comes, younger kin may not only be miles away geographically, but of different social status. The more frequent tensions or problems resulting from such mobility tend to make irreconcilable the sharing of dwellings by the two generations. I believe that proper design of joined dwellings, taking a clue from recent sociological research, could reduce the incidence of frustration stemming from such status differences, but that is a design and not a capital problem. At present there are 70 per cent of those over sixty-five years of age in our mobile society trying to maintain themselves in independent households. Our question is: "How can the about-to-be-aging of an urban industrial culture provide for themselves the same assurance of satisfactory shelter in their later years which their rural forebears knew?"

Lacking urgently needed market and sociological research concerning the varying housing needs of the aging, we can assume for the time being that the pattern to be established will not be as simple as in rural cultures. Some will want to live with

or near younger kin, some will want to live in normal neighborhoods away from kin, some will want to live with fellow oldsters
and away from all youngsters. Some will seek out one sort of
neighborhood and design, others will demand another. Depending on local attitudes, some will want only ownership and others
only rental housing. But in any case the common denominator
will be assurance of good shelter as income declines.

Problems of Rental Housing Among the Aging

The insecurities of rental housing are exaggerated in the later
years because of the fear of eviction, increase in rent, or just the
unpleasant bickering with a landlord about premises which may
not be well kept. We know that the important thing in designing
housing for the aging is to create an environment which will
help reduce the psycho-social isolation that the elderly experience
upon retirement, upon the final move from their former friends
into a new neighborhood, upon the loss of family ties. But insecurities of ordinary rental housing cannot aid in the creation
of the desired atmosphere no matter how ingenious the design is
in inducing them to come out of their shells and continue participating in life.

Financing Rental Housing

With these things in mind, perhaps one of the more significant
contributions which can be made in advising the about-to-be-aging
of proper customs for housing of older people in our new culture
will be to suggest ways in which the aging, before their retirement, can make provisions for housing in their later years. In
discussing special capital sources for financing rental housing for
older people, I am proposing four sources of capital for such
housing which the about-to-be-aging can arrange, and which will
give them, when aging, assurance about their housing equal to
that of their more fortunate contemporaries who own up-to-
standard homes, and equal to that of their rural forebears who
knew what accommodations they might customarily expect in a
Chinese courtyard, an Irish west room, or a Yankee ell.

The test of the success of rental housing for the aging will be not only the degree to which it develops an environment that will reduce the psycho-social isolation, the aging experience in our urban culture, but also the degree to which it attracts private equity capital in sufficient quantity to make this type of special real estate investment something more than a curiosity. Private rental housing for older persons must get its equity financing soundly in hand before sufficient supply becomes more than a dream.

Two sources of such equity financing are now in the control either of the elderly themselves or of those professionally concerned with advising and helping the aging. The first is to be found in the savings of the more fortunate persons who can afford the small 10 per cent equities called for by management co-operatives. The second, a resource for assisting those not so lucky in savings, exists in the many funds and benevolences placed in trust to provide for the elderly in the years prior to the advent of social welfare legislation.

Two other sources of providing capital could also be available to the two groups of elderly, those able to set aside savings, and those not so situated. These two sources can be in the control of the older people only by their exercise of individual or group foresight in their preretirement years. The first of these types of capital has never been used to my knowledge. Yet it involves merely a combination of several current practices. Why should our life insurance companies not offer, in addition to cash annuities, a policy which would guarantee one over sixty-five, and his or her spouse, a life rental in a network of specially designed housing located in favored spots around the country?

The second of these ways of getting capital for housing upon retirement requires group action. It is a technique used abroad, especially in England, but only now being contemplated as a good idea by some in this country. Large business corporations, their trade associations, and labor unions may severally or jointly act to provide housing for their retiring worker-members.

Except for a trickle of speculative investment and of public housing, it may well be that the four sources just cited will be the chief means of financing housing for aging until such rental property has been proved financially sound. The aging have not yet been shown to be a class of tenants with an effective demand large enough and stable enough to attract the usual real estate investor in our metropolitan areas. Statistically, they increasingly represent a potential market, to be sure. But they have as yet to give evidence of developing habits warranting speculative capital being tied up in projects especially devoted to the aging.

The real estate promoters are well aware that the 1950 Census shows that 38 per cent of our households are one- and two-person establishments. They are devoting a larger part of their production of new apartments to fit that size of household. By and large the aging are potential candidates for just such apartments. Few of them, however, can, unless still employed, afford the rentals that such new speculative construction is designed to bring in. Such expensive speculative rental construction, and the less expensive supply of existing small apartments, will, however, serve those among the aging who wish to maintain an independent household not surrounded by too many other old people.

Incidentally, one source of effective demand for rental housing which is little recognized stems from the Old Age Assistance program. That piece of social welfare legislation has presented the indigent pauper of the nineteenth century with a small but effective means of affording free choice of shelter in the open market. The result, in New England at least, has been to remove clients from homes for the aged and to produce customers for lower priced rentals. Too often, however, lack of co-ordination between local public welfare and health departments, causes the Old Age Assistance recipient to be a source of indirect subsidy by public funds of substandard housing conditions. In Massachusetts, we recently launched a drive to get the two municipal jurisdictions to work together and to assure minimum housing standards for Old Age Assistance recipients in existing rental housing. Such Old Age Assistance clients, nevertheless, could also be customers for new rental housing, if the promoters would plan a range of rents such that the lowest equalled the Old Age Assistance ceiling rent relief permissible in the given state.

Off-hand it would seem that rehabilitation of existing dwellings would gain rents less expensive than new construction will now permit. Probably those proposing to use any one of the four special sources of capital should investigate the possibilities in their locality of buying and rehabilitating old properties. In Boston, the Housing Association, a Red Feather Agency of the United Community Services, found, unfortunately, that the building code requirements for fire-proofing means of egress in multiple units upon rehabilitation or change of use, made it more feasible to build anew than to convert a block of five-story row houses. Nevertheless, smaller projects may be able to find existing apartment houses which, the Draisner co-operative management experience in Washington, D.C., indicates, can be successfully handled at modest rentals.

How Lower Rentals can be Achieved

Before explaining in detail how the four special capital sources can be utilized, I wish to point out how housing built with such capital can achieve lower rentals in new construction than the usual promoter-investor offers. Cheaper rents in new construction can be gained in four ways: through the design, through the financing, through limitations of profit, and through the use of redevelopment or other partial tax exemption. In terms of the average FHA insured dwelling in Metropolitan Boston, 37.5 per cent of the monthly rent receipt goes for interest and amortization, and about 21.5 per cent for taxes.

On that basis, if the rate of interest can be lowered .5 per cent, a 2 per cent decrease in the rent can be realized. Such reductions in interest can be justified by elimination of mortgage brokers' fees, by demonstration of sound management as in the case of The Amalgamated Homes Co-op in New York, by reason of partial tax exempt status during the period of amortization, or by use of a mortgage without an FHA guarantee fee. Further, if the usual twenty-year amortization period is increased to the now allowable forty years, the monthly rent can be cut another 9.3 per cent. Finally, if the state law provided for partial tax exemption of limited dividend or redevelopment housing projects, and if that formula yields a tax equal to 25 or 50 per cent of the normal tax, the monthly rent may be reduced 15 or 10 per cent, respectively. By these several financial and tax means a monthly rental payment 23 per cent less than the usual could be achieved.

Such a reduction could be handed on to the tenant by any investor trying to hit the so-called, middle-income housing market. But most promoters are not interested in that market with its limited returns. The four special capital sources under discussion, however, are by their nature content with limited dividends or seek no profit and should take advantage of such means of reducing the rent bill of the tenants or members. The fact that such sources of capital might be found with expectation of speculative profit permits a further reduction in the rent varying according to reserve funds and payment of interest on the equity from 1 to as much as 10 per cent.

The use of design to achieve lessened rents need not mean the construction of inferior accommodations. The average promoter, in order to attract tenants of unknown needs and tastes, often relies on a design which caters to conspicuous consumption. The result is unnecessary and unused square footage in the building and an expensive location. In designing rental apartments for the aging, the common areas which are required to induce them into participation and to overcome the tendency to isolation need not be a source of undue construction cost per unit. The smaller dwelling size suitable to a one- or two-person household, while increasing the square footage cost, will produce an average rental unit cost markedly below that in the average new construction.

Let us assume then that our special capital-promoting group are content that they know their market, the needs of the people for whom they will build, and ways in which they can achieve moderate rents and even a range of rents which may benefit some Old Age Assistance clients. How can they get their equity capital in hand, and what will they run into in seeking FHA guarantees of the mortgage capital?

Co-operative Housing

If they decide co-operative housing is what is wanted, in which they will be mutual owners on a rent-like basis, the initiating groups had better take a leaf out of the book of experience with housing co-operatives. We find that here and abroad such enterprises succeed or fail depending on their utilization of what may be termed "centralized know-how." On their own, trying to gather around themselves the tenant-members, trying to get their equities, trying to get unanimous consent on location, design, and so on, they will age more rapidly and probably fail. They may be able to generate their own management later with the help of a professional consultant. But at the outset they had better put the proposition in the hands of the best builder they can get interested. He does not have to put up much, if any, of his cash to handle the project for them. All he needs to show the FHA Cooperatives Section at the outset is a few prospective co-operative members and a line of credit. After the builder and the initiating group have gotten a site, a set of plans, and the thing looks like a going concern, it is much easier to get the remaining co-operative members lined up. They then would not be buying-in on a pig-in-a-poke basis.

Unused Trust Funds

Our promoters, instead of being aging themselves, however, might be professional or volunteer people concerned with the aging. Such persons in our part of the country are frequently holding sizable sums of money, which their annual reports suggest they have no use for, and which could be the foundations for nice equities for noninstitutional housing for the aging. In one city, I know of three Nineteenth Century Homes for Aging Men, Women or Couples. One is nearly bankrupt and is a burden on the local community fund. The other two have between them $1 million in invested funds. Even in a year when they renovate their kitchens, they can only use half their income and have to reinvest the rest. Using 10 per cent equities under FHA Title II, sections 207 or 213, they could build some fine modern housing for the aging with that extra $500,000.

In Boston, two directors of the Home for Aged Colored Women walked into my office one day and said they were troubled because, since Old Age Assistance had reduced their clients to only four, they had sold their real estate and had a quarter of a million dollars lying idle. We agreed that the great need was for noninstitutional housing. We noted also that, while they could not greatly expand their equity by mortgage borrowing, if they purchased an old hotel to form another old-fashioned institutional home they could expand the equity ten times by building the noninstitutional type of apartments.

It took two years and three new members on the board before a vote was passed to transfer the funds to our new nonprofit trust, the Commonwealth Housing Foundation. That trust, incidentally, was set up to provide centralization of know-how for this source of capital for housing the aging anywhere in the state. But this first project will be in Boston's Sound End, on a downtown redevelopment site. By vote of the old home and by the decision of the court in sanctioning the transfer, the project will be nonsegregated. At least 50 per cent of the initial tenants will be sixty-five or over and not more than 50 per cent from forty-five to sixty-five. The project will contain about three hundred units for four hundred persons. It is presently estimated that the cost will not run more than $15.00 per square foot, and in any event we are planning that the average dwelling cost will not exceed $5,000. The break-even rent, utilities included, it is estimated, will be about $52.00 to $55.00. Since we are going to try to have 30 per cent of our tenants recipients of Old Age Assistance, we will use a range of rents from $42.00 to $65.00 a month.

Our experience so far with FHA regulations indicates that new rental housing for the aging market, planned to meet their size of household and their needs and not that of other customers, can not be undertaken sensibly until the FHA realizes that the aging represent a bona fide market and works out regulations accordingly.

Corporations and Labor Unions

Briefly, a third promoter group interested in housing the aging should be either the large corporate employers or the labor unions. As a gesture of good will and good public relations, why should management not reward long-term employees by having retirement housing built for them by putting up the small FHA 207 equities at 10 per cent? Or, again, why would it not be good policy for a labor union to use part of its welfare funds for such equities? Better yet, why do not labor and management get together and hand over such equity funds to neutral nonprofit trusts, like our Commonwealth Housing Foundation? Foresight and group action by the about-to-be-aging are called for to establish this as a pattern in our culture. The results could be good housing and related facilities, planned to suit the several types of demand of the aging.

Life Rentals in Place of Cash Annuities

Finally, why should our life insurance companies not make use of FHA Title VII to provide housing for the holders of a new form of annuity policy guaranteeing shelter rent for life in an integrated chain of projects throughout the country? The yield insurance guarantees of FHA Title VII would assure the fiduciaries of income from their investment in the housing and against loss of the principal. Such a guarantee would cover their risks in the early stages of selling such a program, and in the event maintenance costs rose in the future to a level higher than anticipated at the time the annuity premiums were fixed.

Conclusion

These four special sources of rental housing capital are suggested as ways of expanding the private market for new housing for the aging. More particularly, they are submitted as possible means by which the aging, or the about-to-be-aging of our industrial culture, can establish customary patterns assuring their shelter in the years of lessened income.

A PROPOSED PLAN
FOR FINANCING HOUSING
FOR OLDER PEOPLE *Chapter XIX*

BY CHARLES H. SILL

> *Charles H. Sill is lecturer in real estate, School of Business Administration, University of Michigan. He was formerly president of the real estate firm of Sill and Hadley, Inc., and executive vice-president of Drennan and Sill, Inc. His publications include* Real Estate Clinics *and* Michigan Savings and Loan League Clinic, *as well as numerous articles for the Mortgage Bankers Association of America. Mr. Sill is a past president of the Detroit Mortgage Bankers Association, has served on the Board of Governors of the Mortgage Bankers Association of America, and is a member of the American Institute of Real Estate Appraisers.*

THERE ARE two basic requirements for the solution of the increasingly important problem of providing adequate housing for America's aging population. One is an efficient, workable plan; the other is the development of a source of financing.

Financial Sources

As for financial sources, there are in our country today vast amounts of capital, as yet untouched, for safe and sound investments. For our purpose, the question that must be answered is how to divert and utilize this capital. Owing to the fact that this capital consists mainly of the savings of millions of individuals, this money is seeking proper security to afford safety for the individual's savings. The plan I propose offers just such security and safety for investment.

Savings departments of banks offer a more restricted source of capital. Owing to close supervision and regulation, both on a state and national level, these departments are limited as to their activity in investing. They must maintain large cash reserves to offset withdrawal demands, for when an individual deposits his savings with a bank there is ever the option of withdrawing them at any time.

Saving and loan companies, on the other hand, are widening their activity in furnishing funds for investment in residential properties. Owing to their corporate structure and more liberal control, they are in a much better position for lending activity; their funds are not as readily callable as those of the bank. Shares are purchased in the corporation, and this money may be returned on demand, but not if the demand should be overly great.

In both the saving and loan associations and banks each individual deposit is insured by the Federal Deposit Insurance Corporation up to and including $10,000. There are, however, several new organizations in our country today that control even larger sources of capital that will provide a much better source for investment in the financing of housing for the aged.

The first of these sources of investment capital are the credit unions. These unions are made up of member deposits through controlled savings, and the prime factors here are safety and low interest rate. I know of one such group here in Michigan, which owns its own bank and savings and loan association to facilitate its investment problem, and its capital assets alone are over $60 million. Combine these credit unions on a nation-wide basis, and it would be very hard to estimate the tremendous amount of capital involved.

Still another source, and perhaps one of the most likely, are the labor unions. Vast amounts of funds are rapidly building up from the dues paid in by the union members. In the main, a check-off system of dues collection is used here. The employer deducts the union dues from the employee's pay just as he does social security and federal taxes. The unions have recently been purchasing prime real estate, such as office buildings and commercial properties, with an eye toward sound long-term investments, and a great deal of pressure is being brought to bear on the labor unions to provide adequate housing for their retiring members. As an example of the extent of the potential pressure that may be brought against the unions, in 1952 alone, the General Motors Corporation at Flint, Michigan, retired approximately 750 men, and many of them, no doubt, need adequate housing. The labor unions, then, may be directly involved in providing housing for their retiring members, and are a lucrative source of capital.

The life insurance companies offer the biggest and widest source of investment capital, for they control a major part of the capital wealth in our country today. Owing to the nature of their life contracts, they are constantly seeking long-term investments that will produce a minimum return. In connection with the nature of the life insurance company's business—the investing of other people's funds—the security must always warrant the investment. What better security could be offered to any investor than housing for the aged?

These are the major sources of capital. But it must be remembered that they are worthless without a sound and attractive plan of investment.

I believe the solution of housing for the retired to be relatively simple and quite workable. When, a few years ago, our nation faced a serious rental shortage, the federal government enacted through the Federal Housing Administration a provision called Section 608. Section 608 was a 100 per cent financing system, set up on a 6 per cent return basis with a long amortization period, and an interest rate of 4 per cent, leaving a 2 per cent margin for management, maintenance, and taxes. This section of the Federal Housing Administration is no longer in operation, so in order to attract sources of capital discussed above it will be necessary to seek and obtain legislation, once again through the Federal Housing Administration, to insure the loans for this type of housing in order to protect the investor against loss in case of default.

The Plan

The plan I have in mind is this. There are several large and wealthy foundations, such as the Carnegie, Rockefeller, Ford, and

Kellogg foundations, who would be asked to sponsor the project. Then each project would be set up as a separate corporation, and anyone who wished shelter in the project would purchase shares of stock in the corporation. The number of shares purchased would determine the size of the unit available for shelter. These units would range in size from bachelor units to one- and two-bedroom units. In the center of each project, arranged to its architectural advantage, would be a community center. This center would consist of a modern and up-to-date infirmary, with a qualified doctor and nurse in constant attendance. Also, there would be in the center a large and comfortable lounge and cafeteria. The cafeteria would be managed by a competent dietitian. There would also be a well-planned and stocked commissary department. All services and articles in the center would be offered to the occupants at a fair and reasonable cost.

With modern, architecturally designed projects of this type, carefully planned and supervised, set up as a corporation, sponsored by a foundation, and insured against loss by the Federal Housing Administration, I can see no reason, whatsoever, why capital from the sources cited above should not be readily available for this sound type of security investment.

I feel confident that this type of planned project would in every way afford the type of shelter and secure living for the aged that the American people have worked for, desire, and above all are entitled to.

Getting Community Action

PART V

ESTABLISHING AND MAINTAINING
HOUSING STANDARDS   *Chapter XX*

*Jack Masur, M.D., is assistant surgeon general and chief
of the United States Public Health Service, Washington,
D.C. His former positions have been director of the Clinical Center of the National Institute of Health (1949-51),
chief medical officer, Office of Vocational Rehabilitation;
attending surgeon to the Surgical Department, United
States Public Health Service, Office of Civilian Defense;
and lecturer in hospital administration at Columbia University. Dr. Masur is a Fellow of the American College
of Hospital Administrators, a Fellow of the American
Public Health Association and of the American Medical
Association, and Diplomate of the American Board of Preventive Medicine and Public Health.*

PROVIDING housing for the aging is no new venture of the twentieth century. Last summer in Brussels I met an old friend, a
Dutch physician and director of an excellent, small hospital, who
brought this fact forcefully to my attention. Throughout the
meeting there were some long discussions about the new and
highly important developments in the housing of the able-bodied
aging. I noticed that my Dutch friend seemed impatient with
the discussion and asked him what was wrong. He said, "I'll tell
you about it later."

About two weeks later, we were on our way to visit some health
officials in Holland; we stopped in the city of Delft and he showed
me the cathedral and other sights in the town square. Then he
took me around the corner and down a pleasant street. He stopped
before a small door in a neat, red brick wall, opened the door, and

stood aside for me to enter. We stepped into a beautiful garden, surrounded by a quadrangle of single-story rooms. He took me along the walk and told me to look into the rooms as we passed. Each room seemed to have different furniture, and about the room were knick-knacks of all sorts—photographs, pottery, books. My friend explained that these rooms were the homes of elderly women who had brought in their own furniture and other possessions so that they would feel at home. Some of them were out visiting friends, he said. Others were shopping or working a few hours. I expressed a great deal of satisfaction with such an arrangement for the care of able-bodied aged ladies. Then he took me to the cornerstone and pointed at the date—"Established in 1607."

He said, "Now perhaps you will understand my impatience with the great new thinkers who have arrived at the principle that it is highly desirable to provide older people with the opportunity for some independence of living and some self-reliance. We Dutch thought it was a pretty good idea three hundred and fifty years ago."

The Problem

Many of us now are faced with the task of establishing standards of care for the aging in institutions as provided by the recent amendment to the Social Security Act. The Ways and Means Committee of Congress outlined the problem as follows:

> Tragic instances of failure to maintain adequate standards of care and adequate protection against hazards threatening the health and safety of residents of institutions emphasize the importance of this function of State government. . . Persons who live in institutions, including nursing and convalescent homes, should be assured a reasonable standard of care and be protected against fire hazards, insanitary conditions and overcrowding.

This amendment will support the efforts of public and private agencies to strengthen institutional care, services, and programs.

But we have, each of us, a responsibility that reaches beyond this immediate requirement of the Social Security Act, which applies only to a limited number of the aged. We are concerned with housing for all the aged. We are concerned with the able-bodied who live in public and private institutions, with the sick in nursing and convalescent homes and in hospitals, and with the great majority of our elder citizens who live in private homes.

The Need for Standards

A beginning has been made in the establishment of standards of care through such organizations as the American Association of Nursing Homes, and many state organizations. Most states have limited standards for the licensure of homes for the aged, though many such standards hardly deserve the name.

I have heard it said that we must have much more information available in the field of geriatrics before we can set up standards. Obviously, we need to know more about chronic diseases, about the physiological process of aging, the effect of diet on longevity and on glandular activity; and we need to study the work capacity of older persons. We must learn more about the psychology of aging. We must learn more about what older people want.

But there is already a considerable body of knowledge, and we dare not defer or delay constructive action indefinitely on the pretext that we need additional information, data, and guidance, and try "to document the matter beyond a doubt and then beyond a shadow of a doubt."

In fact, for any constructive action, one of the necessary, early steps is the establishment of standards. Standards are implicit in the American tradition and do not necessarily imply regimentation, but let us not forget, however, that we are dealing with the needs of people. We owe a lot to our engineer colleagues for their contributions to standardization—one of the really great contributions to modern living. But man cannot be standardized.

Unless we believe in the theory of spontaneous generation, we must realize that the establishment and maintenance of adequate standards in a field as complex as this is an enormous task. No matter how great the need, no matter how fully you and I may understand the importance of such standards, the task of transposing them from thought into reality is enormous. Still, it has been done in other fields, for example, in hospital care.

In 1940, when the Hospital Survey and Construction program

was being seriously discussed by the hospital and medical professions and by the United States Public Health Service, this same problem arose. There was no uniform pattern of standards for hospitals, and there was grave doubt as to the possibility of establishing such standards on a systematic basis, although, in legislation passed by Congress in 1946, provision was made for minimum standards. Many felt that such provisions would be an invasion of states' rights, of the rights of local communities and private interests. Nevertheless, a few far-sighted hospital people insisted that standards could be established.

They called upon leading physicians, hospital administrators, architects, and interested laymen, and asked them to assist in drawing up hospital care and construction standards. These, with innumerable variations to make them adaptable to all state and local conditions and needs, were made the minimum requirements of the federal legislation. Communities applying to their states for funds under this program, popularly known as the Hill-Burton Act, were required to meet these standards. And in a short time, states and communities throughout the country had accepted and carried forward these concepts to practical application.

Major Steps in Developing Standards

With certain variations, the three major steps taken in the development of standards for hospital construction and care can be used to develop standards of housing for the aged.

First, you who are directly engaged in the care of the aged can select what you believe to be the minimum standards. Your knowledge and experience are invaluable. Though you may feel that your information is incomplete and inadequate, you are the only experts in the field.

There are several sets of standards available which can serve as guides. The Welfare Council of New York City has issued a pamphlet called *Suggested Standards for Homes for the Aged.* The Methodist Church and the Lutheran Church have set up standards for the management of their own homes and hospitals. The National Committee on Aging is now working on a set of standards, and a subcommittee of the Committee on the Hygiene of Housing of the American Public Health Association is developing a special report on housing for the aged. This latter committee has also established a guide, *The Basic Principles of Healthful Housing,* which can serve as an excellent framework for developing standards for aged persons.

Practically every health department in the country has had experience with the development and administration of standards programs for hospital and related institutions. Obviously the state health department can be a key official agency in the formation of these standards.

The second step is vital. It is really a check and balance on step number one. When a set of standards has been drawn up, a group should be called together which represents all interests concerned with care for the aging: physicians, psychiatrists, welfare workers, and interested laymen, representatives from the health department, fire department, building inspector's office, and any other branch of the municipal government concerned with either shelter or care of the aged. This step can lend prestige to your efforts. It can contribute to the workability of your standards. And it can establish a foundation of professional and official support that is essential to the acceptance of your proposals.

May I sound a note of caution here. Don't, under any circumstances, limit the membership of such a committee to a single group of health officials, welfare authorities, or architects. It is invaluable to obtain the support of industrial, labor, religious, civic, and other local organizations. All of them have a direct concern with the problems of the aging.

The third step is to give the standards legal status in order to prevent abuse by unprincipled persons. Here, again, you must have the backing of all the above-mentioned interested groups. Ultimately the translation of the standard from paper to reality depends upon widespread public understanding and active support.

Need for a Broad Approach

I must emphasize that we are concerned with housing standards for all of our older people, and that it is essential to approach the problem on a broad basis. Housing is so complex and is woven in so many ways into our whole pattern of living that significant progress in providing housing for a major segment of older persons can only be achieved as basic progress is made in providing decent housing for the nation as a whole. We in the health professions have learned that we do not make significant progress in improving the health of man by fragmenting the body. The general medical diagnostician, usually called the general practitioner, is still necessary to evaluate the patient as a whole to assure that the specialist treats the patient for his entire disease rather than merely for some of the symptoms. As the great Boston clinician, Dr. Shattuck, once said, "It is more important to know what kind of a man has the disease than to know what kind of a disease the man has." In many respects, so it is with housing.

There is a general awareness in the financing of housing that unless a substantial decrease in the unit cost of housing for aged persons can be achieved, programs for special types of housing can make only small headway. But substantial reduction in the cost of housing for aged persons will be achieved only in the measure that we reduce the cost of housing for all people. Extensive revisions and improvements are needed in designs, materials, construction methods, financing, and even perhaps in our concept of housing if real progress is to be made in cost reduction.

Relationship of Proper Housing to Medical Care

Another basic consideration that is just beginning to be recognized is the important financial and therapeutic relationship that housing has to medical care and hospitalization. Although this relationship is important for the general public, it is particularly significant for the aged, infirm, and chronically ill.

Recent pilot studies in home care for prolonged illness indicate that patients who do not need hospitalization, but require more care than just outpatient clinical services, are more comfortable in their homes than in a hospital and may be expected to get well more quickly. Furthermore, the economic considerations are even more striking. Today, hospital costs are about $20,000 per bed. Family housing may be provided for as low as

$3,000 per person. If the average cost of hospitalization per patient day and the average cost of home care per patient day are compared, the cost of care for a patient at home is one fifth to one third the cost of hospitalization.

We are particularly interested in good housing for all of our older people because we realize that medical care facilities are seriously overcrowded and must be saved for those patients who need hospitalization. Furthermore, the lower cost of home care will allow more funds to be used for better housing, education, and food. Unfortunately, home care involves several difficulties, particularly for the low-income persons who most need its financial advantages.

According to the 1950 housing census there are at least 16 million dwellings that have one or more basic health deficiencies. For example, more than 12 million urban and rural dwellings have no bathtub or shower, and nearly 8 million urban and rural dwellings have no running water piped inside the structure. Surprising as it may seem, only about 40 per cent of these health deficiencies occur in rural farm areas. The millions of American citizens living in such housing know that it would not be adequate, let alone suitable, for use in home care of a patient. Hospital administrators are all too familiar with the need to postpone the discharge of a large number of patients because they would have to return to housing that is totally unsuitable as a post-recovery or convalescent environment.

The question is: what is to be done to bring about conformity with even the present established standards of housing for the population as a whole—the simple basic requirements necessary for elementary decency, cleanliness, and health?

Need for Rehabilitation of Substandard Housing

We are all familiar with the attack on housing conditions made through new construction, redevelopment, public housing, and special institutional housing. But the opportunities for improving existing substandard housing by the application of health regulations have been given far too little attention. Certainly we need to produce a tremendous volume of new housing. Some authorities estimate the national need for new housing to be ten million or more units in the next decade. We also need to attack the housing problem by preventing accelerated rates of deterioration of dwellings and their environment and by rehabilitating existing substandard housing that has a sound frame and foundation. In short, prevention, rehabilitation, and production are all necessary to improve housing conditions. As we make progress in this area, we shall make progress in the provision of decent housing for aged people as well.

It has been demonstrated in more than a score of communities in the last few years that such action is practical and productive of immediate results. It is no panacea. It is not the end. As we progress we shall find more and more varieties and refinements to introduce into the program of housing for the aged. But meanwhile, the rehabilitation of substandard dwellings is a necessary and salutary beginning. With this fundamental approach in mind, we may then turn our attention toward other needs. We can begin to consider standards for institutions and for care of the aged.

Importance of Public Support

As you take up the task of developing standards, you must face one important fact. Before any effective standards can be established you must interest the public in the problems of the aging. The formulation of public policy in this regard is essential. The practical extinction of child labor is only one case in point where public opinion supported public action to smite this evil.

During the past few years there have been dozens of magazine articles and books on the aging—even a play, George Bernard Shaw's *Widowers' Houses*. Today there is far more interest than there was at the end of World War II. But this appearance of interest does not constitute the backing necessary to transpose a set of professional standards into a practical and acceptable way of life.

What suggestions for specific action can be offered? First, I suggest that you look to your state health and welfare departments as the official agencies to provide leadership in establishing and maintaining standards. Second, crystalize your ideas about standards of facilities and care, and set them down in detail. Third, recognizing that public understanding and support are essential, seek out all interested persons and groups concerned with the problems of aging and enlist their help. Perhaps action can best be achieved by forming a local organization which can serve as a rallying point for all who are interested in the problems of aging. When these organizations spread to other communities, and to the states throughout the nation, they will form a voice that must be heard. Finally, in our democratic American way, this voice will provide the support necessary to give legal status to the establishment and maintenance of the standards which can then serve as the springboard for national action.

To interest the public in making a reality of a standard of decent shelter, we must mean business. We must close our ears to the counsel of despair and disillusion. Throughout history there have always been timid souls who would not venture to walk to the rise of the next hill. There have been Jeremiahs whose fears of disaster paralyzed their will to act. There are enough of these people today to form powerful social forces, but the majority force in society is the force that has a will to grow and to live.

Alistair Cooke, in his book *One Man's America* tells a story which illustrates my point. He tells of a historical day in Hartford, Connecticut, the 19th of May, 1780:

The day has gone down in New England history as a terrible foretaste of Judgment Day. For at noon the skies turned from blue to gray and by mid-afternoon had blackened over so densely that, in that religious age, men fell on their knees and begged a final blessing before the end came. The Connecticut House of Representatives was in session. And as some men fell to their knees and others clamored for immediate adjournment, the Speaker of the House, Colonel Davenport, came to his feet. He silenced them and said these words: "The Day of Judgment is either approaching or it is not. If it is not, there is no cause for adjournment. If it is, I choose to be found doing my duty. . . I wish, therefore, that candles may be brought."

Let us then light the candle and do our duty.

THE NEED FOR COMMUNITY
SERVICES TO THE AGED   *Chapter XXI*

BY JANE M. HOEY

> *Jane M. Hoey, M.A., is director of the Bureau of Public*
> *Assistance, Social Security Administration, Washington,*
> *D.C. Formerly she was assistant director and secretary of*
> *the Health Division, Welfare Council of New York City*
> *(1926-36). She is coauthor of* Study of National Social
> Agencies in Fourteen American Communities *(1926), and*
> *of many articles in various professional journals. Miss Hoey*
> *is a member of the American Association of Social Workers,*
> *the American Public Welfare Association, and the National*
> *Social Welfare Assembly.*

Attitudes Toward Aging

PERHAPS IN ANOTHER FIVE YEARS we shall be able to abandon the fiction that our interest in aging is altruistic and freely admit that, age being an inescapable period of life, when we plan for the aging we plan for ourselves.   For Americans, particularly, this is a hard step to take.   Youth worship has become almost as entrenched here as ancestor worship in the Orient.   But East and West, to the defiance of Rudyard Kipling, have met many times before and, on the question of age, may come together again to mutually accept the indisputable fact that every age has its own inherent compensations.   And as the East begins to admit youth into its counsels, so may we begin to look upon age as the privileged, not the problem, period of life.

One of the greatest obstacles to a healthy attitude toward aging is the fact that so many people—including the aged themselves— have assumed the abnormal symptoms of advancing years to be the normal characteristics of that period.   When we see an eighty-year-old who is strong, vigorous, keen, and a center of busy interest, we regard him as a phenomenon and marvel at how he has kept his "youth." In our grandmother's day, babies who didn't continually fuss and cry were considered equally amazing, and for the same reason, good health was the exception rather than the rule. Colic and other pains were then considered a natural part of infancy, just as feebleness is now taken for granted among the aged.

As long as we consider old age synonymous with helplessness, we are going to keep on pushing the possibility of our own old age far back into the recesses of the unconscious. And as long as we do this, the wholehearted, widespread effort to develop community services which would save us from that fate will be inadequate.

There are many, of course, who are converted to this view, who know that the late years can be good years and who are working for the measures that will make them so. Our problem is to reach those whose eyes are still tightly closed to their future, whose interest in developing community services is in the nature of tepid charity rather than urgent need. If we are going to get them to open their eyes, we must help them to dissociate age itself from the miserable company it keeps.

Need for Economic Security in Old Age

One of age's most disreputable companions is poverty. Thanks to social insurance and public assistance, I suppose our older citizens today have more money in their pockets than any previous generation of elders. But social security payments have not kept pace with the increasing cost of living. Even with the 1950 and 1952 amendments, the Old Age and Survivors Insurance monthly benefits range from $25 to $85 for a single individual, $37.50 to $127.50 for a couple without other income and resources—hardly enough to purchase the essentials of life. Further, the average monthly payments from Old Age Assistance is only $45.[1] Alto-

[1]This figure varies according to states from $21.00 in Mississippi to $70.00 in Colorado. Of the low income states, nine have an average income of under $30.00; of the high income states, six average over $60.00. When the increase from the recent amendments is included—$5.00 a month for adults, $3.00 for children—somewhat higher payments are possible.

gether, a third of all the people over sixty-five—and that includes three million who are working—have incomes of less than $500 a year; and half of that age group have incomes of less than $1,000 a year. As long as old age means that one has only a fifty-fifty chance of escaping dire poverty, we cannot expect to make it palatable.

While incomes are so low, suitable housing is out of the question. I recently saw a report from Kentucky where they made a study of the living conditions of the people receiving Old Age Assistance. Half of the houses, or rather shacks, were in such a bad state of repair that it was surprising that their inhabitants had not burned to death or suffered fatal falls. Three fourths had no running water and 80 per cent had no inside toilets. A third had no electricity. Anyone at any age would find life in those houses scarcely worth living. And Kentucky homes are exceptional only in degree. Many other states have housing just as disreputable.

We Americans are often criticized by others and we criticize ourselves for being too materialistic. But having enjoyed a comfortable home in our younger days, or at least the hope of attaining one, it is unrealistic to expect that we should ever imagine ourselves living in shacks that lack even the fundamentals of health, let alone comfort. Only if we realize that living in these conditions is a possibility will we gain the incentive to reduce the currently good chance of our being the next inhabitants of those hovels of the aged. Five hundred dollars—the top total income of one out of every three people over sixty-five today—will not buy anything better.

Public housing and pensions come to mind immediately as measures that might reduce our risk of an ill-housed old age. But these raise another problem, that of being considered a burden. Being a burden either to relatives or to taxpayers is another one of the hardships that we have come to regard as inseparable with age. It is normal and natural that in old age, as in any age, we should want to attain our economic security by socially useful and personally satisfying means.

Employment of the Aging

Throughout the nation, only one in three persons over sixty-five is still actively contributing to production, and undoubtedly a good many of these are engaged in the low-paid, unpleasant jobs which younger workers scorn and which, by no stretch of the imagination, can be said to provide personal satisfaction. A study of the employment status of older workers, recently issued by the Labor Department, revealed that 50 to 70 per cent of employer orders for workers received by local offices of the United States Employment Service carried maximum age limitations. Bad as the job prospects are for the person over sixty-five today, they are likely to be even worse when some of us attain that age unless attitudes and policies toward older workers are changed. In 1944, a person over sixty-five had one chance in four of working; now he has only one chance in three.

Leaders of labor and management alike are agreed that there are no insuperable obstacles to increasing work opportunities for the aging. Many communities have developed projects in this field that have yielded most encouraging results. One can pick up any of the growing number of excellent books that are appearing on aging problems and find the answers that have evolved from these projects: specialized counseling and placement services, research on better ways of fitting jobs to the workers and workers to the job, education of industrial management, stimulation of certain types of homework, nonprofit sheltered workshops, vocational rehabilitation, the establishment of permanent hometown job finding services for older workers. We know how to lift the employment barriers, but we just have not come to grips with the hard, cold fact that each year we delay, our chances of an idle old age are increasing.

Need for Health Services

The prejudice against employing the aged undoubtedly stems from another one of age's unsavory companions, namely, impaired physical and mental health. Here again, our problem is how to separate age from the bad company she keeps. It is a particularly tough problem because, in most cases, their association began way back in youth or middle age. If we have not attained, before sixty-five, the mental and emotional adjustment that makes life interesting and filled with friendships, it is unlikely that the hard shell of loneliness will be cracked in our old age. And if we have yielded to extra poundage and ignored the warning symptoms that some medical repairs were needed, we, like so many aged of today, will find it easier simply to "set" than to get out and enjoy life. Since we have allowed feebleness to become an almost universal characteristic of advanced age, it is important, through research and specialized medical and rehabilitation services for the aged, to mitigate their hardships. It is equally important, however, to save the oncoming generations of oldsters from this fate. The isolated case of the man or woman who is vigorously busy throughout life must become the usual case. That means, of course, that we must strengthen preventive and curative health services for all age groups and that within the framework of our total health services, we must develop special health services for the aged. With good physical and mental health, I believe most people, whatever their age, can carve out their own satisfying and useful niches in life.

Housing Needs

Health services, however, are by no means our only weapon against infirmity. In fact, they might be called our second line of defense. The first defense is a wholesome home environment. I do not intend here to make any practical proposals about housing for the aged. But I do want to insist on the need to build happiness into the model homes of the future. I mention this because so many people have been surprised at one of the results of the Kentucky housing survey which I mentioned earlier. When these old people, living in such miserable shacks, were asked whether their housing was better or worse than formerly, their answers had no relation to the physical properties of the housing. Some with quite adequate housing thought it was terrible, while others, living under incredibly bad conditions, were not disturbed. This mystified the researchers until they hit upon the idea of grouping the answers by living arrangements. Thirty-four per cent of those who were living alone were disturbed about their housing, but only 15 per cent of those who were living with their children had complaints. When we hear complaints about children neglecting their parents, it is well to note that the 1950 census reported 76 per cent of persons sixty-five and over living in family homes with one or more relatives. It was not the rickety stairs and the cold drafts, it was their own state of happiness or unhappiness that made the house seem good or bad.

But how often even the best-intentioned people, perhaps particularly the best-intentioned people, forget that the inside feelings are always more important than the outside furnishings. In that connection, I have great respect for one public welfare agency out West that continues to assist a group of aged ex-lumberjacks to live in a boarding home, despite community protests that public funds were going into an "unfit" home. The boarding home, in fact, does look unfit. One of the inmates is raising rabbits and there is tangible evidence of their accidental visits to the parlor. Another is hatching baby chicks under the kitchen stove. The bedroom of another is deep in sawdust and woodshavings. Meals are somewhat haphazard and not always well balanced. Life is casual, easy-going, sloppy if you will. But the eight old men who live there love it.

Of course we need standards for homes for the old people who cannot live in their own homes. The new amendment requiring states to set up a standard-setting authority, if they wish to receive federal public assistance funds for the aged and infirm who are in institutions, is a great mark of progress that will help to protect thousands from inhuman and unsafe living conditions. But let us keep our standards flexible. Let us be sure our ex-lumberjacks, as well as our genteel old ladies, can spend their final days in the kind of surroundings that symbolize home for them. And, remembering that one's own home is the very best place of all, let us be increasingly imaginative in finding ways to enable people to stay at home, even when their mental and physical powers are diminishing: ways such as meals on wheels, homemaker services, home medical and nursing services, counseling for those families and their aged relatives who live together but do not like it. With the advent of the Old Age Assistance program, the shadow of the poorhouse no longer looms over every prospect of growing old. But many who are using this aid to maintain themselves in their own homes are suffering unnecessarily, simply because their communities have failed to provide those extra and relatively inexpensive services that make all the difference between existing and living.

Need for Recreational Services

Fear of loneliness, according to Lord Amulree, is the first of the three main factors which interfere with an old person's happy enjoyment of his home; the other two factors being fear of ill health and fear of poverty.[1] I do not have any statistics to tell you what percentage of today's misery among the aged is due to loneliness, but I believe I can safely predict that the percentage will rise steadily unless there is a change in the trend of recreational interests in this country.

The more our workaday lives become mechanized, the greater our need for leisure-time activities that release our creative talents, if we are to continue as human beings and not mere animate adjuncts to our machines. Yet, more and more, we are turning to the television, the big sports arena, the professional entertainer; we are passive observers of other people's fun rather than active creators of our own. Looking at it superficially, one might say that this growing tendency to sit and be entertained is preparing us for the days when that is all we may be able to do. Unfortunately, this kind of recreational fabric is too thin and shoddy to wear through all our years. The soap opera heroine becomes a diminishingly satisfactory substitute for the boon companion we crave; the comedian's joke that sent us into gales of laughter at seven or seventeen gets a little boring after we have had seventy years of its varying versions. In recreation, as in friendship, we receive in proportion to what we give. We can appreciate the professional's music, but for the full savor we need also to be able to make our own. To engage ourselves actively in the arts and crafts is not only revitalizing in itself, but provides the solid

[1]Lord Amulree, *Adding Life to Years* (London: Bannisdale Press, 1951), p. 24.

ground of mutual interests upon which stimulating friendships are built. These cultural values are ageless. But if interest in them has never been awakened or cultivated, it cannot spring full born in our later years.

The aged of today have an advantage over the aged of the future in that they began life in the craft days, and many of them are now finding comfort in their quilting clubs, their woodworking groups, and other handicraft groups. Many more could find friends and fun through these activities if local communities were more alert to bringing them together. Councils of social agencies, churches, schools, and settlements are doing much to organize these groups. But more needs to be done, especially in areas where housing is poor. People living on low incomes are particularly in need of these community facilities, for many of them have no place to entertain guests in their own homes, and do not even have the money to enjoy the solitary pleasures of books, radio, or television.

The Need to "Do for Others"

The social relationship of the aged need not, of course, depend entirely upon recreation. They, like other groups, should have the opportunity of "doing for others." Many of them are serving as volunteers in the Red Cross, in mental hospitals, and in other civic and charitable enterprises. But, again, many more could be recruited, to the mutual advantage of themselves and the organizations they serve.

As we develop more and different types of social programs, we will be in a better position to test their values against basic principles. For example: do they help the aging person to live with his increasing limitations? Do they discover and develop new talents? Do they open up for the aging new experiences for living with their families and communities? Do they add information and counteract misinformation about the processes and limitations of old age?

Our birthdays are passing. We are going to want those answers sooner than we think.

Spiritual Needs

Against the inner loneliness that comes at times to all of us even when we are surrounded by warm friends and doting relatives, there is, of course, but one protection—faith in God, our religion. Age is the time of all times when we have the depth of experience and wisdom to savor the deep wells of the spirit wherein lies eternal strength. Just as youth might be considered the period when joys of physical prowess reach their height, so age is the time when the philosophical and spiritual richness of life reaches its full fruition. The special meaning of religion to the aged is well recognized by churches and synagogues. Yet the spiritual needs of the aging have not been fully recognized in the programs designed for their care, a serious defect in this modern world where many of the aging have been uprooted from the religious traditions and contacts of their more active days. Practical suggestions to remedy this defect have been made by many more qualified than I. All that is lacking is the will to action. In the meantime, the inner religious impulses of many aged persons are blocked off from the religious institutions through which they should normally flow.

Conclusion

Old age is moving into new company. It is a hopeful sign that it can be separated from those miserable companions—poverty, idleness, loneliness, ill health—which have given it such a bad reputation. Once we have made it respectable, there is no reason why we need to dread its inevitable visit. Rather, we can look forward to entering the final stage of life with the five prerequisites for happiness:

1. Economic security obtained through socially useful and personally satisfying means. This includes adequate social insurance for support in retirement and public assistance when needed. In fact, these income maintenance programs are so important that they might well be described as the backbone of all community services for the aged. As more and more people are assured of an adequate income in their later years, they themselves can become

increasingly effective in creating the other conditions for a satisfying life.

2. Sound physical and mental health.
3. Pleasant living arrangements.
4. Happy social relationships.
5. Spiritual inspiration and comfort.

Community services can be provided which will assure everyone an opportunity to attain these goals. Such services will be provided if we see them as our own needs—not as needs of others who have reached an unfortunate period that we, in some vague and miraculous way, will escape.

ORGANIZING
THE COMMUNITY *Chapter XXII*

CARL L. GARDNER

Carl L. Gardner, M.C.P., is secretary of the Chicago Plan Commission. His previous positions included director of Land Planning, Federal Housing Administration; chief land planning consultant, Federal Housing Administration; and lecturer in city planning, Dartmouth College. Mr. Gardner is also secretary of the City Planning Advisory Board, Chicago; member of the Board of Governors, American Institute of Planners; past president of the Chicago Region Chapter of the American Institute of Planners; member of the Board of Directors, Chicago Building Congress; and chairman of the City Planning Committee, Chicago Civil Defense Corps. He has published numerous articles on city and regional planning.

RECENT COMMUNITY efforts around the country to stimulate interest in, and get action upon the problems of the aging, differ in many important aspects. This, obviously, is to be expected. The variations of geography, economic circumstance, and social history, among other things, require that each community organize for action on a basis best suited to its particular needs. As we all know, too, the challenge of the care of the aging population is an evolving thing. There are few American guideposts. Yet experience, to date, reveals that a rather definite pattern of community organization has developed despite the relative infancy of these investigations. The accomplishment of such workers in this field as Dr. Wilma Donahue in bringing this subject to the fore in recent years has focused an extensive amount of technical thought upon the subject.

Suddenly, it seems, our oldsters as a class, because of their greatly increasing numbers, are the subject of special political consideration. Expansion of their Old Age and Survivors Insurance benefits was urged recently in the platforms of both major political parties. Political favor is sought by some who have promised to abolish the "work clause" of the Social Security Law, which limits the earnings that men and women drawing old age benefits may receive. The question of providing for the needs of older people has gained increasing political importance, and, to ease the pressure upon the public treasuries for more and more old age assistance, the public should be informed of the political dangers involved.

Community action, which has been successful in other fields of civic endeavor, has followed, generally, a basic pattern. City planning and important development programs, adoption of zoning, the suppression of crime and corruption, the overhaul of outmoded local government, and other worthwhile measures have been achieved in this way. The plan of community organization to which I am referring is simply one of good public relations. No program, however important, will avail much without well-ordered support. It is ironic that our recent history is replete with examples of thoroughly sound and justifiable projects for community betterment which have been either scuttled or rendered impotent because of sheer apathy or because their aims and objectives were not understood. Therefore, if a civic program is to succeed, proper communication of the facts and recommendations is vital.

Community Organization in the Philadelphia Charter Commission

Perhaps the plan of community organization which "rings the bell" can be best illustrated by the recent work of the Philadelphia Charter Commission, which drafted and secured adoption of a city charter in the face of apparently insuperable odds. In Philadelphia, where it is reported that city government was riddled with corruption, a spectacular reform was effected through the co-operation of a great number of citizens' organizations. The

Charter Commission conducted a series of public hearings at which civic groups were invited to express their views.

Advantages of public hearings. Such participation has three distinct advantages. First, it is productive of all manner of ideas and suggestions, and if later some of the suggestions are adopted—as they are sure to be, because nearly everything conceivable will be suggested—the groups will take pride in their participation. Second, in educating the members of the commission, group leaders educate each other. They hear opposing points of view and gain a new appreciation of the magnitude and complexity of the commission's task. They become less dogmatic and more inclined to recognize the need for justifiable compromise. Furthermore, the heads of the groups report back to their membership that they have appeared before the commission and presented recommendations. The matter was in many instances reported in the groups' publications, and thus still more people learned that a good city charter was in the making and that the commission was composed of a pretty intelligent group of sincere and hard-working people. Where it was found that large groups of people were inarticulate and insufficiently versed in the matter to offer help, the "trial balloon" technique was used: if the community group was unable to resolve its wants, speakers for the commission would formulate a statement of the needs and then let that group say what was wrong with it.

Means of community education. In the early stage, leading newspapers published helpful articles on the commission, and reprints were made available. Radio and television programs were given, and magazines told the story. Schools picked up the project and made it a practical bit of education in civics. The school children took the problem home to their parents, and so the education of the people continued. Finally, a tentative draft of the charter was published, and again many public hearings were held and many sound changes accepted by the commission. This unremitting concern for the suggestions and opinions of the people created confidence in the commission and its work, and prevented the feeling that the commission was trying to "jam something down the people's throats." It forced the critics of the charter out into the open and the commission was able to pull the props out from under the opposition. In the latter stages of the campaign for adoption, much help was obtained by securing the endorsements of outstanding men and leaders of groups—labor, Negro, political parties, etc. Those people who did not understand the charter and the problems involved and who would not care to study the matter in detail, might nevertheless follow the lead of prominent persons. A speakers' bureau was formed, printed publicity was distributed, cartoons in comic-strip form were published, and in the end the charter was adopted. The Charter Commission understood that its appeal must be made to many and diverse groups, each interested in a different phase of the subject—and therein lay part of its success. Another part was because of the completely democratic process of participation by many groups and many people.

Chicago Community Project for the Aged

Similar methods were used by the Community Project for the Aged of the Welfare Council of Metropolitan Chicago. This project began as one of four which were financed by the Wieboldt Foundation of Chicago in commemoration of its twenty-fifth anniversary. It carried on its work through a staff, with the assistance of an advisory committee. The advisory committee was composed of persons (1) representing many fields of social work which corresponded with the different facets of the problem; (2) persons engaged in studying psychiatric, medical, and sociological aspects of the process of aging; and (3) representatives of governing boards of social agencies.

Objectives. This community project set up for itself four objectives:

1. To study problems confronting older persons in Chicago.
2. To conduct a program of community education.
3. To carry on demonstration programs and to stimulate other agencies to undertake them.

4. To prepare a plan of community services for older people in metropolitan Chicago.

Means of community education. In the four short years of the project's existence it was extraordinarily successful in its program of public education. Some of this was direct, as in conferences of the staff with representatives of all the agencies which in one way or another had a responsibility (whether or not previously recognized), for the welfare of older people. Much of the education of the public was indirect, as in stimulating the press to report activities and events in this field.

In carrying out a program of community education it was recognized that the nature of the work required an approach both general and specialized. To create a favorable climate for the development of adequate services for older people, it was decided that the general public needed to be given two kinds of information. First, the public needed to be made aware of the problems growing out of the increased life span. This information included clear-cut and simple statements regarding the increase in older age groups; the effect that urbanization mobility of population and housing shortages have had upon older people; and the difficulty of accumulating savings over a long period of rising prices. The public needed particularly to learn that years are no accurate measure of age, and that people do not become old, worn out, feeble, or incapacitated as soon as they used to. Emphasis was laid upon the probable inability of our economy to support in nonproductive roles all of the old people we are going to have in the future, and the consequent necessity of extending opportunities for productive work to older people.

The second body of information which was communicated to the general public concerned itself with a realistic appraisal of the services available now for older people in metropolitan Chicago. This information pointed out the deficiencies at the present time, and suggested the new or expanded services required.

Specialized information was directed to the following groups, among others: over-all planning and financing bodies, employing and personnel groups, labor unions, civic organizations, churches, and political units.

The experience of the Community Project for the Aged was that many community agencies and individuals, as well as commercial, publicity, and news organizations, were more than willing to co-operate, provided certain conditions were maintained. The first of these conditions was that there should be a specific reason for a message to the general public; (2) the facts should be clearly set forth, with a qualified source indicated, from whom additional material could be obtained; (3) it should be made clear why the message was of interest to the members of the organization to which it was sent.

Other means of getting the facts before the public were audio-visual material for use with community groups, a speakers' bureau under some appropriate agency, articles in professional and trade journals, newsletters regarding items of interest, committee reports, and personal interpretations.

Co-ordination of all the channels through which information was sent out into the community was needed in order to avoid the negation of one message by another. For example, if organization A pictured all older people as racked with chronic illness, or emotionally maladjusted because of rejection by the community, organization B would have a hard time selling the older worker to prospective employers. The special aspects in the field of the care of the aging must be balanced in order to build a balanced program in any community.

The Chicago Plan

The work of the Community Project for the Aged of Metropolitan Chicago culminated in a program published in 1952, under the title *Community Services for Older People, The Chicago Plan*, from which I have freely quoted. The central principle of the Plan is the integration of services for older persons with the existing structure of welfare agencies. Naturally and logically, the Welfare Council is charged with the greatest share of the responsibility for co-ordination, promotion, and leadership in the development of the Plan from blueprint to reality. In co-operation with the Welfare Council for the effectuation of the Plan are the governmental agencies at federal, state, county, and city levels;

the churches, each denomination of which maintains one or more homes for the aged; and an impressive list of private agencies.

Conclusion

Despite the many difficulties that we face, we are moving forward in providing for better working and living conditions in our urban centers, not only for the aged but for the aging—in other words, for all.

There are certain fundamental conditions which hold great promise for better city living:

1. A prosperous and sound economic base, modern transportation, adequate housing, unpolluted air to breathe, police and fire protection, places to play, homes for the aged and ill, sound municipal health services, a bearable tax rate—all the things that make a good physical and material base for an urban community.

2. The constant stimulation to the cultural and spiritual growth of the community that comes from human institutions such as the press; radio and TV; well-staffed schools; great universities; schools of medicine, law, music, art, and architecture; museums; art galleries; and strong churches.

3. Co-operation and understanding among all the people of all races, creeds, and nationalities who go to make up the city.

We are ever approaching these goals. There is a new spirit abroad of pride in the community. Local organization of the community to provide adequate housing for the aging, through democratic and co-operative processes, is an integral part of this march forward.

PROGRAMS
IN ACTION *Chapter XXIII*

WILMA DONAHUE

WHAT AMERICA has done to house its aging has been slight in comparison with the need. In January, 1952, Hertha Kraus wrote in a discussion on housing our older citizens that "there are practically no new developments in this area. We scan the literature and meet the same old friends: a few cottage colonies developed for the elderly by public enterprise . . . ; fewer than three hundred apartments designed for the aged in public projects . . . ; even a smaller number of apartments for the aged under the auspices of voluntary agencies."[1]

But perhaps we should not try to measure our effort by the yard, for what has been done has often been the hard, wood-clearing work of the pioneer, the groundwork, the earth base of a new movement. This work has been difficult because each program undertaken has had only a slender body of knowledge from which to draw. In each case there was the need to be demonstrated, the opposition to overcome, the plan to be determined, the finances to be arranged, and the standards to be developed. Indeed, all the problems that arise between the conception and the reality had again and again to be solved and interpreted anew because the findings of one venture had not been immediately available for the beginning of the next. Despite these difficulties, much has been gained and it seems worthwhile to describe the various housing experiments that have been undertaken, even those that are "old friends" so that some general conclusions can

[1] Hertha Kraus, "Housing Our Older Citizens," *Ann. Amer. Acad. Pol. Soc. Sci.*, 279 (1952):129.

be drawn, and above all, can be made available within the covers of one book. The analysis cannot be exhaustive, but trends and directions which housing the aging has taken will emerge from a review of programs in action.

Fraternal Organizations

Several fraternal organizations have made a serious attempt to meet the housing problems of their aging members. The Masons, the Odd Fellows, and other similar organizations have established homes in various parts of the country. The Loyal Order of Moose has developed an extensive colony for old people in Florida. Mr. Wesley J. Leinweber described this project in considerable detail as a part of the program of the Michigan Conference on Aging. The following is an abstract of his description:

Moosehaven. The Moose fraternal program of aid to children and the aged resulted in the establishment of "Mooseheart" in Illinois in 1913 where services to both these groups were originally administered. When, in the early 1920's, it became apparent that it would be more desirable to provide the services for the aged in a more hospitable climate than prevailed in Illinois, the fraternity moved to establish a home for the aged in Florida. The Moosehaven of today, a model community for old folks, was founded in 1922 for members of the Loyal Order of Moose who had reached the age of retirement. It is located on the west bank of the St. Johns River at Orange Park, Florida.

The community's operations are financed with funds allocated by the Supreme Lodge of the World, Loyal Order of Moose, out of dues received by the 1,600 member lodges. The Legion of the Moose and the Women of the Moose lend financial support towards capital expenditures in the expansion of the community.

The main Moosehaven campus has an area of sixty-eight acres and has a river frontage of over quarter of a mile. Residences are so located that all have an open view of the St. Johns River. The major houses on the main campus accommodating twelve to fifty-eight persons each are one story buildings of brick veneer construction. Each has its own dining room, kitchen, a spacious living room, and several large screened porches. Two smaller homes are located on the ninety-acre Moosehaven dairy farm, one mile distant from the main campus. The total housing capacity of the Moosehaven community, including the hospital and the convalescent units, is 374.

The administrative offices, an auditorium with a seating capacity of three hundred, and the Moosehaven Laboratory for Gerontology occupy one large building on the grounds. Other buildings include a commissary through which all food and clothing supplies and shoe repairs are handled, an industrial shop in which are located maintenance and repair departments, a hospital, and four private residences for staff members.

Moosehaven has its own water supply system. Electric power is obtained from the electric company of a near-by city. All buildings are heated by individual oil burning systems, and cooking is done by gas.

The home and community life at Moosehaven is made a matter of concern to all residents. The operation of the community is based on fraternal and democratic practices. Each house, by vote of members, selects a three-member house committee which services for a three-month period. This committee, with the supervisor of the residence, is responsible for the general operation of the home. The house committee chairmen are ipso-facto members of a community committee which co-operates with the administrative staff in formulating and carrying out the program of activities for the community as a whole.

Through a town hall meeting, held once every three months, problems and issues are brought before the entire community; and each resident is privileged to speak from the floor on any matter or issue that comes up for discussion. The issues are voted on and the results are used by the administration for its guidance and direction.

Activities at Moosehaven include both work and recreation. The residents participate in the community's operational and maintenance programs; jobs requiring one, two, or three hours a day are classified under more than fifty titles. Each resident draws a monthly financial allowance, the amount of which depends upon the amount and type of work done, and the number of hours devoted to it each day. All those who are unable to accept job assignments because of health or other reasons are given what is termed a "sunshine allowance." About 40 per cent of the residents are not physically able to participate in the work program. The residents carry on many hobbies and crafts. Most of the work is done in their living quarters, but some is carried on in special hobby shops. The finished articles are put on display at the reception center for visitors to buy if they wish.

Most recreational programs in the community are carried out through Opportunity Lodge (the Moosehaven fraternal unit) to which all male residents are automatically eligible. The recreational program for women is provided through a local unit of the Women of the Moose and a sewing circle.

One important activity of the community is the monthly publication of the *Moosehaven Booster,* a newspaper which reports the events which have taken place at Moosehaven during the month. On the staff of reporters is a resident from each home unit, who reports the incidents and items of community interest that occur in his particular house. Through the *Booster,* the administration brings to the community's attention matters of policy and program, and seeks to cultivate an understanding and an esprit de corps among the residents in furthering the general welfare.

Medical services are extensive. The hospital has a twenty-five patient bed capacity with private and double rooms and wards for men and women. In addition there is a convalescent unit which accommodates fifty-three persons. Medical services include a dispensary, a laboratory, X-ray and diathermy rooms. A physician and a staff of nurses provide medical care and nursing service twenty-four hours a day.

A very special feature of the Moosehaven community, one in fact which does not exist in any similar community, is a gerontological research laboratory. The research aim of the laboratory is the investigation of the physical, nutritional, social, educational, and emotional factors contributing to the improvement and maintenance of mental health in the aging population. In addition to its research, the laboratory staff endeavors to be of direct service to the Moosehaven community through the administration and interpretation of various diagnostic tests and by offering counseling services to residents.

This community has been reported in detail because it offers an excellent example of a well-built, well-staffed old age housing project complete with a program to meet the psychological as well as the health and physical needs of the aging. (Further information may be obtained by writing to Wesley J. Leinweber, Superintendent, Moosehaven, Orange Park, Florida.)

Religious Groups

Traditionally, organized religious groups have concerned themselves with the total welfare of their members and have been in the vanguard to provide housing and other types of services needed by their older people. Some of the best programs of the country have been developed under the inspiration of religious leaders. Unfortunately, this chapter cannot discuss all the examples; those that are included are chosen not because they are necessarily the best but because they are representative of the best.

Home for the Aged and Infirm Hebrews in New York. On March 13, 1870, the B'nai Jeshrun Ladies Hebrew Benevolent Society adopted a resolution which led to the establishment of the Home for Aged and Infirm Hebrews in New York. The core of this resolution was a simple determination to "provide some means to care for the aged and infirm of our persuasion, destitute . . . daily increasing in numbers, many without friends or any visible means of support." Today, the Home, which claims to be the largest voluntarily supported institution for the aged in the country, is providing modern, comprehensive care for nearly one thousand older people.

How this vast project has been financed through the years may be indicated by the following figures from an annual financial statement. In 1951, the total operating expense of the Home was $1,651,808.04. Of this, about one third was met by a subsidy from the Federation of Jewish Philanthropies of New York.

An amount somewhat in excess of a second third was received as contributions from relatives and friends of residents. Scarcely more than one fourth of the total expenses of the Home was met by what may be called "public" money—federal, state, and city funds administered by the New York City Department of Welfare.

The Home comprises a group of buildings of which the nucleus is the Central Building on West 105th Street in New York City. This building has accommodations for 364 residents and includes an infirmary of seventy beds. Central Building is like a small community in itself with its own kitchens, laundry, tailor shop, beauty parlor, barber shop, synagogue, library, open-air garden, occupational therapy shops, smoking and gamerooms, and a spacious clubroom equipped for motion picture, theatrical, and television exhibitions.

Within walking distance of Central Building are two groups of apartment residences with private accommodations for 150 men and women. Married couples occupy double rooms; single persons have rooms of their own. The residents share a communal dining room and common sitting rooms for recreation. They arrange house rules and entertainment themselves and, in general, have a greater degree of independence than is possible in the Central Building. Yet at the same time they may rely on the Home for medical services and supervision for special services such as housekeeping aides, and for custodial care when necessary.

In addition to the apartment project, there is a home care program which serves about sixty people in their own homes. As in the apartment project, social service workers from the Home visit these aged persons regularly, and homemakers provided by the Jewish Family Service, in co-operation with the Central Bureau for Jewish Aged, ease cleaning and shopping tasks. The Home's services, including its medical department, are available to those on home care. Nursing service, when required, is supplied by the Visiting Nurse Service. These nonresident members of the Home are assured of accommodation in major units of the Home if they need more supervision or professional care than can be efficiently provided in their own dwellings.

All of the facilities and services provided in the Central Building are also furnished in Kingsbridge House, a two and three-quarter million dollar development which was opened in 1950 in the Bronx. Kingsbridge House consists of six spacious interconnected modern buildings set in five landscaped acres, and with special accommodations for almost four hundred residents of varying degrees of functional capacity. For those who are able to get about easily, single and double rooms are available in one building. For those whose activity is more limited, the same kind of accommodations are set aside in the two main buildings where regular nursing care is at hand and where there is easy access to the clinics. An excellent library, a recreation hall, and an occupational therapy building are additional structures on the grounds. A new service for older persons of means who can afford to pay for long-term private care was started as an integral part of Kingsbridge House. This facility, called "Private Pavilion," offers to its ninety-eight guests residential accommodations which compare favorably with those in apartment hotels and nursing homes. In addition, the residents have ready access to a complete range of medical, recreational, and social facilities paralleling those at the Central Building.

The integrated socio-medical programs of the Home for Aged and Infirm Hebrews form an important part of the total care that is given. In 1950, a physical rehabilitation program to care for the handicapped aged was started and has achieved considerable success, even among patients once considered virtually hopeless. The social service program has long been under way. Its activities begin with a study of each applicant in an effort to determine if and how the institution can help him, and then interprets to the applicant and members of the family what it will be like to live in the Home as compared with the community. After the applicant is admitted, the social service staff help with his intramural adjustment and maintain a close relationship with the resident in the institution and with the family and friends of the resident on the outside. Finally, as a part of the psychological care that is offered, there is an elaborate program of occupational therapy and recreation.

The Jewish homes for the aged throughout the country are of a uniformly high standard and in general have been foremost in the development of new types of programs and services. Sheltered workshops which have been incorporated in a number of these homes are among their more recent programs. For example, the Montefiore Home in Cleveland has recently added a wing to the main building for this purpose. Here the resident can work as much or as little as he wishes each day. He is paid a standard wage, a part of which he may keep and a part of which he returns to the home toward payment for his care. The feeling of usefulness that this program has engendered in the aging residents, the better physical and mental health and the greater happiness that have resulted, make this activity a valuable addition to the social plan of the home.

The day-resident program is another innovation which has been well developed in Jewish homes such as the Drexel Home in Chicago. This plan provides opportunity for older people living in the vicinity to take part in the daily activities programs and to have at least one good meal a day at the Home. By this means, the facilities of the Home with its social, recreational, and medical programs are made available to older people who would otherwise have to spend their days in lonely isolation and neglect in their own residences.

Mary Margaret Manning Home. The Mary Margaret Manning Home is operated by the Carmelite Order in New York City. It is a very large plant consisting of a number of floors and wings and incorporating many unique features. There are accommodations for both men and women and for married couples. Throughout the building there are kitchenettes where light meals and snacks may be prepared; there are a generous number of sitting rooms, small porches which open to the outdoors high above New York City's life, wide, well-lighted corridors, special recreation rooms, and libraries. Some of the more special features of the Home include a small theater, a well-equipped hobbyshop, and a snack bar looking very much like a modern bar in any restaurant. The beautiful chapel situated in the center of the building adds an air of deep quietude to the Home. Medical services are provided in the infirmary and hospital units and the Sisters offer continuous nursing care. One special feature of the medical service is a large and unusually well-equipped rehabilitation center under the guidance of a physician skilled in physical medicine. This rehabilitation center is open to people outside the home as well as to the residents.

Pilgrim Place. Pilgrim Place, Claremont, California, sponsored by the Congregational Church, is of special value as an example because it demonstrates how a community for retired persons can be made an integral part of a city or town. The village is restricted to retired missionaries, ministers, and other Christian workers, although they need not be of Congregational persuasian. It is situated on twenty-eight acres of land within walking distance of the shopping center of Claremont, and within easy commuting distance of eight colleges. The community consists of residence halls with small apartments for single men and women and of small homes which are either privately owned by their residents or by Pilgrim Place. Because Pilgrim Place is a nonprofit organization, rental charges are kept somewhere between one half and two thirds of commensurate commercial values. In addition to the living quarters, an infirmary and nursing home has recently been built on the grounds. One resident, suffering from a heart condition for which he felt a need for continuous nursing care, has built an apartment as a wing to the nursing home. Here he lives as independently as he would in any other part of the village, but has the security of medical supervision and care at his beck and call. The homes built in Pilgrim Place conform to specifications of one-story structures with frame, stucco, brick, or cement block exteriors. Houses vary in style, and as one drives along the avenues of the village it seems no different than driving along any city street. The naturalness of the setting, the absence of institutionalized program features, and the freedom of the residents to live independently make this project one of great significance.[2]

[2]"The Over-65 Have Housing Problems," *Amer. Builder,* Nov., 1953, pp. 58-64.

Methodist homes. Many of the homes sponsored by religious groups, which heretofore had only one large institutional-type building, are now adding apartment units, and are making provision for detached cottages built adjacent to the large home. At Charlotte, North Carolina, the Methodist Home for the Aging has a large well-equipped central building. In it are common dining rooms, an excellent infirmary, sitting rooms, recreation halls and theater, chapel, occupational therapy shops, and store. The building houses approximately one hundred and fifty people in individual rooms complete with private baths. Nearby is a row-house development in which there are one- and two-bedroom units. The residents of these apartments may prepare breakfast and supper in their kitchens but are expected to take their noon meals in the main dining room. Land has been set aside for privately built houses which will become the property of the Home upon the death of the surviving member of the occupying couple. At the present time there is one owner-built and occupied cottage.

Great attention is given to the planning of social and educational programs which will meet the needs of the residents for participation in interesting activities. Sociability between the residents of the apartments and those in the central building is fostered; the opportunity to visit in the private homes and apartments is of great value to the more institutionalized resident. Standards are high and every effort is exerted to make this home one where maximum health and happiness are maintained.

A housing project under the auspices of the Oregon Methodist Homes, Inc. and under the direct supervision of the National Methodist Board of Hospitals and Homes will be opened in December, 1954, at Portland, Oregon. Willamette View Manor will be a large apartment-type building and will be operated as a modern hotel club for retired people. Emphasis is placed on the fact that it will not be an old people's home in the usual sense of the word. According to its organizers, it will provide luxury, security, freedom from care and responsibility, and a homelike community spirit.

The cost of the building and operation will be shared co-operatively by the residents of the home. Those wishing to live in the home will share the construction cost of their own apartments by the payment of a founder's fee. The amount of the fee will depend upon the size of the accommodation chosen. At the present time it is possible to secure apartments at a substantial reduction below the cost to buyers after the completion of the project. There will be sixteen different types of living quarters from single rooms to deluxe apartments which may be had with or without pullman kitchens. For those occupying the smaller rooms, there will be community kitchens located conveniently on each floor. Each apartment will be a complete living unit with private bath, telephone, connections for radio and television, and an emergency buzzer to the nurse's headquarters. Public facilities will include a main dining room, recreation room, and hobby and craft rooms. A number of cottages will be built for those people who prefer more privacy but who will use the facilities of the main building.

The cost of living in the home will, at present price levels, be $100 a month. This sum may be paid monthly, annually, or on an annuity basis with life care paid in advance. The cost of the prepaid life care will be based on the life expectancy of the applicant. Meals, hospitalization, recreation, and free access to all other benefits of the home will be provided regardless of the method of payment.

Presbyterian Village. In Detroit, Michigan, a new program is underway sponsored by the Presbyterian Church. After making a decision that they should develop a plan which would help solve the housing needs of the able-bodied, the frail, and the sick, and after a careful study of the facts and trends in the aging population, the planning group produced a blueprint for Presbyterian Village. This community is to be located on a plot of about thirty-five acres which lies outside the city limits but which is in the midst of a new suburban shopping center and community. Four types of housing are planned: row housing of one- and two-bedroom units; detached cottages built by individuals (later to become a part of the church property); apartment-type buildings providing single rooms or suites and including a central dining room; and an infirmary hospital unit to provide for outpatient services, rehabilitation, long-term care, and acute illness. In addition to these several types of housing arrangements, the Village will also include buildings housing recreational rooms, hobby and sheltered workshops, a church (already built), and dormitories for medical and staff personnel. The Village is planned to provide for the maximum in independent living and at the same time to furnish complete care and shelter for those who need it.

Trade-unions

For the most part the efforts of trade-unions to provide housing for their older members have resulted in the building of the conventional old age home. In different parts of the country are to be found homes for retired and disabled members of such trades as printers, carpenters, actors, conductors, and soldiers.

With the widespread application of compulsory retirement among industrial workers, there is a growing need for more housing within the price range of a limited fixed income and with features important to easy living in old age. Union members are pressing their leaders to look into the possibilities of converting the homes which they already own into assets which can be liquefied toward the purchase of more suitable homes for their retirement years.

A description of the more traditional union home and of two other developments now under way are given to illustrate the changes in trends.

Carpenters. The Home of the United Brotherhood of Carpenters and Joiners of America is one example. This home is situated in beautifully landscaped surroundings at Lakeland, Florida, and consists of one large handsome structure and several small service buildings near by. To be admitted to the Home, the applicant must be at least sixty-five years of age and must have been a member of the Brotherhood for thirty-five years or more. The attitude of the home appears to be essentially paternal. All the necessities and comforts of life are furnished the residents, including clothing and tobacco.

The Home was created by a general per capita tax from the membership of the Brotherhood throughout the country.

Upholsterers. Although the Upholsterers' International Union of North America has so far done no more than buy, clear, and dedicate 340 acres of land in Florida, it is worth noting that they have planned a complete village for their retired workers. The village is also designed to serve as a vacation spot for younger workers and their families. The present plans call for an infirmary, individual cottages of different sizes, community center, craftshop, and other facilities needed to round out life in the village. This forward-looking group is, as an initial part of the project, hiring personnel who will work on intake policy and help design the psycho-social program as well as the medical services of the community. Also, the Union has plans under way to institute a program of preparation for retirement for all their employees. It wishes to ensure that the workers will be ready to experience the best possible returns from their later years regardless of whether they are spent in the Florida village or in their own communities.

The Retail Clerks Union, Local 770. The Retail Clerks Union, Local 770, with headquarters in Los Angeles, has taken leadership in establishing various social programs for the benefit of its membership. For example, it sponsored the Permanente Hospital in Los Angeles and trained its members to make the most intelligent use of this facility. Then the Union sent out a questionnaire to its membership requesting a listing of other problems which the union should undertake.

Although the average age of the membership is only thirty-two years, the problem which was given priority by the largest number of the group was that of finding some way to care for the older family members. In many instances, the fathers and mothers of the workers were ill, or they needed a type of sheltered care which the family was unable to provide either within their own living quarters or in homes and hospitals, which were beyond their means.

In order to help solve this problem, the Union has drawn up a plan which will provide a convalescent service for old people. Land has been purchased within a block of the Permanente Hospital and the first units of the home will be built this year. It is planned to have all the services in the building emphasize the importance and possibilities of "getting well" and returning to the community. The buildings will be only one story high. Groups of rooms will be built as wings opening off a central corridor which will house the nurses' stations. A patio will separate the wings and each room will have full-length glass windows and a door which will open onto the patio. From the beginning, patients will be encouraged to go outside, in beds if necessary, or in wheel chairs, and under their own power when possible. Activities and rehabilitation procedures will be employed continuously, because it is not anticipated that this home will be a permanent one for old people but that it will be a place where they can be reinstated to a functional level which will allow them to return to their own homes and families.

Other Housing Projects Under Voluntary Sponsorship

In all the plans of housing for old people we note the same trend toward independent congregate living arrangements with provisions for special services such as housekeeping, shopping, and medical care. The Commonwealth Housing Foundation project at Boston already described in a previous chapter in this book is an example of this type.

Tompkins Square. The best-known example and the one with the longest history of successful operation is Tompkins Square House in New York City, operated on a nonprofit basis by New York's Community Service Society, a voluntary agency. The apartment building includes forty-four single rooms and eight two-room apartments, for both single and married people. The rooms are furnished or unfurnished as desired; they have no kitchen equipment, although kitchen and refrigeration facilities are available in the building for the use of each resident. There is also a cafeteria which serves three meals a day at cost and requires a certain minimum of patronage from each resident to keep it solvent.

Other facilities that the residents share are common sitting rooms, a roof garden, and a basement laundry. The director of the residence is a registered nurse with experience in health and welfare work, who, in the event of need, is able to give some care and assistance. Hospitalization and bedside care, however, are arranged by the resident himself. This project has been described many times during its more than twenty years of operation, and it has served to stimulate the thinking of many communities in their efforts to provide housing for their older citizens.[3]

Santa Barbara Rainbow Cottages. The American Women's Voluntary Services (AWVS) in Santa Barbara, California, have built, as a demonstration, a row-house project of rental units. They hope to show that low rent housing built by private funds is not beyond the realm of possibility. The AWVS collected enough funds through private donations to build fourteen individual units divided between five buildings. Each living unit consists of a living room, bedroom, bath, and kitchenette of the pullman type. The over-all cost of building the houses was $57,638; cost per unit was $4,177. Land and grading cost another $6,000. After almost a year of operation, it is estimated that there will be a net profit amounting to between 3 and 4 per cent, although the apartments rent for only $30.00 a month including utilities. Residence in the project is restricted to people with incomes of $80.00 or less a month.[4]

The construction of the houses is frame with stucco exteriors topped with cedar shake roofs. Each of the five buildings is painted a different pastel color. The residents have given the name "Rainbow Cottages" to the project. Inside, the walls are plastered; floors are cement; bathrooms have shower stalls with seats. A stove and refrigerator are furnished, but otherwise the

[3]Nathan Shock, *Trends in Gerontology* (Stanford University, Calif.: Stanford Univ. Press, 1951); Geneva Mathiasen, "Housing for Older People," *Enriching the Years* (Newburgh, N.Y.: New York Joint Legis. Comm. on Problems of the Aging, 1953), p. 98; R. W. Hill, "Public Housing and Our Aging," *Birthdays Don't Count* (Newburgh, N.Y.: New York Joint Legis. Comm. on Problems of the Aging, 1948), p. 255.

[4]"The Over-65 Have Housing Problems," *op. cit.*

apartments are unfurnished. The rooms are adequate in size: the living-dining area is 10½ feet by 16½ feet, and the bedroom is 9½ feet by 9 feet. Two closets and drawers for linen are built in, as is also an ironing board.

The location of the project is on a city street handy to the shopping district. An additional feature is a community center which was also provided by AWVS. It is open not only to residents of the housing project but to the older people of the whole community. Here an extensive social, recreational, and work program is carried out. The director of the center serves as the rent collector for the housing project. The community center building also houses a large automatic washer and dryer which is used by the Rainbow Cottage residents.

Medical care is not a part of this project. In fact, the older people living in these units have the same relation to the medical care facilities and services of Santa Barbara as they would have if they were living in any other part of the community. The AWVS has under consideration the possibility of establishing a nursing home within a block of the project. This nursing home would be available for the use of other citizens in the community but the Rainbow Cottage residents would have priority.

This is one of the most interesting of the new housing experiments, and it will be a very useful demonstration to those who are planning low rent housing projects. Further details about the plan can be obtained by writing the American Women's Voluntary Services in Santa Barbara.[5]

Peabody Home. Peabody Home for Aged Women in New York City provides a delightful residence for a carefully selected group of old ladies. Of special interest is the use of this facility to provide nonresident aid for women who will at some later time be admitted to the Home. The conditions which led to the evolving of this program are common enough. The number of applicants for admission became so great that it was apparent that the Home could not take care of them, unless the Home was prepared to make an enormous expenditure to enlarge its facili-

[5]American Women's Voluntary Services, 209 East Islay Street, Santa Barbara, Calif.

ties. This was not feasible, but at the same time there was an awareness that the need was immediate and that something had to be done. A study of the applicants indicated that at least 80 per cent did not immediately need the protective care of an institution. Ruth Laverty describes these applicants as "anxious, bitter, and resentful against a world that seemed to have no place for them. At the time of application some were potential suicides, others had become hypochondriacs and adherents of strange cults or food fads in their confused search for security, and still others expressed their frustration in difficult behavior, much to the exasperation of relatives, friends, and neighbors. They were women who needed immediate help and guidance, but not necessarily institutional care."[6]

The nonresident aid program was designed to help these aging women to continue living as independent members of the community but with greater security and better adjustment. When the time comes that a nonresident requires the care of an institution, Peabody Home is obliged to take her in.

Trained caseworkers visit the nonresidents each month, or more often if necessary; their intention is not only remedial and alleviative, but, if possible, preventive. Financial advice is given and in many instances money is provided for telephone, carfare, and for recreational, religious, educational, and cultural activities. Help is also given in finding suitable housing and employment when feasible. Health measures are employed; the nonresidents are given a thorough annual physical examination by the Home physician; hospitalization and extended care are given by the city department of welfare; and when the nonresident requires continuous medical supervision, she is admitted to the Home.

Public Housing

Although some public housing was provided for older people as long ago as fifteen years, there has been virtually no expansion of this type of project until within the last two or three years. Re-

[6] Ruth Laverty, "Non-Resident Aid: A Community Program for the Aged," *State Govt.* (Chicago: Council of State Governments, 1952).

cently, several states and communities have taken steps to build a few housing units especially for the use of older people.

Public housing in New York. In 1939, at the request of the Welfare Council of New York City, provision was made for fifty-four one-person apartments in the Fort Greene Public Housing Project then under construction. Each apartment has an area of about 150 square feet divided into a large living room, kitchen, and bath. The older people have proved to be very good tenants, and keep their homes clean and neat. Of course, many older couples are also accommodated in the public housing projects in the normal course of caring for those citizens needing places to live and having insufficient funds to rent privately owned property.

The experience at Fort Greene and the growing need for more housing for old people with small financial resources have led to a further development of public housing plans in New York State. In 1951, the Commissioner of the New York State Division of Housing issued an order to the effect that all local housing authorities using State Loan Funds for public housing must make provision for the aging in all future projects. Two standard apartment plans have been drawn up for use in the state-aided projects. These are recommended by the commissioner for use in private developments also. One of these units is designed for couples and the other, a smaller unit, is intended for the use of a single person or a remaining spouse. The larger unit has a kitchen-living room, separate double bedroom, and private bath. The smaller apartment includes living-bedroom, separate kitchen, and private bath. Both types of apartments have special adaptations to suit older people, such as the elimination of thresholds, substitution of electricity for gas in cooking, shelves placed at easy-to-reach levels, mechanical operation of windows, seats in the bathtubs and shower stalls, and a sunny exposure to add cheerfulness to the setting. Rents for the apartments are from $32.50 to $37.00 a month; the maximum income of tenants will be $2,200 a year.

Other special facilities which are planned for the public housing units accommodating older people are special day centers within the buildings where programs will be offered similar to those developed at Hodson and Sirovich Centers and others under the auspices of the New York City Welfare Department. Also, in order to offer a preventive health program and to give full medical care at clinic rates, it is planned to include a geriatric medical center in each project for four hundred families or more.

It is planned to provide about fifteen hundred apartments for old people throughout the state. At present there are 585 such units in use or under construction.[7]

Public housing in Chicago. Like other public housing developments, the Chicago Housing Authority reports that it is housing approximately 2,000 persons aged sixty years or over in apartments where they are mixed in with other families. The Authority, with the co-operation of the Committee on the Aged of the Welfare Council of Metropolitan Chicago, has put aside in the Prairie Avenue Courts project thirty-six one-bedroom units in a seven-story elevator building for rental by couples who are at least sixty years of age. These units are a part of a building housing other families in all age groups. The Committee on the Aged is co-ordinating the services of local health and welfare agencies and hospitals in an attempt to prevent illness, mental deterioration, and idle loneliness. If successful, this approach can be copied by other large metropolitan areas having a constellation of services available for the care of people with limited funds.[8]

Co-operative Housing

Co-operative housing should be a feasible method by which older people with some means can provide themselves with the kind of housing they want. There is considerable interest manifest among professional and occupational groups (especially women's groups)

[7]H. T. Stichman, "The Aged and Public Housing," *Enriching the Years* (Newburgh, N.Y.: New York State Joint Legis. Comm. on Problems of the Aging, 1953). Pp. 105-7.

[8]Albert G. Rosenberg, "Chicago Develops a New Approach in the Housing of the Aging," *Aging*, No. 6 (Washington, D.C.: U.S. Dept. of Health, Education, and Welfare, 1953).

in establishing co-operative housing plans through which space can be purchased for occupancy after retirement while the individuals are still employed.

The 1950 legislative provisions permitting the use of public funds for co-operative housing has given some impetus to the development of these types of projects, although there were a number of plans already in operation before the legislation was passed.

There are many types and degrees of co-operation possible, and examples of some of them are described below:

Melbourne Village.   Although not a co-operative enterprise in the sense that property has common ownership, nevertheless, Melbourne Village just west of Melbourne, Florida, is conducted along essentially democratic and co-operative lines. The land is bought by individual purchasers and homes are privately owned. All residents of Melbourne Village are life members and as such have the following privileges: a warranty deed to one or more Melbourne Village lots, a vote at the annual membership meetings, a share in the ownership of all community property, access to the park areas, use of recreational facilities and community buildings, and the benefit of discounts on products bought on a co-operative basis.

Costs include a $500 membership fee and the purchase price of a lot for building purposes. The cost of land is nominal, being $250 for a plot from one-half to one acre in size; additional lands can be purchased at a cost of 1 cent per square foot.

At the present time there are ninety families living in Melbourne Village and two hundred and fifty parcels of land have been sold. Most of the residents fall in the category of the older age group, although the Village was not designed specifically as a retirement community. In fact, many of the older men work in nearby Melbourne. As one man remarked, "We have to work in order to stay young." Jobs in which these older men have found employment include bookkeeping and accounting, sales positions in local stores, and various industrial jobs at a nearby guided missile base.

The Village has one community center which is used for educational and cultural programs for which the residents take complete responsibility and in which they take great pride. There is one commercial venture in the village,—a large hydroponic garden complete with infra-red lamp to guard the plants against sudden frosts.

There are no special restrictions on the kinds of houses that can be built in the village except that they must have 400 square feet for one person or 575 square feet for two and must be of acceptable materials. Most of the homes are modest one-story structures ranging in price from $7,500 to $15,000. The villagers have a homestead exemption of $5,000 and county taxes are low.

The general spirit of the Village is one of co-operativeness and pride. There are many hobbyists in the community and much emphasis is put upon nature study and outdoor activities. I must admit that it was a pleasant experience to pick oranges, grapefruit, guavas, bananas, orange blossoms, azalea, and other fruits and flowers in the yard of one of the villagers on a mid-January day.

Ida Culver House. The Ida Culver House for retired teachers was recently built as a co-operative venture in Seattle, Washington. The House accommodates thirty-eight residents. Rooms that have private baths can be bought at a cost of $3,750, those that have a bath serving an adjoining room are priced at $3,000. Each resident pays $50.00 a month to cover the costs of board and other services provided in the home. A room reverts to the home again upon the death of the owner and is resold to another retired teacher.[9]

Claremont Manor. Another and somewhat more elaborate plan is that of Claremont Manor in Los Angeles. This home is a branch of the Pacific Home which is sponsored by the Methodist Church of Southern California. It has accommodations for two hundred people. Costs in the home are relatively high; single rooms are bought for $5,000 and suites cost $7,500. The residents also pay a life-care fee based upon their age when they enter the home which guarantees complete care including all medical ex-

[9] Geneva Mathiasen, "Housing for Older People," *Enriching the Years* (Newburgh, N.Y.: New York Joint Legis. Comm. on Problems of the Aging, 1953), p. 99.

penses as long as they remain residents. This project is said to be self-supporting.

Facilities in the home include a main residential hall, bungalows housing eight to twelve people, a clubhouse, administrative building, and chapel. Like most church sponsored homes, Claremont Place is not restricted to members of any one denomination.

Canadian Projects

The housing of older people has been developed more extensively in foreign countries than it has been in North America. This chapter, however, will not deal with old age housing as it is today in Great Britain, the Scandinavian, and other countries of Europe. For detailed reports there are several excellent reviews of these foreign activities which have appeared in the literature during the last few years.[10]

However, because the problems of Canada's aging population are similar to those in this country, and because the Canadian government has made funds available for the development of housing for older people in local communities, two special developments will be reviewed here.

In March, 1948, there was opened in Burlington, Canada (near Hamilton), a low-cost apartment block which was made available to old age pensioners, widows on mothers' allowances, and certain war pensioners. Since then a second block has been built and a third is under construction. The apartments are modern in design and situated on a pleasant street in the heart of the town.

These projects represent a co-operative effort on the part of the town of Burlington, civic organizations, and the federal government. The town, the Lions Club, the Canadian Legion, and private citizens provided 10 per cent of the cost; and through the Central Mortgage and Housing Corporation (a federal government

---

[10]Albert Abrams, "Trends in Old Age Homes and Housing for the Aged in Various Parts of the World," *No Time to Grow Old* (Newburgh, N.Y.: New York Joint Legis. Comm. on Problems of the Aging, 1951), pp. 265-82; Kraus, *op. cit.*, pp. 130-31; Shock, *op. cit.*, pp. 50-51; B. S. Rowntree, *Old People, Report of a Survey Committee on the Problems of Aging, and the Care of Old People, Nuffield Foundation* (London: Oxford Univ. Press, 1947).

body set up for the exclusive purpose of financing residential undertakings), the federal government provided the remaining 90 per cent by way of a low rate of interest mortgage amortized over a period of forty-seven years. The apartments rent for $16.00 and $21.00 a month and provide a revenue sufficient to maintain the property and retire the mortgage. To administer the property, there is a board representing the town and interested civic organizations.

Another Canadian experiment is a cottage project developed by the New Vista Society of New Westminster, British Columbia.[11] The Society is composed of a small group of private individuals who got together because they were interested in housing old people, and in order to ensure the continuity of the project, incorporated themselves as a nonprofit society under the provincial laws. No officials are paid for their services.

The Society's first project was a row of six duplex cottages built on a large, pleasantly landscaped lot, 480 feet by 40 feet. Each duplex is 45 feet by 24 feet; each unit has a living room, bedroom, utility room, kitchen, and bathroom. A second row of six more duplexes of slightly less accommodation has been built. Both projects are small, occupying two sides of a street block with approximately 500 feet frontage on each side of the street. They are situated in the middle of a residential area, with stores, churches, and public transportation close at hand.

To be eligible, the tenants must be either too old or too infirm to work, and must have an income no higher than the government's old age pension rate of $50.00 a month. Not all the tenants, however, are old age pensioners. Some are superannuated or on limited war disability pensions, or have a limited income from private sources; but all are subject to the $50.00 maximum.

The projects are partly financed by donations from private individuals and firms. One third of the financing comes from the Provincial Government, which makes it a policy to contribute that proportion to reliably sponsored, low rental housing projects for

[11]E. E. Winch, "A Housing Project for Low Income Citizens," *No Time to Grow Old* (Newburgh, N.Y.: The New York Joint Legis. Comm. on the Problems of the Aging, 1951), pp. 284-86.

senior citizens. To complete the first project it was necessary to make a $10,000 loan at 3 per cent from the Central Mortgage and Housing Corporation, to be amortized over a period of twenty years with an annual payment of $672. The mortgage and the up-keep of the property can both be covered by the $20.00 monthly rent charged on each cottage.

The second project is similarly financed, except that it was necessary to borrow a larger percentage of the cost with repayment spread over a longer period so that rents could be kept down to the minimum.

The Private Entrepreneur

As already pointed out in earlier chapters of this book, the building industry has set as its goal that of housing adequately all segments of the population. There is little question but that the most difficult aspect of this task is the housing of the old age group and that the greatest barrier to the immediate achievement of the goal is finances. Fortunately, there is a sizable number (65 per cent) of older families who already own their homes; and if some means for liquefying these assets can be found, they will become potential buyers of new and more suitable housing. The more difficult group for the private builder to serve is made up of families who do not have capital assets in any form and who have limited fixed incomes. This, however, is an important and challenging problem to the private builders because the numerical size of the group is great; and because, at least in this country, an endeavor is always made to meet the needs of all people through the normal channels of commerce rather than through government subsidization.

At the University of Michigan Conference on Housing the Aging, of which this book is a report, Allen Brockbank, then President of the National Association of Home Builders, pledged that the building industry would take steps to solve the housing problems of the older people of this country. This was not an idle pledge because within three months the Association took up the problem in one of its major meetings on the west coast. Later in the year, a special committee met in Chicago at the annual meeting of the Association to discuss what the industry could do. Recommendations were made to the executive committee to the effect that a permanent committee should be appointed, and that every encouragement should be given builders to help meet this problem. In addition, it was recommended that the Congress be memorialized with regard to the need for changes in legislation which would make it possible for older people to have the same privileges of insured loans as do younger age groups. During the ensuing year, the Association has continued to explore the situation and to hold meetings for the education of its membership as to the size and characteristics of the older segment of the population. Also, in both the official publications of the Association and in a number of trade magazines, articles have appeared discussing the problem and suggesting methods for solution.

Few private enterprises have so far been developed, but one or two will serve as examples of possibilities.

Florida Sun Deck Homes. The Florida Sun Deck Homes Company has established a virtual city of one thousand, five hundred homes which is to be expanded into a $40 million community. The company considers its effort the "first large-scale attempt to tackle the problem of housing and healthful comfort for retired people."[12] Leisure City, as it is called, is situated just off the Florida Keys, 24 miles south of Miami.

The basic unit of the "Sun Deck" home is three rooms occupying a space of 30 feet by 28 feet on lots varying in size from 80 by 100 feet to 100 by 128 feet. The company describes the structure of the houses as monolithic, solid concrete and steel, "constructed to withstand the natural hazards such as hurricanes, termites, fire, excessive heat and humidity."[13] To expand the home into five comfortable rooms, many buyers are using the space and the ready-made structure of the carport which is a part of every basic unit. In general, the structure is simple and strong, and requires practically no upkeep.

The cash price of the basic unit is $5,280, an amount low

[12]Advertising pamphlet, Florida Sun Deck Homes Company, 1430 duPont Building, Miami, Fla.
[13]*Ibid.*

enough to provide for an FHA loan under Title I of the Housing Act. If the purchase is to be financed, a down payment of $690 is required and the buyer must have an income of at least $140 a month, which may be from pensions, annuities, income investments, wages, or any other means. The monthly payment, which includes interest, repayment of loan, taxes, and insurance is $31.85.

Ormond by the Sea. This is another retirement village which is being built by venture capital. It lies eight miles north of Daytona Beach and extends from the Halifax River on one side to the Atlantic Ocean on the other. Two basic plans are available, a one-bedroom unit for $5,250, and a two-bedroom unit costing $6,950. There is more than the difference of one room to be considered, however, because the one-bedroom plan is heated with gas and has no equipment whatever, while the two-bedroom house has oil heat and is equipped with electric refrigerator and electric stove. Construction is concrete block without a basement. The carport has been designed for possible conversion into a utility room and sun porch.

Mortgages of $3,000 are available on the one-bedroom home with monthly payments as low as $25.30; mortgages on the more expensive home can be obtained up to $4,250 and monthly payments are $35.83. Two hundred and forty-eight homes were already occupied in 1954.[14] There is no evidence that recreational or community activities are being developed; it is expected that the residents will avail themselves of the recreational opportunities and community facilities offered at nearby Daytona Beach.

Flexabilt. A house which can be a lifetime home for the young couple who buys it has been a concept which has intrigued the imagination of builders for some time. A number of experiments and demonstrations have been developed which permit the interior arrangements of the house to be changed in accordance with changes in family needs. It is natural that when builders began to give consideration to the housing of older people and espe-

[14]Advertising brochure, Kinsella and Wittenberg, Owners and Builders, Box 1953, Ormond Beach, Fla.

cially the housing of three-generation families, they should consider the flexible house.

An example of a house that adjusts to family needs is the Flexabilt Home designed and built by Mr. Frank Robertson and his son in San Antonio, Texas. The keys to the flexibility of the home lie in two components: a wall of movable panels that can be folded back or removed entirely, and closet sections mounted on casters that can be easily rolled into position. The advantage is that these sections can be moved easily and quickly and provide a secure, snugly-fitting, and relatively soundproof wall. Within a day's time the interior can be entirely remodeled.

The home has 1,250 square feet of living space, including two bathrooms. The only permanent interior walls are those around the bathrooms and kitchen, and those separating the halls from the bedroom unit. By shifting wall units seventy-two different room arrangements may be made. It is possible to turn the house from a one- to a four-bedroom single-family dwelling, or into a two-family residence, with one of the units designed as an efficiency apartment. Thus a newly married couple might require only a studio apartment and prefer to rent out the extra five-room unit. When the family grows, the house can be re-arranged so that the young couple can take the amount of space required for their needs and rent the remaining apartment or occupy the total house themselves. When the children are gone, the couple can again rearrange the house and move into the smaller space, and have a steady income through rental of the larger apartment.

Ryderwood. An entirely different approach by private enterprise has been made by a group of investors in Los Angeles. A corporation called "Senior Estates" was organized in 1953. The corporation bought a ghost lumber town in the state of Washington including four hundred houses, business buildings, a recreation hall, and public utilities. The exteriors of the houses were rehabilitated, but the interiors have been left just as they were when purchased. The two-bedroom houses are being offered for sale at $2,500 each with a down payment of $200 and monthly payments of $20.00; the three-bedroom units cost $3,500 with $300.00 down and $30.00 a month payments.

In addition to the purchase price, the buyer must be prepared to restore the interior of the house. It is expected that most of this work will be done by the older couple themselves and that there will, therefore, be a minimum outlay of money required. There are no restrictions upon the interior remodeling.

Purchasers may sell their houses to anyone approved by the corporation, or in case of death the corporation reserves the right to buy the house back. In this way it is hoped to maintain the characteristics of the town as a community of retired people.

Residence in the village is restricted to people with yearly incomes between $1,620 and $3,000. The corporation is encouraging the residents to establish businesses along the lines of their previous skills in the hope that, in this way, the older people themselves can supply most of the needs of the community. One may wonder what will happen if the community thrives and the business enterprises succeed to the point where the owners have more income than is allowed for residence in the village.

Medical care is being provided through a clinic operated by a registered nurse working under the supervision of a physician who gives one day a week to the community. It is probable that in time a more adequate service will be needed and that some provision will have to be made for at least nursing home care.

This experiment was entered into entirely as a business venture and the purchasers expect to make money. If they meet with the expected success, similar projects may be attempted by other private entrepreneurs in other parts of the country where abandoned property is available.[15]

Custom Designs

To date there have been no large-scale ventures in providing custom built housing for older people. What has been done, generally, has been done to order at the particular request of an aging couple who had the money to pay for what they wanted

[15]"Ryderwood, Washington, A Thriving Community for Retired Workers," *Aging,* No. 9 (Washington, D.C.: U.S. Dept. Health, Education, and Welfare, 1954).

in a home for their later years. The homes that have been built under these conditions give exciting promise of things to come.

In general, these ideal homes for easy living have certain characteristics in common regardless of whether they cost $10,000 or $20,000. They are almost without exception one-story structures without basements. Cabinets and easily accessible storage space are built-in features. Room for guests is provided either by having a number of bedrooms or by using sliding or folding partitions. Living and dining space are usually combined, but bedrooms are separate even in the smallest units. Special attention is given to draftless heating and ventilation, and to providing moisture proof floors. Convenience is the keynote and is obtained through the use of functional design and the elimination of all unnecessary details.

Most of the custom built houses that have been described do not include many of the features recommended as essential by experts in housing of older people. For example, handrails on bathtubs and bath seats, and handgrips near bathtubs and toilets are not mentioned. It may be that most older people who are having homes built are not yet frail enough to appreciate these features which are reminders of advancing age, and hence are unwilling to make provision for them. The author is inclined to agree that an array of handrails and grab bars in the bathroom and along halls are not things of added beauty. It seems desirable, however, for some provisions to be made in the plans of the house which will make it possible to add these features at a later date should the necessity arise.

Architects who are giving attention to the problems of housing for older people are finding this a challenging new field for their efforts. It is hoped that low-priced, easy-living homes for the aging will become a dominant preoccupation of architects and builders alike, and that in the near future we will have both custom built and large-scale developments to meet the needs of all groups of the aging.

Conclusion

In summary, it can be said that there are already many evidences that the difficult task of finding housing for older people has become a concern of older people themselves and of those experts and groups who can help bring about an expansion of housing facilities for them.

Throughout the discussion, we have included reports upon the kinds of programs which are being developed in conjunction with the housing projects, because so much more than mere shelter is involved. The best of housing, devoid of services and programs to meet the social and psychological needs of the aging, would be little improvement over the present situation.

The job of providing housing for old people can not be done by any single group. It will require the best talent of architects, builders, planners, economists, physicians, and those who understand the social requirements of the aging.

Hertha Kraus has said that housing the aging is a great challenge to America. She points out that "adequate housing for the aged must develop at the crossroads of two important programs: better housing in better neighborhoods within the reach of all income groups, and more adequate services to meet the peculiar needs of a large and growing senior consumer group commonly characterized by waning ability and a proneness to multiple handicaps."[16]

It is our hope that this volume may serve as a timely source of communication between the researchers, the planners and builders, and the older people themselves.

[16]Kraus, *op. cit.*, 289 (1952), p. 133.

REFERENCES

ABRAMS, ALBERT J.   Old Age Homes and State Loans.   Enriching the Years.   Newburgh, N. Y.: New York State Joint Legis. Comm. on Problems of the Aging, 1953.
Trends in Old Age Homes and Housing for the Aged in Various Parts of the World.   No Time to Grow Old.   *Ibid.*

ALT, EDITH.   Standards of Care for Older People in Institutions. Sec. I.   Suggested Standards for Homes for the Aged and Nursing Homes.   New York: Comm. on Aging of the Nat. Social Welfare Assembly.
Ibid. Sec. II. Methods of Establishing and Maintaining Standards in Homes for the Aged and Nursing Homes.   New York: Comm. on Aging of the Nat. Social Welfare Assembly.

Are You Selecting a Nursing Home?   Milwaukee: Central Agency for the Chronically Ill. (n.d.)

BAKER, CALVIN L., M.D.   Housing the Aged in Rest Homes.   Journ. Ohio Assn. Nursing Homes, 1, No. 3 (1952).

BLUESTONE, E. M., M.D. Medical Care of the Aged. Journ. Gerontol., 4, No. 4 (1949): 305-9.

British Medical Association.   The Right Patient in the Right Bed. 1st suppl., Rep. Comm. on Care and Treatment of the Elderly and Infirm, 1947.   Pp. 29-35.

Buildings for the Handicapped and/or Aged.   Bull. Amer. Instit. Architects, Nov. 1951, Jan. 1952.   Washington, D.C.: The Octagon.

Committee on Problems of the Aging and Research Department of the Welfare Council of Metropolitan Los Angeles.   Housing for the Aging. Special Rept. Ser. No. 34, Los Angeles, Calif.

GOULDING, WILLIAM S.   Housing for Older People.   Canadian Welfare, 28, No. 6 (1952).

GROSS, MIRIAM Z.   Our Firetrap Hospitals.   Colliers, 128 (1951): 28-29.

GROSSMAN, BEN L.   Older People Live in Institutions.   Journ. Ohio Assn. Nursing Homes, 1, No. 4 (1952).

GUMPERT, MARTIN, M.D., and others. Where and with Whom Should Older People Live? Round Table No. 703. Chicago: Chicago Univ. Press, 1951.

HILL, RUTH. Group Living for the Elderly. Proc. Nat. Conf. Social Work, 1948. New York: Columbia Univ. Press. Pp. 410-18.
Housing the Aging. Nat. Assn. Home Builders Correlator, Sept., 1953.

JOHNSON, RALPH J. and M. ALLEN POND. Health Standards of Housing for the Aging Population. Journ. Gerontol., 7, No. 2 (1952).

KRAUS, HERTHA. Community Planning for the Aged. *Ibid.*, 3, No. 2 (1948): 129-40.
Housing Our Older Citizens. Ann. Amer. Acad. Pol. Soc. Sci., 279 (1952): 126-38.
Older Persons Have Special Housing Needs. Journ. Housing, Jan., 1950. Pp. 17-20.

LAVERTY, RUTH. Non-resident Aid—Community Versus Institutional Care for Older People. Journ. Gerontol., 5, No. 4 (1950).

LAWTON, GEORGE and MAXWELL STEWART. When You Grow Older. Public Affairs Pamph. No. 139. New York: Public Affairs Comm., Inc., 1947.

MATHIASEN, GENEVA, and others. Housing for Older People. Enriching the Years. Newburgh, N. Y.: New York State Joint Legis. Comm. on Problems of the Aging.

MONROE, ROBERT T., M.D. The Community Resources Essential for Old People. Diseases in Old Age. Cambridge: Harvard Univ. Press, 1951. Pp. 359-402.

National Old People's Welfare Committee. Age Is Opportunity; A New Guide to Practical Work for the Welfare of Old Age. London: Nat. Counc. Social Service, 1949.

Neighborhood Villages for the Aged Proposed. Amer. City, 66 (1951):162; A Reply. *Ibid.*, 67 (1952):151.

NICHOLSON, EDNA and LILLIE H. NAIRNE. Private Living Arrangements for Elderly People. Proc. Nat. Conf. Social Work, 1946. New York: Columbia Univ. Press, 1947. Pp. 477-90.

POLLAK, OTTO. Social Adjustment in Old Age; A Research Planning Report. New York: Soc. Sci. Research Counc., 1948.

ROBBINS, IRA S. Housing Our Aging. Age Is No Barrier. Newburgh, N. Y.: New York State Joint Legis. Comm. on Problems of the Aging, 1952.

SCHENDEL, GORDON. To the County Home to Die. Colliers, 124 (1949):22.

SILK, LEONARD S. The Housing Circumstances of the Aged in the United States, 1950. Journ. Gerontol., 7, No. 1 (1952). Pp. 87-91.

STEINHAUS, HENRY W. Financing Old Age. Young at Any Age. Newburgh, N. Y.: New York State Joint Legis. Comm. on Problems of the Aging, 1950.

STICHMAN, HERMAN T. The Aged and Public Housing. Enriching the Years. *Ibid.*

SWARTZ, P. W. Organized Community Planning for Old Age. Journ. Gerontol., Suppl., 6, No. 3 (1951):154.

Vancouver Housing Authority, A Report of. Housing for Our Older Citizens. Vancouver, B. C., 1949.

Where Age Is Youth, Old Man's Town. Coronet, 26 (1949):20-21.

ZEMAN, FREDERICK E., M.D. The Medical Organization of the Modern Home for the Aged. Journ. Gerontol., 5, No. 3 (1950): 262-65.

INDEX

Age structure, of American population, 1–4

Aged, who are the? 1–12

Aged population, characteristics of, 8–12; geographical distribution of, 5–8; household relationships of, 8–10; predicted increase of, 3–4; sex and marital status of, 8; sources of increase in, 2–3

Allegheny County Infirmary, 147–51

Attitudes, toward aging, 226–27; of older persons toward housing, how to change, 89–90; of older persons toward housing problems, 75–76

Banks, mortgage loans issued by, 158–59

Birth rates, and changing population structure, 3–4

Building industry, approaches toward housing the aged of, 64–71; position of, 48–54

Canadian housing projects, 264–66

Case histories, of aged residents in improvised rural housing, 95–100

Chicago Community Project for the Aged, 239–42

Chicago Housing Authority, study conducted by, 87–89

Chronic disease, as research category, 109–10

Chronic disease hospitals, 112; offering sheltered and medical care to the aged, 173–74

Chronic illness, management in cottage housing, 96–97

Chronological age, as a determinant in housing problems, 13

Claremont Manor, 263–64

Commonwealth Housing Foundation, 81–83

Communal living arrangements, see Congregate housing

Community action, 215–72; organization for, 236–42

Community considerations, in developing housing for the aged, 198; in planning urban housing for the aged, 39–47

Community participation, in nursing-home services, 130

Community services to the aged, as aids in improving family relationships, 79; needed, 226–35; need for comprehensive approach in planning of, 121–22

Congestion, in homes of old people, 15

Congregate housing, for the aging, 72–90; conversion of dwellings into, 83–87; independent, needed by old people, 59; institutional, 79–81; noninstitutional, 81–83

Convalescent homes, 116–31; see also Nursing homes

Conversion, of dwellings into congregate housing, 83–87

Co-operative funds, as source of capital for rental housing, 206–7

Co-operative housing, 261–64

Corporations, investment in rental housing by, 208–9

Cottage housing, improvised for retired aged in rural areas, 92–99, 101–3; management of chronically ill in, 96–97

County infirmary, cost of care in, 146; current defects of, 143–46; need for community interest in, 147; need for high turnover of population in, 143; place in community of, 142–43; program in Allegheny County, 147–51; role in long-term illness and disability, 141–51

Credit unions, as source of investment capital, 211